GunDigest Guide to
MODERN SHOTGUNNING

L.P. BREZNY

Published by

Gun Digest® Books, an imprint of F+W Media, Inc.
Krause Publications • 700 East State Street • Iola, WI 54990-0001
715-445-2214 • 888-457-2873
www.krausebooks.com

To order books or other products call toll-free 1-800-258-0929
or visit us online at www.gundigeststore.com

ISBN-13:978-1-4402-3947-2
ISBN-10: 1-4402-3947-9

Edited by Jennifer L.S. Pearsall
Designed by Dave Hauser
Cover Design by Dave Hauser

Printed in China

L.P. Brezny has worked in the test and development end of smoothbore shooting sports for better then 50 years. In that time, he has developed new load designs that are currently in use by the shooting sports industry, including those ranging from subsonic rounds for deer hunting to winged target ammunition, and he has made contributions to both large and small companies, in terms of their load development projects.

While working with Minnesota Steel Shot at the onset of non-toxic load development, Brezny assisted in testing and designing "supersonic" heavy wad systems that saved 10- and 12-gauge barrels from total destruction by the heavy iron (steel) shot pellets in use at that time. It was in that period that Brezny turned much of his focus to the 10-gauge magnum, that large-bore and its ammunition becoming a specialty of his.

Brezny was the first to work with modern chronograph equipment and shotgun loads and, as such, began to measure the exact velocity of shotgun pellets in flight. Some said it could not be done, but, today, thanks to Brezny's in-depth work and research, the old black-powder equivalent rating for shotshells has been replaced with true muzzle velocities generated.

With actual known velocities in hand, Brezny's testing turned to how much energy, penetration, and wound channel damage was required to terminate live game. As that knowledge grew so, too, did his development of new chokes to optimize loads to their peak performance levels.

Brezny designed and commercially built the first and current Metro Gun Systems, which consist of an extra section of barrel with special porting installed. Coupled with the author's load development, this system is as silent as a 12-gauge can get. Other advancements the author has made in this area include the newer .724 Orion, a 17-inch suppressor "can" that fits the muzzle of a threaded shotgun barrel. This 12-gauge silencer holds subsonic ammunition report to under 72 decibels (about like a car door closing).

Prior to his long career as a firearms writer and ammunition developer, the author was a street police officer for 23 years via the S.F.P.D. in the Minneapolis/Saint Paul metro area. Eventually ranking as a sergeant, he worked as a training officer with young rookies and spent a great deal of time teaching the use of the shotgun as a combat tool on the street. Also, as a high-school teacher of 36 years, Brezny ran hunter education and shooting programs directly through the Minneapolis Public Schools, during a time when shooting was still an accepted primary and secondary school subject, and he's logged an additional 17 years working in other youth shooting training programs.

Today, L.P. lives in the Black Hills of South Dakota, among the rocks, tress, and native wildlife. A "back 40" test range occupies most of his days, giving way to writing projects on subjects that are just about endless.

The author with a suppressed shotgun of his own design, about to head afield in his home stomping grounds of South Dakota.

INTRODUCTION

the modern shotgun is a small wonder, when observed from mine, a ballistician's point of view. While being random in terms of projectile control (or lack of it), the shotgun's functioning system retains some very predictable elements that make it one of the very best and most flexible gunning tools in use today by hunters and target shooters, as well as in military and law enforcement applications.

How flexible is the shotgun, how lethal? In its time, the shotgun has often been used by war-time armies, as was the case in Germany, during WWII, for instance; those who knew they were to come up against them on the battlefield wanted them declared illegal for combat! As law enforcement tools, there are no better weapons to be considered, when a team or even a single officer is confronted with multiple targets in urban settings and at close range; merely the sound of a pump gun's action in the dead of night, slamming home a chambered round, strikes fear into the heart of any intruder with at least half a brain in working order. Of course, for the sportsman, when the targets are rising game birds, descending waterfowl, or incoming deer or coyotes, the shotgun can also answer the call, providing the correct ammunition is applied for such purposes in the field.

There was once a question asked of Alaskan bush pilots, regarding exactly what gun they would consider as a survival tool to be carried in their aircraft, if only a single choice could be had. The answer was, *overwhelmingly*, a 12-gauge shotgun. Why? Because the shotgun is flexible in terms of bringing down everything from bears to rabbits, as well as it is dependable, in that its action, even in a repeating pump gun, always seems to work. Haul along a mixed-fruit salad of slugs, buckshot, or fine birdshot and you're in business, when it comes time to keeping the Dutch oven full of meat. Indeed, when one of the survival-themed television shows aired awhile back and the participants were issued guns, the single gun that worked out the best, in terms of just keeping these people supplied with some form of protein, was a simple .410-bore shotgun. (At the time, I wondered why a .410, but knowing a few television writer types and also knowing their understanding of the real gun world, that whole issue becomes still another story. I'm sure you can imagine as well as I can.)

All this brings me to purpose to this book, but first let me clarify what it *won't* be about. What this book will not be about is a reconstruction of the shotgun's history. Nor will it be a basic evaluation of shotguns as the tools of the upland, waterfowl hunter, or clay bird shooter. While elements regarding upland, waterfowl, and other related target shooting subjects will indeed surface within the text, the primary purpose of this material is really to give the reader some insight to the massively extensive and flexible adaptations associated with a modern scattergun.

The world of shotguns, and mainly the study of smoothbore ballistics, started for me almost 50 years ago, back in the heart of the Midwestern United States. In those days, hunting land access was easy, game was plentiful, and lead shot ruled the land. For the roughly first 15 years or so I hunted and shot there, I never chambered a single factory load in my shotgun that I could remember; you don't know smoothbore ammunition or scatterguns until you have built your own ammunition from scratch. That's the start of a full-blown learning curve and, in my case, the start of a drive toward a long and eventful career of both making shotguns work better and pushing the loads that supply them fly harder and further then any previous time in American smoothbore history.

Being at the very onset of the non-toxic revolution, and with a decade already behind me in high-performance lead shot load research, I was right in the driver's seat, when my writing and field work began to turn to reporting on load performance. Tacking on my research time involving the development of totally new types of specialized non-toxic ammunition for long-range waterfowl and varmint applications, and you could say that I was positioned at a point in firearms history that proved to establish my long and eventful travel down the road of smoothbore ballistics learning and advancement.

During the past 35 years, I have been involved in the testing, development, and field application of new shotshell load designs; believe me when I tell you that ordnance development, as in highly upgraded ammunition, has pressed forward at an almost unbelievable pace. I've also regularly participated in actual, real-time testing of completely new shotguns being released for public sale by the firearms makers. So, much of the writing in this book will expose you to those real-world field-testing examples, because that's what's truly pushing the modern shotgun technology today. Related shooting gear associated with the modern smoothbore firearm will also be included, as required.

Over the course of this book, I've made sure you will be introduced to hard data ballistics that will show you how different load designs function and what you can expect of them when they meet their target, doing away with the minimal (and not very useful at that) shotshell box-top information. Why? That box-top info is produced by measurement systems at the shotgun's muzzle—and nothing to my knowledge ever gets shot at, in terms of published ballistics, quite that close to the muzzle of a shotgun. You have *distance* between the muzzle and whatever it is you're aiming at, and it's that distance, in a few to many dozens of yards, that matters far more than what's going on directly in front of the bead.

If there is an element of subject elimination within the text here, it is in the areas of clay target shooting and studies in lead shot ballistics. I admit that clay shooting is not my area of expertise, but that's not the reason you won't find much information on it. The reason you won't find much info on those two subjects is that, for the most part, lead shot is, without question, *on the way out!* That includes lead shot as we currently see it being used for clay target games and field sport shooting. As for the sporting guns themselves, what's new with them—backboring, extended chokes, stock weights, barrel weights, adjustable stocks, and the like—are tried and true features and, so, aren't really new at all.

Finally, it's of particular note that specialized shotguns for the military, sporting games (3-Gun, for instance), and police have evolved to enter the realm of mainstream field application. The use of silencers (noise suppressors) on shotguns, for instance, is very new. This includes my own design developments in this area, which have centered on the current-production .724 Orion 12-gauge silencer system, as well as the established Metro Gun System, both of which are designed to produce very quiet shotgun shooting. The information you will obtain here covering shotgun silencers will be some of the first on this subject—and accurate to the letter. Overall, and taking interesting developments such as these and others and viewing them as a reflection of what truly defines today's *modern* shotguns, what I can assure every reader is that, if you review this work in detail, you will come away a better informed shotgunner, no matter your choice of use for these ever-popular firearms. And doesn't that make all the difference? Enjoy.

TABLE OF CONTENTS

DEDICATION

To my father, Nick Brezny, who introduced
me to the wild side and never once left me
by the side of the road. Thanks, Dad.

ACKNOWLEDGMENTS

You could say my shotgun education started in 1972, about the time I started hunting long-range geese with a 10-gauge on open federal and state refuge lands throughout the states of Minnesota and Wisconsin. In those days, there were few decoys ever used, so you lived by your ability to remain flexible, think like a rocket scientist in building effective, long-range shotshell loads, and were willing to spend a lot of hours over a reloading bench while dreaming up the next mile-high waterfowl killing device.

From those days to the present, I have relied on a massive number of outstanding hunters, as well as many other individuals, when it came time to help me down the road to better understanding ballistics science and how that led to at least some degree of success, in terms of better loads for field use. This was especially true, as we all started down the road of improving non-toxic loads.

Of those individuals who made this all possible, my first thank you goes to my old friend Ross Metzger of SHOTData, who has always been at my side (and often ahead of me) in understanding the math of basic ballistics, as well as how projectile performance is measured as it passes through the air.

There is another good friend and an actual student of mine, Paul Wagner, out of the metro area of Minnesota, who gets a thanks. Paul introduced me to pass-shooting for geese, when I was way back in my early twenties. Also on the team were Gordy Herman, George Herman, and the whole Rochester waterfowl crew. They don't have any idea how much I learned from watching those very dedicated goose hunters work at their craft. We loaded 10-gauge shotshells all week long and shot them all weekend.

Gratitude to the old handloading master Dave Fackler, top gun at Ballistics Products, in Minnesota. The Saturday mornings in Dave's handloading supply store, where we spent much time rolling over new load ideas, will always be fondly remembered.

The grassroots outfit known as Minnesota Steel Shot Reloaders, Inc., headed up by my old friend and now departed Don Vizecky, played a major role in the development of modern steel shot ammunition. Don felt I was on the right track to a better handload, much of the time.

Also in the research end of the deal is Tom Armbrust, the head man at Ballistics Research, in McHenry, Illinois. Tom was indispensable in keeping my head on my shoulders, as I developed new shotshells with him and as we then tested some of the very early—and, I should add, successful—non-toxic loads in 12- and 10-gauge.

Federal Cartridge, the outfit right in my backyard, allowed me to learn my way, down in Test Tunnel No. 3 and in the conference room upstairs at the ammunition plant, alongside good friends like Bill Stevens (now departed and surely missed), and Mike Larsen, the driving force behind my own Metro Gun, the only silent production shotgun system built in America today. Those two guys were always in my corner on each and every project I came up with, across the board. I miss them a whole lot today. The sport shooting information age ain't what it used to be, friends, believe me.

Winchester Ammunition's Mike Jordan actually cracked the door that allowed me to move into the mainstream of the shooting world, which, in turn, allowed me to move my material out to publishers. Mike is one of the best smoothbore shots I have ever seen bar none, and I thank him for the many seasons of wingshooting we had together over the years. I learned from Mike, and even though Mike had hunted worldwide, we shared the art of calling and gunning the American crow. As he once said to me, "Brez, crow hunting is wingshooting at its best," and boy oh boy was he dead-on correct.

Many thanks are owed to my publishers and editors who, over many years, have put up with my somewhat eccentric and, admittedly, different ways of looking at ballistics, not to mention general shooting subjects. And I owe a special thanks to my readers—without you, I would never have moved off first base in this business. I hope I have been of some help to you in improving the smoothbore shooting sports.

Last but not least goes thanks to my friend, now passed, Grits Gresham, the sport shooting pen of *Sports Afield*, as well as many other publications over his lifetime. Grits came north to meet this long-range 10-gauge shooter and put into words many of my ideas. I thank him, you, and all the others heartily.

CHAPTER ONE

FROM TANKS TO MODEL 870s
They're All Just Pieces of Pipe

The author with 1,000 pounds of South Dakota buffalo taken by way of a 20-gauge 3½-inch wildcat shotgun.

One of the very first shotguns I ever owned was a very old, 34-inch barreled, side-by-side 12-gauge with twist barrels, open hammers, and set up for nothing but blackpowder. That may seem to date me a bit, but, rest assured, the blackpowder generation was *not* mine! That gun, in fact, was but one way my dad had of settling down a kid of nine years of age, when it came to hunting pheasant in southwestern Minnesota. In those days, Dad, a young, upstart railroad engineer, simply didn't have the cash to buy an extra shooter just so his kid could tag along on those fall and winter outings.

That old blackpowder cannon of my early years was an unwieldy piece of steel that one of my uncles had insisted to my aunt was unfit for taking ditch chickens at any level. As such, he required a new pump gun from the local Sears store sporting goods department. His about-useless blackpowder gun, having thus been relegated to the status of relic, was going to be retired. I guess the bottom line in the family was that, if it was good enough for the wall, it might as well make a starter gun for a kid like me.

In truth, I didn't care. I was now in the field with what to me was a beautiful piece of steel, several

Orman Dam, West River, South Dakota. Ducks hunters set up for the morning shoot and teal are already in the air.

rounds of old and water-swelled 2¾-inch paper loads of No. 4 lead shotshells in my pocket, and ready as rain for that first rising cock pheasant. Regardless the guns or loads with which I was hunting, just being out there and hunting meant all was very right with the world, at least though my young eyes.

With my uncle on my left and Dad to the right, I fought the tall grass that seemed to be trying to tangle my legs with every step. But then, at the sound of thundering wings and the sight of that bright red head and long tail of that first rooster catapulting out of the grass, I went into automatic mode. One of the gun's heavy iron hammers came back, the barrels were leveled at the now departing long-tail and, with a blast of thunder and a great deal of white smoke, it was clear that, somehow, I had connected on that bird, even though I could see nothing of it through the dense cloud of blackpowder smog.

Thinking back on seeing Sandy, our well-seasoned English setter, return with the bird, I know that, to this day, I am not sure if it were me or my dad who was the most excited. As for my uncle and that brand new J.C. Higgins he'd talked my aunt into, he had a look on his face that read like a book—it was something like *I didn't know that gun could do that!* Over the course of that first morning hunt, I counted a second clean one-shot-killed rooster. As for uncle, well, he went zero for several. Even counting back, now some 58 years ago, I can still see his face as he looked down

on the old double gun and knew he had to admit to my aunt that it had not been the gun, but the guy shooting it. The half-pint behind the hammers had clearly illustrated that fact.

***

For all their history, for all the stories we share about them, shotguns are not much more than a section of pipe, some kind of detonation system and a stock or furniture on which to hang its several pieces of steel. Only after that most basic of definitions will all the other elements of gun design and action type start to come into play. Still, it is those elements that make shotguns as different as snowflakes. To be sure, what works for one shooter may be totally wrong for another. That blackpowder relic worked for me at the time, and enough so that, within a year, it had been replaced with a brand new Winchester Model 24 side-by-side that Dad and Mom had put under the Christmas tree. As Dad said to me, "You shoot a double well, so I figured it was a natural choice." He was right. Twin-pipe scatterguns are still favorites of mine, to this day.

Because shotguns are not much more than a butt-stock and pipe (or pipes) with some steel receiver parts thrown into the mix, what sets each apart from the other are the wide range of action designs. Most shooters are clearly aware that the basic actions include hinge, auto, and pump guns. Hinge guns make up the single-shot break-open and the side-by-side and over/under twin-barrel shotguns. Auto-loaders stand alone as self-stuffing, magazine-fed gun systems; pump guns are actually much like autos, except the shooter manually works a slide system to feed ammunition from the magazine to the shotgun's chamber.

Again, that's what everyone knows about shotguns. What people don't often understand is that a shotgun in any of those action designs is cloaked in a number of very different configurations. Such design framework is tied to military and police applications, but, as developments filter down from military research and other development folks, it's the sporting shotgun shooters who truly benefit from these high-tech advancements.

Need an example? Remington Arms retains a division that goes under the title of Government Products (MPD). This is not a sporting division of Remington, but one that is military and government related. In this division, shotgun creations take on a look and feel wholly different from the standard bird gun

This young man will know a very different world of shotgunning from what his father has experienced. Advanced design and flexible uses are the hallmarks of our new age of smoothbore shooting.

Yes, these are shotguns, the top model a stand-alone, the bottom a rifle paired with a shotgun attachment.

most of us sportsmen take afield. Even the good old tried and true Remington Model 870, one of the most used pump guns in the world, comes to the surface with this military label, labeled the Model 870P; the "P" stands for "police."

That's just one example. As we move on into other areas of this book, it will be easy to see how other military developments in gun design have played into the civilian market. Whether you're a turkey hunter, waterfowl hunter, or deer harvesting individual, military design has indeed come calling, as it's applied to our general-purpose field guns. The bottom line is that, today, you carry military technology quite often when you take afield a sporting gun, and, in most cases, you don't even know it.

Such is the case with a shotgun based on the ever-so-versatile AR-15/M16 platform, including the collapsible stock, red dot sight, extended magazine, and muzzle break (see the photos at the top of this page). There's even an option to mount a shotgun under a dedicated rifle barrel, as in the setup in the bottom picture. Taking the process a step further, you can regard military special assault equipment, such as that found in an auto-loading M-37 grenade launcher, for instance, as a shotgun of sorts, in that it uses a smoothbore barrel, though also a very large, 40mm shotshell-like round that can employ a variety of projectiles ranging from anti-personnel shot to high explosive (HE) shot and much more. Even heavy armor, as in the M 1-A1 Abrams tank and its big, ultra high-velocity 120mm gun can and does shoot anti-personnel canister shot (i.e., it's a damned big shotgun). When this world-class tank-buster really gets serious, it will pound out its sabot-encased, anti-tank smoothbore darts just as both the old and currently designed sabot slugs and bullets fly from game shooting sporting guns today. In Vietnam, the famed American M-60 tanks often fired big

shotshells filled with large steel balls (called "beehive rounds"), in their application to jungle fighting infantry support rolls. If you called these outfits "shotguns on tractor treads," you'd be close to the truth. Naval guns and land-based artillery in the range of 105mm cannon will also use canister shot loads for deck clearing or against infantry, and, today, the Navy even uses new tungsten-based 20-caliber shot encased in very big shotshells for such work.

If you can remember back about 20 years ago, a film called *Dogs of War* was released, in which the lead charter made use of a drum magazined 12-gauge shotgun that spit out a wide variety of ordnance. These ranged from HE and fragmentation rounds to high explosive armor-penetrating projectiles. Many who viewed the film thought the gun was a Hollywood gimmick. It was real. Called the "Manville gun," after its builder C.J. Manville, this 18-shot, rotating-drum gun was a fore-runner of the currently designed, military-type M32 40mm force multiplier, a new cross-munitions assault system that packs more punch as used by one man than that of a full military support fire team in combat. This modern off-shoot of the 1936 Manville, which shot almost all gas munitions at the time, will shoot to 440 yards and deliver HE/fragmentation munitions into buildings, blowing holes in walls and taking down armor-plated reinforced steel doors in the process.

What this all boils down to is that, though I started this discussion based on a single piece of pipe, shotguns have moved and continue to move well beyond that simplicity. It's a discussion we need to have, if we're to make the most out of the incredible tools we now find in our hands.

(top) The M1A1 main battle tank is also a smoothbore shotgun, when canister shot is fired down the tube. This is indeed a very fancy piece of high-priced pipe. (U.S. Army photo)

(above) Canister shot makes this a very large shotgun. (Jerome Bessler photo)

(right) The M-32 Grenade Launcher is an upgrade from the basic design of the drum magazine shotgun—bigger, with more punch to it. (U.S. Army photo)

CHAPTER TWO

THE SHOTGUN'S FOUNDATIONS

as I have previously indicated, the shotgun as it exists now, in terms of design and function, has really changed a good deal from the days of muzzleloading and breech-opening blackpowder guns. Even turning to examine guns produced well into the age of smokeless powder illustrates that, indeed, we have turned several corners in terms of gun design, when you consider such an old and established shooting system as is the scattergun.

Look backwards a bit. Exposed-hammer lock systems were slow to use and the barrels lacked ejectors. Most problematic, gun stock configurations were often steeply dropped at the butt, a shape that tended to kick the daylights out of the shooter. My family kept a single-shot 12-gauge of such crafting in our duck camp for years, and we would pay anyone a dollar for each shot of duck load they'd run through it. Takers we got if they were new to the camp group of hunters, but old-timers wouldn't go near the thing.

We've come a long, long way from the shotguns like the one this Confederate soldier carried.

Today, our guns so much more evolved, we have a wide range of stock designs that cover ground all the way into the six-position AR-15/M-16-style collapsible systems used on military and police firearms and, of late, the newer Mossberg Flex stock system that allows a quick change in fore-ends and buttstocks on the company's Model 500 pump gun. Why the modifications? Because turkey hunters who sit all bunched up at the base of a

A modified Remington auto-loader using the ATN high-capacity rotary magazine Xrail system. Shotguns are flexible tools, with just a little imagination put to use! (ATN photo)

tree, or duck hunters who need to hold up in a layout or ground blind, have found these modifications to be outstanding in providing them the ability to keep an open sight, bead, or scope on an incoming trophy gobbler, duck, or goose. I currently own the Mossberg 835 pump-action that wears a right-handed thumb-hole turkey stock, as well as a Remington 870 that mounts a pistol grip and collapsible six-position stock system. Both are a joy to use in a turkey woods and a major improvement over a standard shotgun stock. If there is one area of concern regarding today's major variations in stock design it is that, in most cases, the static-position stock systems, wonderful as used by turkey and varmint hunters working calls for coyotes, are not a good design for shooting moving targets on the wing. For this type of shotgunning, the more conventional, standard pistol grip stock or a configuration selected from Mossberg's Flex-style stock is best.

Stock materials, too, have changed on working guns (the term "working" separating these guns from other sporting shotgun types), because the use of polymer or plastic stocks and other non-wood materials has greatly reduced the need for refinishing or wood replacement. That's a boon, when these materials are applied to hard-going duck, deer, or some other general-purpose shotguns that end up in a bush plane's cargo bay or the bottom of an open water hunting/fishing boat. Let's face it, friends, some guns see a whole lot of use while others get looked at more often than shot. Working guns are the former and, to my way of thinking, if it is not a workhorse, I don't have too much use of it.

Today, unlike any other time in America, or even in the world's history, the shotgun can be seen as having undergone dramatic changes, enough so that they may be regarded on a whole different level to the scatterguns of even a mere 20 years ago. Building on stock design and material improvements, steel in barrel material, receiver alloys, and hardened action parts, for instance, have gone space age. These things all come at a cost, of course; the advanced waterfowl auto-loader of today, by example, will sell in the price range of $1,220 to $1,450, with nary an eye blink by the dealer or the customer. But what are you getting for such hefty price tags?

As a basic design, these guns all do the same thing: They get pellets out of the muzzle and on toward your intended target. Beyond all that it's a game of bells and whistles. Yes, certainly, design has kept pace with the times, and the modern autoloader, of course, is now many steps ahead of those well-designed but now outdated smoothbores from old John Browning. Today's auto-loaders features things like the development of the single, non-adjustable gas valve that allows it to shoot various load types without making any changes to the gas system. Other elemental changes can be found in the materials used in the receivers of the modern shotgun. New alloys, poly-carbon materials (in the Remington Model 105 Auto CTI, for instance), and improved sighting systems make up much of what was not available even a decade ago. Still, a closer look will also tell you that Browning's designs were so outstanding that many of the elements in those now outdated guns of his can still be found in modern production shotguns. Yet this isn't a game of two steps forward and one step back, rather a melding of old and new to produce some spectacularly useful and dependable shotguns.

A few years ago, I was hunting the big Black Bayou of Louisiana, with some local Cajun gator hunters that, to the man, were shooting single-shot H&R Topper 12-gauges wearing nothing more than an old-school fixed choke. Judging by the lack of bluing, loss of wood stain, and general nicks and dings, their guns had seen their better days about 25 years before my hunt. Those Toppers, in their heyday, sold for about

One flexible 12-gauge meets the needs of a weekend with various game on the agenda.

The author with a beaver taken during a night hunt with, of course, a shotgun.

Purpose 870 to start the lineup, with Mossberg's 500 or 835 following next. Want to move up in price just a bit? For a few extra dollars, you'll add a bank vault-tight lifetime action to the mix in the well-aged and still very effective Browning BPS.

When I was informed that Remington had been sold, in 2007, I promptly went out a bought a brand new 870 Wingmaster. It is still in the box two years later. Why? Because I didn't want to ever be without a very sold working 870, even now well into my senior years of duck shooting. That's just how I feel about that shooting icon as an American tradition, and, bottom line, you can't beat a Remington 870, no way, no how. In terms of cost, value for the buck, service afield, and, yes, great mounting and balance, the 870 ranks as king of the hill.

Years ago, I had a friend who worked the summer turkey shoot events (clay bird variety), across southern Minnesota. He made a pile of money and prizes in the 27-yard trap events. His choice in shotguns was nothing less than his trusted, 30-inch barreled 870 Wingmaster. My friend shot that scattergun so much, he actually wore the trigger thin enough it required replacement before completely breaking. That's more than a few rounds, to be sure, but most likely no more

$65, including a gun case and shells thrown into the deal. Yet, I am quite convinced that each of those shooting tools had seen more game die than I will ever even recall during my lifetime in the out of doors.

From those Toppers, leap forward to today's 870 Remington, which, though virtually unchanged in its mechanics from its original introduction, now includes all the added attractions needed to fit many dozens of roles in the field, be it that for the everyday hunter or a hiker's survival tool to personal-defense and law enforcement defender and dedicated clay bird shooter. That's a lot to ask from one gun, and it doesn't get to do all those things without a lot of add-ons.

There's a little reminiscing going on here, a little nostalgia, but I do have a point and it is this: You don't *need* all those bells and whistles to field a hard-working and effective field shotgun. I cringe when I see a young man put down money he does not have to get into a gun he can't afford, just so he can "keep up" with the crowd. My advice is to think before you leap. A high price is not everything in the effective working field gun market. So, on that note, let's take a look at the foundation guns that should take a place of honor in your arsenal.

SHUCK AND JIVE

One of the best guns you can own in this modern world of advanced design and complicated shooting systems is a generic 12-gauge pump gun. What it might come with—a plastic stock, a set of sling swivels, recoil pad, and a barrel length that your comfortable with—will be covered later in the book, but those are extras. I want to talk about the foundation, the workhorse you can *live* with.

Your choices in this area boil down to a few. There's Remington and its age-old 870 Wingmaster or Special

Perhaps oddly, in terms of price, value quite often is less as applied to the hard-working shotgun. The non-working gun will have the most value attached to it, because of its add-on elements. Taking a finely built, work of art double gun, for example, you can drop the better part of $10,000 up front, and, to be fair, that's an amount some folks never miss when taking ownership of such marvels. These are good looking guns, to be sure, but, too often, shooting them is very limited, if ever.

I consider the ownership of such artwork to be a collector's-level engagement. Be advised, for the most part, these upper-end shotguns are not the stuff of this author's writings. Sure, the artwork-laden smoothbore can certainly be said to be a piece of pipe that's been taken to the uppermost levels of gun making art. At that level, such fine guns are priced correctly for what they represent—but so many hang on the wall or stay tucked safely away in a dark vault someplace. Yes, I can admire such work, but my guns are working guns. They see daylight every day.

An M-16 coupled to 12-gauge under-barrel for dual-purpose door breaching work and close-quarters shooting (right). Creative is the word, in a get-it-done assault system. (U.S. Army/Wikipedia photo)

(below) The new Remington Versa Max goes to work on a clays course at the Remington ammunition factory. It is a very well-made, state-of-the-art autoloader.

Above, one of the newer entries as an auto-loading shotgun today, this one a Browning Maxus. It's shown here, below, being field-tested as a prototype.

than the gun owned by the guide I hunted with in Arkansas, for flooded timber ducks. He had an 870 that was so old it was totally silver bright and pure as a mirror across its steel surface. He told me that if he shot it anyplace other than deep in the timber, where the overhead branches cut the reflection, he'd have to paint it black or green.

In a final tribute to my choice in shotguns, I will tell you that one of the most wealthy men in Arkansas, a fellow I have hunted with several times for flooded timber mallards, shoots his personal 870 that he *hand-painted* with a spray can of green and brown paint. This same hunter owns rifles and shotguns that figure into the tens of thousands of dollars, but he fields the old pump gun all the time. And with that, I rest my case for this old girl of the swamp, bush, and field.

IF YOU CAN'T GET ALONG WITH A PUMP GUN ...

To be sure, there are hunters who can't work a pump gun worth a darn. Why is this the case? To my way of thinking, these guys or ladies just don't shoot enough. If they did, the pump would go to work quite naturally for them. I have seen a practiced and acclimated marriage between shooter and pump gun work out far too many times for it to be pure fiction.

When the deal just won't come together, and sometimes it won't, then a different option is definitely in order. First up is the auto-loading shotgun. Why an autoloader, you ask? Because such is as close to a pump as you're going to get and, when it is working, it will do all the work you do to make a pump gun work for you. I guess you could say, "If you can't, it will."

Federal loads and Benelli guns pair with a literal boatload of hunters for a massive field test undertaking in Texas. Manufacturers take this stuff very seriously nowadays.

"Gas guns," as I call them, have their actions function through the use of a small amount of the expended gas from the round fired in the shotgun's chamber. This gas will open valves, push rods and, in the end, open the bolt far enough to allow the spent or hull to eject itself from the chamber and then allow a fresh round from the magazine to be picked up and replace it.

There are other, newer systems of auto-loading, designs found in the likes of the Benelli Super Black Eagle, the newer (2013) Browning A-5, and others, that, rather than making use of spent gas, work on a recoil system much as you'll find in a .22 auto-loading rifle. They employ a rotating bolt blowback action of sorts. This system is also somewhat like the original Browning A-5 long-recoiling barrel, that gun ejecting the cooked-off round, then replacing it in the chamber with a fresh shotshell without the aid of any barrel gas whatsoever.

The author with a West River Machine Welding/Karl Koenig custom-made Winchester Model 1300 using a Remington thread pattern and employing the author's own 724 Orion suppressor. At its heart, this is still a basic pump-action, despite its fancy appearance. More and more shotguns are becoming "black guns," while the country is on a war footing.

Regardless the system you select, the main thing you need to completely understand before putting down your hard-earned money is that any autoloader, no matter the brand or price tag, will require maintenance beyond that of a pump or hinge-action gun. Autos need a good deal of care, so, if you can't take the time to care for that gun system, forget it, because it is bound to let you down at some point in time.

Auto-loaders will range in price from $400 to more than $2,000, depending on brand and action type. In general, the higher priced guns will retain some better materials, as well as advanced design features overall, will have a reputation for positive function, and will offer a more varied level of finished treatments (camo patterns, for instance), stock configurations, and flexible load applications. That does *not* mean that many lower priced guns aren't worth your consideration. I have both in my working gun rack and have found that guns like the Mossberg 935 Ulti Mag 3½-inch

The side-by-side (right) has never been as popular in the U.S. as the over/under (below), but both are serviceable and available in prices ranging from just several hundred to more than $100,000 and higher.

semi-auto 12, just as well as a Winchester 3½-inch Super Mag X3 (this latter being one of the newer and better auto-loading guns in the commercial market today), will get the job done every day afield. In fact, at one point I hunted with the Mossberg 935 gas semi-auto in Argentina, on a three-day dove shoot that involved as many as 15 cases of shotshells a day, and without a single failure to function. That gun was flushed with solvent at the end of the day by Mossberg engineers, after having been disassembled to only a basic field-strip level, and promptly returned to work pounding hundreds of 2¾-inch low-grade South American-manufactured, slow, dirty-powder dove loads.

That remarkable Mossberg aside, remember that I told you that a clean semi-auto is a working semi-auto. Lacking that care, an auto-loader isn't much better than a single-shot scattergun, because it won't work for long. I speak from experience. This past year, in a duck blind out here in my hunting grounds of western South Dakota, I shot mallards coming into a stock tank, during first light and at 12-below zero. Hunting alongside four other hunters, of the five guns that came up to meet the incoming greenhead ducks, three failed to fire. All three of these guns were auto-loading 12-gauge magnums, and all three failed because gunk—debris, lube, carbon buildup, etc.—in the bolts, followers, and trigger mechanisms had frozen hard, locking down tight the actions, firing pins, and triggers. As to what did work: one 870 Express pump gun and a new Savage Stevens over/under Model 512 Gold Wing.

BREAK-OPEN SINGLES AND DOUBLES

With the thought covering that Savage stack barrel just mentioned, the last action type that is of a major consideration among sport shooters is the single-barrel or twin pipe hanged-action shotgun. Of the latter, this is where the prices go up, due to the level of hand fitting required of many of these guns during manufacturing. However, be advised that these guns are currently coming into the USA in record numbers and are being sold at very affordable prices in field gun configurations. Over the past several years, I have fielded

The author's old-school shotgun, above, is still turning out results in the field. It's just a piece of pipe, but one with great balance—and history to boot!

reliable, steadily working gun. The point here is that double guns no matter what their price are all at the high end of working gun priceless and they can quickly go off that chart, if you let that checkbook get away from you.

Again you have to ask the question, what do you get for the buck? Well, for one, double guns offer more flexibility in terms of choking for game, as they accommodate different choke tubes in each barrel. Too, doubles are a very dependable shooting system, because the actions are enclosed and stay relatively dirt free. Finally, in terms of balance and pointability, nothing tends to get that job done better than a smartly crafted stack-barrel or side-by-side.

In talking with European manufactures some time ago, I was informed that, in the Eastern Bloc countries, hunting quickly increased after communism went south. As such, double guns are, even today, greatly in demand and selling very well. Across the big pond, of course, doubles have always been the favored shotgun, largely because that was the double's home base. Of course, in some countries, auto-loading firearms are simply not allowed for use by the general public, but back here at home, during the 1920s, gun makers and importers couldn't come close to meeting the demand for double guns across the range of military, law enforcement, and sporting purposes. In all, their popularity is widespread.

The double doesn't rule everywhere. At the lowest end of the shotgun market, at least generally, is where the single-shot shotgun ranks No. 1. While ultra high-end single-shot trap guns can run a price tag off the charts, the simple H&R Topper, as shot by those gator hunters, or a Rossi Combo Gun, T/C Encore, or a New England Firearms Pardner, can all be put in the gun rack at a very reasonable cost. And they're great starter guns for youth and novice shooters hunting afield their first few times, as their single-shot nature makes them safer to use as training aids.

a number of them and found them to pass my acid-tough, hard-core swamp and field testing with flying colors.

Let's talk about "affordable" for a minute. To be sure, there are hunters who want to field a Krieghoff or high-end Browning. Those folks are going to go light in the wallet, but they're going to have a fine gun. Of course, there are also some for whom cost is absolutely no object at all and might turn to Remington's offering of the classic side-by-side Parker Gun at $49,000. A British best? Now you're at $100,000 and up. To the other end of the spectrum you'll find a Savage 512, Mossberg Silver Reserve, or Remington Premier STS, and you'll still get a modern,

Specialty single-shots do exist. Take, for instance, the Hastings single-shot Snake Charmer, which is a very short (still legal) stainless steel carbine that makes use of a cut-down stock that holds several rounds of 3-inch .410 ammunition. Such a scattergun is ideal for use as a pack gun for campers in snake country. Other manufactures like Rossi offer combination rifle shotgun hunting systems at budget prices, making it easy for almost anyone to get into a working field gun if they are interested in starting to hunt or shoot without a huge layout of cash.

HANDGUNS AS SHOTGUNS

As you can see, I've moved the concept of the shotgun as a piece of pipe a long way off dead center, but there's one final group of shotguns that, by far, outruns everything discussed here, in terms of being in a class of its own. Shotguns as handguns are becoming popular once again, much as they were back in the 1920s and prior to the laws enacted in the 1930s that banned the ownership of any handgun with a smooth-bore barrel under 18 inches and capable of firing a shotshell. That body of legislation was the National Firearms Act of 1934, and the cause behind its need was the abuse of cut-down shotguns and machine guns (machine gun sales also bit the dust in that legislation), by the era's infamous gangsters.

This two-shot Derringer is a shotgun, when packed with 2½-inch .410 buckshot or snake loads.

Today, unlike the old Holland & Holland "Burglar" gun, the Ithaca Model "B" Auto 1925 smoothbore double-barreled pistol, or a 410 Handy Gun (of which I have seen two in my lifetime), we instead have the T/C .45/.410-bore, Taurus' five-shot Tracker wheelgun in .45/.410, S&W's Governor of a similar configuration, and several other smaller brand single-shots. Why are these new handguns that shoot shotshells allowed? Because all of them retain some type of rifling in the bore and, as such, are classed as basic handguns in .45-caliber.

(top, above, and left)The author with a S&W Model 29 and the results of the CCI shot charge in the 44 Magnum. This buzz-worm never had a chance.

Taurus' Judge revolver started the trend in handguns turned scatterguns.

What can you do with these hand "shotguns?" Obviously, the fixed-breech Thompson/Center action or the wheelgun offered by Taurus are very short-range shooting propositions. I owned the T/C .45 Colt/.410 3-inch for years and never got it to do much more than pound barn rats or dust off a rattlesnake or two at point-blank ranges. Currently, I do retain the Smith & Wesson Governor six-shot wheelgun, but, again, this is not your daddy's 25-yard .410-bore. Shooting a short, 2½-inch .410 shotshell out of the gun's ultra-long cylinder, this revolver will, at best, roll up a buzz-worm encountered in a prairie dog's den or, at point-black range, finish off a grass rat wounded by a varmint rifle. These guns require the .45 Long Colt brass cartridge or the special Remington, Federal, or Winchester slugs or copper-plated lead BB 2¾-inch rounds, if firepower is the wished-for result. Regardless the brand or type, all these guns cross-chamber the .410-bore shotshell and .45 Long Colt metallic cartridge, which, again, makes them legal to own, and so be it. (As an aside, if there was ever a case for a gun control law that went astray, such is the prime example of making a .410-bore—which is not a gauge at all but, rather, a caliber—a crime to possess in a smoothbore firearm. If you can figure this one out, let me know, because I can't get my head around such laws.)

(right) Scott Butz, of Realwings Decoys, with the revamped Browning A-5, new in 2013. The old gun lives again.

(bottom) Remington staff testing shot charges in handguns at the ammunition plant. Note the ballistic gel in use for penetration research.

CHAPTER THREE

PUMP, DOUBLES, SINGLES, AND SEMI'S
Which Type's Best for You?

Doubles are fast handling and balance like a dream. This one in the author's hands is a Mossberg Silver Reserve.

While the shotgun may well be just a piece of pipe, as you've just seen, it comes in a wide range of t styles and, as such, meets a number of needs. I have a real strong place in my heart and gun safe for the basic pump-action shotgun—in my area of ballistics research, for instance, I use and just about wear out the 870 test guns that go to the test range, and I have on site better then 16 different barrels and 50 different chokes systems for them, mostly because the 870s are flexible gun systems and I can get review work done on new loads in prompt order, rather than running around searching for the right tool for the job. But that's me. For the new shooter, and even for the more experienced shooter who wants to maybe try something new, let's talk about the actions we reviewed in the last chapter in more detail and the applications to which they're best applied.

(below) A CZ stack-barrel out on the sporting clays course.

(bottom) The author's quick-handling stack-barrel on very fast doves. It's a combination that works.

BREAK-OPEN SINGLE-SHOTS AND DOUBLES

First on the list are the hinge-type actions, those single-shot and double-barrel break-open guns. These are great starter shotguns, especially for young shooters, as single-shots often wear exposed hammers that require manual cocking. Both single-shot and double-barrel break-opens are also easy to observe as being loaded or unloaded, when they are broken open.

I started my shotgunning days with a heavy double gun wearing exposed, "rabbit ear" hammers, and barrels that would only accept blackpowder. I guess that shows my age, but, at the same time, I have seen the total evolution of smoothbore guns from those "charcoal-burning" types right up to the present day wonder models.

My father put that ill-fitting blackpowder behemoth in my hands for local pheasant hunting with the old guys who had returned from WWII. Yet even with that challenges of that gun's poor fit, I did manage to hit something with it. My early adulthood was spent, among other endeavors, with almost 18 years as a hunter safety instructor in Minnesota, and 23 years as a street cop who also did some training of young officers. In both cases, shotguns came right to the forefront, especially when training novice shooters. I always liked working with these new students with light-

The author with a Zabala 10-gauge 3½-inch magnum. This gun is the top of the food chain, bar none.

weight single-barrels in a 12- or 20-gauge, such as the H&R Trapper or Topper models. A bonus with these very simple guns today? While most other shotguns can sport some fairly high prices, the Toppers can be picked up at a price that just about any shooter can afford nowadays. There are also special Pardner-Youth Models chambered in 20- and 28-gauge, and .410-bores that can be had for new youth shooters, and these models are designed, as the label implies, to better fit these smaller-bodied shooters.

On the other end of the break-open shotgun spectrum are the classic side-by-side doubles or "stack-barrel" over/unders. With these, the shooter can get

into a major amount of expended cash up front; on the extreme high end, doubles are wonderful pieces of function and art. On the "everyday" side of things, the doubles built by the brand names like Browning and Beretta, for example, can cost several thousand with ease, and even a general-purpose, no-frills "field" model can run upwards of two grand.

Okay, you've been warned about price, but here's the upside to doubles. In the first place, they make

Sleek and fast. You can't out-gun the two fastest shots in the world.

for great clay target guns, as they have outstanding balance in almost all grades and brands. They are, without a doubt, the dominant choice for serious skeet, sporting clays, and FITASC shooters. Second, they also tend to hold up very well among clay birds shooters and hunters alike when given regular, vigorous use—more bang for your buck, some would say. Now, a couple or three thousand, though the starting price point norm, still isn't in everyone's budget, but, today, that doesn't mean you have to be "stuck" with a pump. Companies like Mossberg now offer some very good stack-barrels and side-by-sides at prices that won't break the bank, those guns coming in under a grand. Best of all, I've found these "bargain" double-barrels tend to shoot very well and point like a dream. Both these facts and their lower price points fully demonstrate the advances made in many modern shotguns.

Something else to consider. Similar to the hinge-action shotgun, the falling block action is a rare bird

if found as a genuine (read "antique") piece, but, as offered in modern iterations through a number of outfits like Interstate Arms and some specialized gun dealers, you have guns such as the Winchester Model 87 Lever Double Coach. That gun, made so popular in *The Terminator* films while tied to Arnold's Harley Davidson, tend to show up quite often out here in western South Dakota. If such uniqueness is your cup of tea and you actually want to use one for sport—in my neck of the woods, we see them used in Cowboy Action events quite often—beware the copycat guns that come from China. In my experience, they are not well made and require a good gunsmith in most cases to get them running correctly.

PUMP-ACTIONS

While I have praised the modern pump-action gun in these pages, particularly the Remington Model 870 and the Mossberg 500s, I must allow a special place for

(opposite bottom) The author shooting the dedicated Ithaca slug gun that was developed, in part, from advanced military engineering back down the line a few decades or three ago.

(right) Eddie Stevenson, a friend and colleague of the author, with his limit of Canada geese by way of a Remington 887 pump gun. Built of almost all plastic, this space-age shotgun is an example of where gun art is going of late, and how the pump gun is becoming "modern" once again.

(below) The author at the bench with a Remington Model 887.

the very old Winchester Model 97 and Model 12, and Ithaca's Model 37. In my mind, these are the real backbone of pump gun development in the United States. These old guns, among a few others, paved the way as a truly American shotgun development; European shooters have never thought much of the corn shucker, for the "lowly" pump is a shotgun that leaves the gentleman's class of high-end English, German, and French hunting smoothbores a far stretch away. But here on U.S. soil, the pump gun has been the hand tool of the American stump jumper and the ridge running hunter who have made up so much of our gun history. These are the places and pastimes the pump continues to excel, but it's also taken on new life for self-defense purposes and in action shooting events such as 3-Gun competition, thanks to a bevy of tactical hardware add-ons that enhance the pump's utility and broaden its flexibility. In fact, you might say the pump has become everyman's shotgun.

I own and shoot a completely reconditioned Winchester Model 97 2¾-inch duck gun with a 30-inch barrel and a super-tight fixed Full choke, and, by way of called in birds, I have dusted off my fare share of trophy-class tom turkeys here in my home in the Black Hills of South Dakota. I'm not the only one who loves these old and still functional pumps. I'll always remember the northern Minnesota bush pilot who said to me, as he laid an old pump gun behind the seat of his Piper Super Cub, " I never leave home without it."

SEMI-AUTOS

Today, with the massive emphasis on war-fighting gun designs, new combat-style shooting games (3-Gun), and the general advancement of the modern shotguns, the auto-loader has moved to the top of the list as the preferred smoothbore of the American hunter and tactical games competitor, and is even making stronger inroads with the serious clay shooters. Why? Because they come loaded with innovations and are more durable than ever.

You'll pay for this. I honestly never thought I would see the day an auto-loading shotgun would be priced close to $2,000. Such a price point had always been left to the stack-barrels. Yet it would seem that the more you put into a modern auto-loading shotgun, the better results you're going to have in terms of service life and overall performance on clays courses or in the hunting field, not to mention in general fit of the gun to the shooter. With today's semi-autos, you're actually getting what you pay for.

A perfect example of this is the wonderfully built Winchester Super X-3. At about a grand and change, this is one hell of a gun buy, bar none, and, as such, I shoot two of them as general service and test guns often. Moving up the food chain, today's shooters will find the Benelli Model SBE (Super Black Eagle), Beretta Xtrema, and the Browning Maxus and re-vamped A-5 as auto-loaders at the top the list of upper end modern shotguns.

(above) The Winchester Super X-3 pictured here at the pattern bench is one of the best buys in an auto-loader today. The author says, "This is my ringneck gun hands down and has been for four years to date, with one pile of roosters fatally seeing its business end."

(right) Tom and Jerome, the author's good friends, with Remington 11-87s. The 1100 and 11-87 have been benchmarks in auto-loading gun design almost forever it seems.

(opposite) Scott Butz turns loose the Browning Maxus on spring snow geese. This shotgun is the epitome of cutting-edge technology in semi-auto shotguns.

A Winchester Super X-3 in a walnut stock.

Remember that short-barreled shotguns, those with tubes under 18 inches and/or overall lengths under 26 inches, will have you paying the NFA tax to be legal.

So what's changed with auto-loading shotguns to warrant such popularity and pricey sales tags? For the most part, it's about engineering advances and raw materials. Today we see titanium, special aircraft-type alloys, advanced plastics, and even carbon fiber materials coming into the initial design phase of the modern shotgun. These materials are often hard to work with, as well as difficult to source as their own initial raw products. Action designs matter, too. Everything from inertia blowback systems on up to the ultra-modern gas valve designs have taken over the marketplace, but not after about 20 years of research and development. I know, as I have owned, tested, and fielded almost every one of them at one time or another.

Remember that auto-loaders require more maintenance than other action types. Yes, the modern auto-loading shotgun can take a pounding and work a very long time under some nasty field conditions and high rates of fire, but, in the end, it will need some specialized care, most of that attention going towards its action and gas or blow-back operating system. Neglect this, and eventually you'll be reduced to a single-shot gun with shell storage.

Or not. Could be that along with the higher price tags and all their mechanical advancements, detailed and frequent maintenance of auto-loaders has actually become a thing of the past. I ran across a fellow, recently, who owned a Winchester Super X3. He asked me about when he needed to take the gun to a gunsmith for general maintenance. I found that he had owned the auto-loader for a period of five years and had never done anything but load it with shotshells. And this guy was not a weekend warrior, but, rather, nearly a professional hunter, as many tend to be, here in the far western side of my state. I was pleased to be sitting down, when he told the story, and, at that point, I

(opposite, below, and above) The author with Kel-Tec's futuristic KSG—Kel-Tec Shotgun—a short-barreled, high-tech defensive firearm adorned with Picatinny rail and a unique dual-magazine tube. It meets regular-Joe specs, at 26.1 inches overall and a barrel length of 18½ inches.

asked to see the gun. When I set my eyes on the black, gritty, spent powder mess, I was flat-out *amazed* that it still functioned—*at all.* I've never seen Winchester/Browning Arms run a test gun through something like what this gun had been subjected to, but it spoke *volumes* for just how darn good these new systems are.

As a last note, and all that said, in my mind, semi-autos are best left to more advanced shooters, as these guns are among the type most likely to develop an unintentional discharge. I never start a new or young hunter out with an auto-loader. To me, that's asking for trouble. Proper gun handling, time over the sights, and flat-out experience all count for a whole lot, when taking up an auto-loading gun. Training before handling them is mandatory.

THE DEFENSIVE GENRE

Included in the list of buyer options today are the fast-emerging styles of shooting game scatterguns, those specifically aimed at action and speed-shooting sports like 3-Gun. Really, we've come to have an entire industry designed around this approach, whether for games or for actual home- and self-defense use.

These are the shotguns for the twenty-first century, those super-short, bullpup-type auto-loaders, three-barrel coach guns, ultra high-capacity alley sweepers, and military police point man and entry door breacher combat pieces. You'll see names like the Atchison Assault-12 (AA-12), Daewoo's USAS-12, Kel-Tec's KSG, Century Arms' Saiga, and Pancor's Jackhammer, among more than 70 others in current, worldwide production that make up the truly impressive list of emerging defensive smoothbores.

There's a lot of variety to choose from in this genre. When you get right down to it, for the most part, a simple side-by-side coach-style 12-gauge, with either exposed or internal hammers, can defend the fam-

It is the guns like this Kel-Tec KSG—not over/unders, not sporting semi-autos, not any other traditon-based design and regardless their refinements—that are leading modern shotgun design today. And why wouldn't they? This gun is just downright cool!

ily quite well. What the new tools you're seeing now bring to the forefront is pure firepower. This is particularly true in the cases of the military/police models USAS-12 and AA-12, whose effects can be devastating against an enemy combatant. The AA-12, actually originally developed in the early 1970s, is a full-auto shotgun in a bullpup configuration. This gun is noted as serving as the platform for Daewoo's USAS-12 design, offered in both selective fire and full-auto configurations. Obviously, these aren't generally available to those outside military and law enforcement realms (though some short-barreled version can be purchased and shot with the appropriate BATFE tax stamp), but they do serve as examples of just how advanced the shotgun can be, when designed for such applications. Expect to see more shotguns like these in civilian-legal versions in the future.

STEP BACK, NOW

Just as we should explore the realm of the super-combat gun, it's also worth a turn back in history to view our older gun systems, the muzzleloaders or, as like to call them, "charcoal burners." Some turn up their nose at the idea of one, I guess because some don't consider them as lethal. However, as evidenced by my Pedersoli side-by-side, as well as my time with the breechloading blackpowder shotgun I had as a boy, these guns will absolutely turn some heads in the game harvesting department. Because blackpowder loads generally run out of the muzzle around 900-plus fps, and because I have developed many specialized commercial loads that don't return much more velocity then that from a modern smokeless firearms, I can tell you that nothing and no one ever wants to ever get in front of something moving that fast, even when driven "only" by blackpowder (or its modern substitutes).

Some time ago, I hunted at a writer event, in central South Dakota, in which a fellow brought

along his English, handmade, rabbet ear-hammered 12-gauge muzzleloader to be used on the hunt. He was writing about the gun at the time and said that, over a good dog, which he also had with him, he could expect many successful shots at or under 30 yards. Being the hunter was a good shot and knew the elements involved in working up a good 1 1/8-ounce load of No. 6 lead shot for this special smoothbore muzzleloader, his hit ratio was, indeed, nothing less then impressive.

Would you want a muzzleloading shotgun as your primary field or clays gun? Are they leading the way as "modern" shotguns? Of course not, but they do hold a valuable place in shotgunning and shouldn't be left off your radar screen. Not only do they make a nice change of pace from the traditional smokeless powder shotguns, they provide a way to explore shooting games like Cowboy Action shooting or vintage clays tournaments, and they may extend your hunting season, where special muzzleloader times are designated.

THE CHOICE FOR YOU

Regardless the action design, brand, or gauge you're thinking about buying, the major question always remains, what type of shooting are you going to do with your gun? Some friends I know shoot nothing but clay birds and are almost never to be found in the field hunting warm targets. Others are waterfowl specialists who spend all their available season scouting and hunting both ducks and geese. Where does that position the modern shotgun and how you choose?

Much of the choice is as simple as you'd think it would be. If you're going to spend vast amounts of time hanging around dedicated waterfowl hunters, buying a high-grade stack-barrel double may not be the best idea. Instead, a well-made and camo-coated or flat black pump or semi-auto will do the job much better (and stay better looking over the long haul). Yes, lots of shotguns can server a number of purposes and applications. Once upon a time they had to, but if anything says we've truly arrived at the age of the modern shotgun, it is that that is no longer the case. There's so much variety, so much specialization, that, if you're going to dabble seriously in one area or another, it will likely pay for you to get involved with a gun dedicated to your particular pursuit. Indeed, it's that idea of dedicated purpose that defines today's modern shotgun. Celebrate it.

SHOTGUN LIFESPAN
Just How Long Will Yours Last?

CHAPTER FOUR

Beretta AL391s have a very long lifeline. Duck hunters and South American dove shooters often gravitate to them, because of this reason. They point very well.

Let's cut to the chase. For the most part, the average hunter won't ever shoot their gun enough to wear it out. That event is reserved for yesteryear's market hunters, professional clay circuit shooters, and possibly old gun writers who live in the outback and shoot at something almost every day. Even at that, it's a real stretch to even think about turning today's shotguns to junk due to shooting in terms of round count. That said, there are some danger signs that indicate a shotgun that is about to give up the ghost, and these signs are especially pertinent to you if you're exploring purchasing a used gun.

Let's say that, for about 30 years, your favorite shotgun has been sending duck loads toward fast-flying mallards, but, of late, you've noticed some wear in places where there hadn't been any a couple years ago. You ask yourself the obvious question: what is the lifeline of this shotgun, in terms of needing major repair? Is it time to replace my gunning tool, or do I hang with it until something breaks down?

When I give talks or answer the phone to reader calls about one of my several ballistic columns, often I'm asked what someone can expect in terms of a reasonable working lifetime from a shotgun? The answer to that question can involve many elements, such as the amount of use the gun gets each season, the types of loads run through it, and the general care given the gun after each hunt. Most know this, but a few years ago an event came together that gave me some new insight into the subject of gun wear and, in doing so provided a new and better answer to the question of shotgun longevity.

During the summer of 2002, I was requested by a manufacture to field test loads in sub-sonic variants, as well as take several new guns afield for function testing. The primary test and the real question at hand was, how well would they hold up to some of the highest volume wingshooting available: doves, specifically the "Macha" roost, the largest in the world and retaining more birds than I had ever imagined existed in one place.

This would be the testing grounds that would produce conditions that could wear out most auto-loading shotguns in less then six weeks of full-time hunter use, an the guns would be rental guns employed by the local outfitters. I remember thinking, *Wow, six weeks and a gun requires rebuilding or worse?* Now, I'd seen Beretta stack-barrels at very high-end sporting clays clubs down in Mississippi, that had had ammo running through them for years of rental service, but even the thought of a gun wearing down in as little as a few weeks was hard to get my brain around.

Hunting with the Trek International Safaris opera-tion, out of Jacksonville Beach, Florida, guided by H&H Outfitters (www.HandHDoves.com), located in Kearny, Nebraska, and managed by Bjorn Terpstra, in Cordoba, Argentina, I was set up in carefully selected blinds located directly on passage routes that held tens of thousands of birds morning and afternoon. Here it was possible to shoot 50 boxes of shotshells before lunch, then another 50 boxes after a couple hours rest. Believe me when I say that I would never have bought into this story if I had not actually been there and taken part in some of the shooting myself. (I say some shooting, because,

The author knows that one way to test the life of a gun is to have a go with it on South American doves.

Hardcore Waterfowl in Uruguay

As if the experience in Argentina hadn't been enough, the country across the bay, Uruguay, several years earlier had gotten the call to test the then-new Kent Cartridge Matrix Impact shot. The hunt was primarily for waterfowl, and the event produced duck guns that got warm fast and stayed that way until very liberal limits of waterfowl were gunned every morning. Later in the day, those same guns would be turned to grouse and pigeon work.

Shooting case after case of the Kent Impact shot, everything held up well—but only if a regiment was generated for cleaning the semi-autos completely each evening, as well as running solvent through extractors and locking block parts on the stack-barrels. We did see extractors lock up and the semi-autos reject feeding fresh rounds from time to time, but these were normal function problems; given the fact that that Uruguay shoot, one held under Trek, Inc., can produce the best and fastest duck gunning in the world, it was hard to ask more of a scattergun. This kind of longevity over hard use and really what amounted to minimal maintenance, is a testament to the modern shotgun.

being the reporter, photographer, and interviewer, I was restricted to the amount of time I was able to spend over the barrel of one of the test guns.)

It was while going through my own series of tests with some Rizzini stack-barrels and my self-designed Metro Gun Systems, and then the hunt in Argentina, that I came to realize that I might have, for the first time, an answer to the question about the lifespan of a shotgun, lifespan in terms of when that smokepole will start to fail or at least show wear and parts failure. Be advised, my friends, that I have tried to run shotguns through what I and most others would consider *extensive* testing, actually working to get the core mechanical systems into trouble during new gun test projects. The problem has always been getting enough rounds through a system to produce some element of failure. Well, Argentina and its never-ending streams of doves fixed that. For the first time, there would be *cases* of shotshells expended each day through the test guns. Hunters who came before and after me would, together, expend a load count of 50,000 rounds in only a few short weeks time through the guns in the Treks/H&H rental department.

My first solid information about such expectations from those rental guns came during a discussion with some of the top guides at H&H Outfitters. With them, I found that it was quite common to need to totally rebuild an auto-loader in less then six weeks time of use. Bags of parts were brought into the country all the time, just to keep those self-stuffers up and working. Now, some would assume the guns were all low-grade junk. Not at all. In fact, some of the best in the business were represented; indeed, Beretta AL391s were at the top of the use list in H&H's rental gun department. What was clearly the problem, since it wasn't gun quality was that the guns not only shot *massive* amounts of game loads, but they went through those loads fast and hard. Indeed, shooters in the field would use a pair of matching shotguns and keep a bird boy loading at his back, while he emptied the magazine of the gun in his hands. With that gun empty, a quick pass back and forth to his loader put the freshly loaded gun in his hands. This was repeated all day long, empty gun exchanged for a loaded gun.

With shooting under these kinds of conditions, the major enemy to gun parts, even whole receivers, is heat stress. These guns are, after all, only steel, and they can take just so much stress before things start to fold. While I did not see a single failure in the Berettas (and I watched one shooter clear better the 47 boxes of shotshells on one morning's shoot), I was told that those Berettas were taken back each and every night to the gunsmith, completely stripped to the bare wood, and cleaned, checked, oiled, and reassembled for the next day in the field. Remember, this and others like it are very high-grade hunting operations, full five star programs,

and their owners and managers don't want guns failing the customer at any time.

By now you're probably thinking that this is all a nice story, but what's this got to do with your gun? How much can that duck scattergun of yours take before you're forced to head for the sporting goods store in search of a new replacement?

The take away from the high-volume shooting in Argentina, the kind of volume you're never likely to experience anywhere else, the first factor I see is that your gun's longevity is about fighting off heat. In general, duck hunters don't shoot fast enough, nor usually in super hot environmental conditions, to build up much heat in a gunning system. That's good news, because, compared to those guns in Argentina, the life of your working gun is thereby extended by massive amounts. I would say at least a third more active gunning time before things start to fall apart.

"A third?" you ask. "A third of *what*?"

About a third of 50,000 rounds, which can add at least another 15,000 shells through your shotgun. By taking the heat factor out of your gun use equation, the gun should run up to 65,000 rounds if it's a top-end shooter from the get go. Shotguns in this group include those from Beretta, Benelli, and Fran-

Thriving Birds in Argentina

While you may think shooting as it happens for doves in Argentina is depleting the resource, nothing could be further from the truth. With 2.5 nesting cycles each year in the Argentine Macha roost, the numbers of birds have been on an increase each year, even with routine heavy gunning. In actuality, the birds are saved from disease through controlled numbers, and they can't be eliminated using hunters and shotguns. Too, being each bird eats one ounce of grain a day and the birds number in the multi-millions, farmers welcome some kind of basic control over the doves that have become varmints in this beautiful country, the Land of Silver. I believe this type of sustainable commercial hunting is a great ecological indicator of what can work when there is little or no general hunting by local folks.

chi, to name three that have been stress-tested down on that never-ending Argentinian string of flying targets.

Okay, but those are semi-autos. What about an over/under? Well, here you can expect up to 100,000 rounds of trouble-free performance, first because the gun can not be reloaded as quickly as a semi-auto, and second (and partly because of the first), it won't build up heat as quickly in general. I have shot, as indicated previously, a Beretta over/under that had been regularly used as a rental gun on the sporting clays course at the Willows

Sporting Clays and Hunting Center, in Mississippi. That shotgun has run through more than 100,000 rounds, and the gun was still in good working order when I used it. While the wood was bleached and stained by skin oils, and while the checkering was almost gone on the fore-end, the guts of the locking system and firing mechanism were solid as a rock. That says a whole lot for stack-barrels of a quality manufacture. Beretta isn't the only maker to be considered here. Indeed, you have a huge selection of upper-end doubles that will get the job done, starting with the Beret-

Want to know what guns hold up? Head to a busy sporting clays or skeet range that has rental guns. If the staff's on top of things, they're keeping logs of the number of times a gun goes out and how many rounds get run through it, plus, of course, the maintenance logs that go along with them. This kind of information nearly always immediately tells you which models are worth your time and money.

tas and moving to the guns from Browning, Rizzini, or Caesar Guerini, among a host of others too long to list here and which I have shot long and hard.

Find an active skeet and sporting clays range that has a rack full of rental guns and talk to the pro shop folks about which ones make the grade. Most well-equipped ranges keep a log of how often each gun goes out and the estimated number of rounds put through them, and the range operators know which guns are down for repairs more than others.

WHAT THIS MEANS FOR YOUR SHOTGUNNING

Knowing the outer limits of a shotgun's life says that, for most of us, a scattergun will likely last the life of the shooter, given some small repairs and parts replacements. During the test hunt illustrated, the extractor on the gun I was using (my own Remington Express 3½-inch mounting the Metro Gun System), gave way and started to become a part-time working unit. This gun's receiver had been shot in South American on another occasion, had hunted ducks and doves in Mexico, and had been maintained as a test gun for my own ballistics projects during the previous four-year period. Nevertheless, it held up well in Argentina (and, indeed, overall), regarding all the major parts in the gun system. Even today, it still shoots well, and that Remington pump gun will see many more rounds through it before it's set aside.

Taking any shotgun into the type of extreme gunning environment as is found in Argentina will, without question, draw life out of the steel that makes up the shotgun's heart. *Massive* shooting will start the countdown toward the gun's demise. Know, too, that while rifles primarily burn out chamber throats, shotguns will start to come unglued in *every* respect, when the day comes around for a replacement.

If you shoot less than a case of shotshells a year, it would require 50 years to equal a few weeks of what a semi-auto rental gun goes through on the Macha dove roost and travel pass in Argentina. Once your gun hits that kind of usage, and just as the Macha guns experience every night, the semi-auto will require parts and refitting. If it's a double barrel, well, it'll be starting to show its age, but will still be in working order.

I haven't talked about pumps much in this particular conversation, but they'll fall someplace in the middle of all this. There's really very little information existing about corn-shuckers and high-stress use. And because of the style and price tag involved in hunting places like Argentina, one of the few places that can produce such high-volume, high-stress shooting, it is very unlikely that much information will ever surface,

When it's all said and done, if you're the average shooter—a trip or three to the sporting clays range each month, dove and duck seasons during the fall— it's unlikely you'll shoot one of today's modern semi-autos or double barrels enough to need more than a parts replacement here and there. Yes, they're that good.

Longevity in a gun is relative, at least in part, to its gauge. It should be obvious that regularly running duck and goose loads through a big 10-gauge like these above isn't the same thing as running skeet loads through a 20-gauge.

in terms of low-grade pump field shotguns and their lifespan. Let's face it, if you have the money to hunt way down south, you are most likely going to rent or own an upper-grade smoothbore to meet the task at hand, and it won't be a pump-action.

As a final note, consider this: Shooting a 3½-inch heavy magnum waterfowl load in your shotgun is like shooting 100-plus rounds of lightweight target ammunition. In other words, the load selected has a direct effect on the overall lifespan of the shooting system.

This is why you'll see old 10-gauge guns start to loosen in the hinge areas, with locks fitting not as tightly as they once did. Everything in our 10-gauge is big-time hard on a receiver. In other words, the 10-gauge's .775 bore ain't your little sister's 20-gauge trap gun. I can even take this argument all the way to the very massive commercial 4-gauges of a generation or three ago and which I've had the opportunity to shoot a few times. These guns shoot 4-inch paper hull shells, weigh upwards of 30 pounds empty, and sound like a naval gun bombarding the beach at Normandy during WWII. The guns I shot, still shot, but all had been re-sleeved, their actions reworked, and their locks tightened after years of heavy load fatigue.

Guns wear out, without a doubt. But, over the long haul, you're going to have to do one pile of shooting to ever see that take place in an average shooter's lifetime, when the modern shotgun is between the hands.

Others Making the Grade

So as not to sit on one brand or type of smoothbore, I'll tell you that another group of hunters who traveled with my partner and me on that Argentina shoot used Remington 11-87s and Browning BPS (Browning Pump Shotgun) 12-gauges. Hunting nearby us, they found that their guns performed well in the field, the group successfully shooting a mixed bag hunt of both dove and grouse. As to the number of rounds spent? Well, they had about enough cash left in their pockets for a cup of coffee and exit taxes, by the time they returned to the airport. Two thumbs up for the 11-87 and BPS.

In recent years, I have hunted Argentina with Mossberg, while testing its new double guns and auto-loaders. I found that because of their ultra-modern technology and materials, what most consider to be budget shotguns are giving a good showing, when applied to massively round counts. For those with more constrained wallets, these are absolutely guns well worth exploring, even for those who'll put the guns to hard use.

THAT THING THAT GOES BANG!

CHAPTER FIVE

In all cases, the type of shotshell you select to use will dictate the success or failure you will experience when shooting a shotgun. For example, hauling a box of 2¾-inch No. 7 steel shot loads into the field for mallard ducks over decoys just won't cut it, in terms of producing the necessary range options and game killing energy required under most field conditions. You'll need to make better choices, if such an activity is on your agenda, but there are so many choices out there now, where do you begin to look?

Let's start by dividing the dozens and dozens of loads available in the sporting market into several categories.

The first are the upland or game bird loads that, in most cases, are still comprised of lead pellets. Of course, waterfowl hunting here in the U.S. mandates the use of non-toxic shot, i.e., non-lead, which comes in all sorts of forms, from steel and bismuth shot pellets to tungsten alloys, the Hevi-Shot brand, and others. But there's a trend here, in the non-toxic realm; more areas of the USA and Europe now require non-toxic shot loads for all sorts of hunting, in the increasing

movement toward "green" ammunition usage. In fact, at the time of this writing (Summer 2013), the state of California has just outlawed any and all lead shot for hunting purposes, regardless the caliber or gauge. As many have been saying for some time now, requirements for total non-toxic shot are coming on fast.

The second group of shotshells the ammunition industry offers, and by far the most used of all, are the general purpose and clay target loads. Here those No. 7 steel shot loads previously mentioned could find a home on the target range or for use as a general farm-yard pest control tool. Clays loads are varied in design, depending on the target sport being shot, while those close cousin general-purpose loads often are marketed as "budget-priced" ammunition. Federal Cartridge, by example, actually offers a special 12-gauge 2¾-inch No. 8 lead shot load called "General Purpose."

The third group of shotshells can be regarded as big-game fodder. Here the shotgun slug or buckshot loads come to the forefront. Slugs are deadly short-range projectiles, and buckshot is an alley-sweeping tool that ranks alone in terms of its ability to inflict effective damage to large warm targets. When evaluating these load types, a move into the police or military market and self-defense propositions are a natural progression.

There's a subgroup of the types of rounds intended for big-game and defense. In military circles, the use of darts (called "flechettes"), buckshot, or advance explosive munitions fired from either standard or specialized auto-loading shotguns come to the front of the class. These specialized guns and loads keep the shotgun as a point man (first guy up front) entry gun.

Because modern military and police shotshell ammunition can be designed to minimize the collateral damage that would be expected from a solid projectile, these are often the tools of entry teams and individual officers in the field. As a street police officer for some 23 years myself, I often relied on the standard, squad-mounted 12-gauge pump gun as my first line of heavyweight defense and, while I never had to actually use that riot gun, I am sure that, at various times, that gun made the difference between the bad guy assuming the position versus starting and escalating a fight in the street (or worse).

Clearly, shotshells today come in a dizzying variety. But, since most lead shot rounds have seen relatively little change over the decades (other than some periodic innovations in wad design and the rare hull change, as occurred with Winchester AA hulls awhile back), and since military and law-enforcement rounds are a genre all to themselves and often unavailable to the general public, I'm going to focus on today's non-toxic shot. It's probably the least understood by the average shooter. Yet it's the one area of shotshell ammunition that's seen an *explosion* in design and performance changes in recent years, and as the case of California illustrates, this is more than a trend for some (and one you can expect more mandating legislating on, in more places, for more game, in the months and years to come). Let's get to it!

NON-TOXIC SHOTSHELLS
Making Waves and Breaking New Ground

CHAPTER SIX

FEDERAL PREMIUM AMMUNITION

BLACKCLOUD™

EXPERIMENTAL
BLACK CLOUD - SNOW GOOSE
12GA, 3IN, 1 1/8OZ STEEL BB @
1635FPS

1¼ OUNCE | BB SHOT

CARTOUCHES

Federal's Black Cloud is at the top of the pile in shotshell design and performance today. Note the "Experimental" label on this box of Black Cloud. Ballistics Research & Development, the author's own business, often got these T&E rounds before anyone else, for use in wet bird review.

a s a ballistics writer for *Wildfowl Magazine, Shotgun Sports, Dakota Outdoorsmen, The Varmint Hunter*, and other freelance endeavors over an almost 30-year period, I have been in close touch with many developments in non-toxic shotshell load applications. What follows are selected field studies, making use of some of the newer types of modern non-toxic shot. I have started with the more advanced non-toxic loads, because these are the "designer" applications, what shooters I know and hunt with refer to as the "king of the hill" loads.

FEDERAL BLACK CLOUD—A DUCK AND GOOSE KILLING MACHINE

It was late in the day, as a flock of mallards descended upon our small section of chopped corn field that lay a few miles east of the Wyoming line. South Dakota in the late duck season can be windy and cold. Both conditions were present, on this not so very nice evening.

As I rolled over in my layout blind, trying to get a better look at the low and fast-flying birds using the 40 mph wind as a booster rocket, I completely missed the pair that had turned into the wind and were now descending from almost straight overhead. The hunter to my left hadn't missed catching sight of the pair though, and, with a swing of his 12-gauge followed by a sharp, high-velocity crack, the drake came to a dead stop against the wind, then dropped like a sack of rocks straight into the cut corn.

That shot made by my partner, to my knowledge, was one of the first kills made with a prototype Federal Cartridge steel shot load dubbed "Black Cloud." That duck had not just been hit by a payload of No. 2 steel, it had been *bent over backwards* by the impact at a strong, 55 yards downrange.

Black Cloud is different and, for the most part, it represents the first real advance made in common steel shot ammunition since non-toxic shot became mandatory for waterfowl hunters decades ago. Before it happened on the scene, Remington and Federal had tried mixed payloads of two and three shot sizes, respectively, in hopes of sweetening up the payload energy. But these "Duplex" loads by Remington, and Triplex loads by Federal, didn't hang on long. For the most part, they were still just basic steel shot loads, with little or no real advantage over a load consisting of just a single shot size. At least that's what the experts are saying. Later in this book, I'll take on that subject and pull it apart to show that doing away with multiple pellet size loads was a mistake and, today, these load types are coming back into use afield. But that's for later. For now, back to the Black Cloud.

Black Cloud is different from other steel shot designs in that Black Cloud's steel shot load in a 3-inch hull makes use of a roughly 60/40 mix of steel and a special Black Cloud pellet. For the first 1¼-ounce test load, for instance, the No. 2 steel is loaded to a 60-percent total payload value, while the new and deadly Black Cloud steel balls, which have a cutting edge ring around the belt or center of the pellet, are loaded

Federal's Black Cloud is a duplex load of sorts, though not of two different shot sizes, but rather of two different shot types. The dark pellets with the mid-line ridge are the proprietary Black Cloud pellets, and they're mixed at a roughly 40-percent ratio to the 60-percent ration of regular steel to produce the full payload.

to about 40-percent of the payload's total value. (Wow! Who would have thought? Are we back into multiplex shot sizes already? Not quite, hang on.)

This new shot type was actually developed some time back, when Federal turned to a different production method for manufacturing tungsten-iron pellets. The new steel pellet referred to here is made like a capsule of sorts, with two halves joined together. The joining leaves this added band around the middle, which looks much like a ring on the planet Saturn. When I first saw this ring, I gave it a name: "power belt." I'd found that, in use with those early tungsten shot pellets, that this belt of steel material would produce some additional damage as the pellet moved through tissue. It would seem that a singular steel shot size that used this " power belt" system, or as Federal calls it, "FS," would be able to inflict damage much as had those early tungsten pellets. "FS," by the way, stands for "Flitestopper," a brand name is becoming a household phrase among wet-bird shooters of late.

TESTING BLACK CLOUD

I have to tell you, the loads I was issued for testing didn't look much like the Federal product you see now—at all. Marked only with an engineering label that displayed the payload weight and velocity, the 3-inch hulls were black in color and lacked any head stamp that would identify them as Federal Cartridge ammunition. I cut apart one of these sample loads and found that Federal had used a very new, high-performing wad labeled "Flightcontrol." Flightcontrol wads were first designed for long-range turkey hunting, and they'd been coupled for that application with Heavyweight shot, another product developed by Federal in recent years. What this wad can do is amazing, to say the least. Here's a general overview of how the Flightcontrol system works.

This wad is designed to fly with its petals at the rear of the wad, versus the common front-opening petals system. When the wad leaves the barrel, the payload is trapped in a solid tube of plastic, with only the back end of the wad opening its petals to start a slow process of releasing the payload. Along the wad's walls are several slits that act as stabilizers, keeping the wad true in flight. In effect, this wad will add about 10 more effective yards to almost all steel shot sizes, because the payload of more than 500 grains is working *as a single unit* much further downrange, as compared to the standard front-open wad system, which starts its release of the payload almost at the muzzle. Now, add the Flitestopper pellets to the mix, which produce a higher level of target damage, and you have a new and far more effective steel shot load that *lacks the added cost of tungsten shot.* (By the way, tungsten shot today is fast exiting the sporting shotshell scene.)

Now, I have been testing a variety of other shot shapes, so as to gain some insight into developing a more effective steel shot load. This new Federal Cartridge Black Cloud Flight-control system, to my way of thinking, makes a whole lot of sense, because it keeps cost down while, at the same time, giving the hunter a truly effective field tool. To be sure, Black Cloud is right up my alley, as I have been a student of velocity, terminal damage, and general performance improvements in both lead and steel shot fodder for better then 25 years. I tried to design just this type of system on the cheap, many years ago, by using a 20-gauge plastic hull inserted, as a secondary payload delivery system, in a 10-gauge hull, as far back as 1979. I almost had it done save for adding the solid gas seal to the 20-gauge tube

Federal Flitecontrol wads after firing, a 10-gauge in the black next to a 12-gauge. These wads stayed together all the way down-range—not your standard wad design at all, to be sure.

insert and those rear-opening petals. After giving up my project in frustration, I simply went to the exclusive use of the 10-gauge magnum and larger shot for just about all my waterfowling needs.

PATTERN TARGETS

During my pattern work with Black Cloud, I relied on three test guns. First was the Benelli Super Black Eagle (SBE) mounting a Modified factory choke. Second was a Mossberg 935 3½-inch mounting the Undertaker Decoy choke, while the third gun was the new Mossberg Reserve Series over/under using the factory Win Choke-style Modified tubes. I chose these guns as they were and are examples of current field guns in use on a regular basis. I also wanted to gain some insight as to their performance to 50 yards against the standardized 30-inch patterning circle. The chart below is an overview of my pattern targets shot at 50 yards with the No. 2 Federal Black Cloud. Note that

I did not shoot these loads at 40 yards, because I was allowing for the 10-yard increase in effective range based on Federal's new wad design.

Three years prior to my testing of the waterfowl loads, I'd gunned some of the first turkeys taken by way of Federal Flitecontrol wads, while in western South Dakota, and realized that, after two birds had met their maker at 60 yards, the world of 12-gauge smoothbore ballistics was about to change—big time.

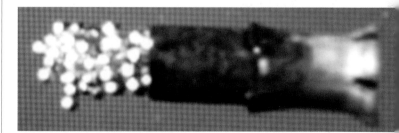

The Federal Flitecontrol wad retains all its payload, even 10 feet off the muzzle. Retained in this manner, the payload acts like a slug of sorts, versus a loose pattern of shot, during its initial yards of travel.

Pattern Black Cloud No. 2, 1¼-ounce, 3-inch 12-gauge

	Pattern 1	Pattern 2	Pattern 3	Average*
Benelli Super Black Eagle, Modified choke:	77%	74%	86%	79%
Mossberg 935, Undertaker Decoy Modified choke:	80%	72%	68%	73.3%
Mossberg Reserve Series (top barrel) Modified choke:	74%	72%	79%	75%

Legend: Elevation 3,000 feet above sea level. Temp 60 degrees Fahrenheit. Wind following five to 10 mph. Ranging via Bushnell 1500 (cross check). Total payload of No. 2 FS = 57 pellets; standard steel = 85 pellets; total payload = 142 pellets (hand count) *Based on three-shot average.

Todd Gifford, a local friend of the author's, in the duck marsh with some spring snows taken with Black Cloud and his Beretta semi-auto.

WORKING WITH BLACK CLOUD

Over-choking Black Cloud is not the way to approach this new direction in steel shot fodder. (In fact, I'm not sure you need any choke *at all* with this system.) Hands-on, recent field-testing examples of shots on puddle and diver ducks on the Texas Gulf Coast suggest that when staying with any form of a standard Modified constriction, Black Cloud will, without question, get the job done. That is why I stayed with the Modified tubes in all three pattern test guns. I also used three guns to illustrate that regardless the gun, this new ammunition will take a liking to just about any smoothbore barrel. In effect, the Black Cloud payload and wad system *creates its own performance values* and, if choked open enough to allow it to do its work, the rest will take care of itself.

Since those first prototype loads, Black Cloud has been improved several times. This is how the current iteration comes packaged.

REAL TIME TESTING

We can talk about the effects of terminal or at target ballistics all day long, but the actual hunting of warm targets counts for a whole lot in load review. During the period I had Black Cloud in house for testing, two hunts were arranged. As you can see from the pattern data on the previous page, the new ammo was devastating on paper, but, when reviewing the actual hunt results, other outstanding observations came to light.

The first hunt with Black Cloud took place over deep, warm, natural springs, just across the Wyoming border, in South Dakota. This was our late season honey hole of sorts and tended to produce great greenhead shooting that could either be in your face or at pass-shooting ranges, with lots of in between "normal" ranges. For my purposes, I wanted to experience normal range decoy hunting with the Black Cloud.

My partner of the day was a local hunter from western South Dakota, and he'd scouted the warm spring hole well, for we were set up in a grass blind with the sun to our back and wind in our face. With first light, mallards started to dump into the hole, first as singles, later in numbers. Allowing the birds to drop in and then flare over the decoys, I asked my partner to take his shots at about 45 to 50 yards, as the birds left the area, so as to duplicate the paper pattern ranges. (We worked out the range with the Bushnell 1500 laser rangefinder.) For the most part, all the ducks gunned were killed within 45 to 50 yards downrange. Truly, this was the perfect range application of the No. 2 steel at high velocity combined with the added energy of the Black Cloud system.

With pack ice covering about half the hole and warm water openings out in front of us, the wad recovery was an easy process. In fact, we could spot the spent Flightstopper wads on the ice as far away as a ranged 80 yards. Yes, wad distance after dropping its payload was to an extreme range of 80 yards, and all of those spent units flew at least to the 60-yard range. If you think wind was a factor, not so, as there was just enough air moving to keep the birds in check and coming in at a predictable angle.

With birds recovered and in the freezer for later review, a second hunt took place three days later. For this one we'd turned south of Rapid City, South Dakota, on the road to Nebraska, hunting a well-scouted honey hole that was the exclusive killing fields of my hunting partners, who had spent days surveying the area for wintering mallards. These local guys had hit a dead-sure spot, one that contained more darn birds then I could possibly start to count. At dawn on the morning of that memorable hunt, we parked our trucks alongside a river that sported steep banks, and also a lot of brush that allowed the building of some workable blinds. After driving everything with feathers off the river in the pre-dawn light, we set up on the water with several dozen Canada floaters and three-dozen mallard blocks.

The hunt was letter perfect, with our party gunning limits of greenheads and a few gadwall thrown in. As birds approached, we used some strict fire control, working hard to keep our gunning within the 50-yard envelope and, at times, closer. As it had been on the first test hunt, Black Cloud failed to let the shooters down. In total, for the two hunts, 18 mallards had been taken with a very small amount of test shot, and that says darn little missing was going on. To be sure, the loads did what they were designed to do.

During the day on that second hunt, we depleted the supply of Black Cloud on hand, so I decided to offer up loads in Federal tungsten-iron from the old lots of 1⅛-ounce payload weights. For added comparison, we did some back-to-back shooting with some Wolf Ammunition No. 2 steel loaded in a 3-inch hull to 1¼-ounce payloads. I was interesting to see the difference between the Black Cloud steel, standard steel, and the now-obsolete tungsten load. For one, there were some birds that required additional shots before coming down, when standard steel was applied; be advised that Wolf steel is actually a really good product in a general-use steel shotshell. It should not be construed

A good day on ducks. The Black Cloud definitely proved itself in the field.

that there was anything wrong with these loads, rather that the Black Cloud was just that much *better*. In fact, the birds taken with the Black Cloud resembled the tungsten-hit birds a good deal of the time. The tungsten loads pole-axed the birds, without question, but so did the Black Cloud.

When ducks taken by way of Black Cloud were reviewed for damage, I found that, when matched to those birds shot under the same conditions but with the standard steel No. 2 pellets, the Black Cloud birds were far the worse for wear. Black Cloud No. 2s produced deep wound channels. In fact, penetration overall seemed to be more extensive. This echoed what we witnessed at the shot. A duck's reaction to being hit was as if someone had been standing

Kent's Fasteel seems to get faster every year. Its velocities now are downright astounding.

on a platform up in the sky with a baseball bat. Large mallards would simply come to a complete stop mid-air after contact with the payload of Federal Black Cloud.

Federal shared ballistic gelatin testing with me, which further illustrated that Black Cloud, by way of the cutting edged ring pellets, was indeed doing more damage than standard steel. Based on that testing, I ran a few rounds of my own test fodder into blocks of Perma Gel (a newer ordnance gelatin offered by the company of the same name), and also found the gel produced a good "smoke" trail, indicating serious damage being inflicted within the wound channel itself.

OTHER STEEL PLAYERS

Federal ATK and its Black Cloud loads have been riding a run that has nearly prevented the company from keeping pace with the demand. But it's not the only player. Today, Kent Cartridge moving up the velocity of its Fasteel loads a notch or two year by year, and Environ-Metal, Inc., bringing out its Classic Doubles load for those high-end twin pipe smooth-bores, active waterfowl load development is breaking totally new ground, in terms of the number of brand names offering non-toxic shotshell ammunition today.

There are several outfits I am pleased to see stay in the fight for better steel shotshell performance. The first of these that I'd recommend are the folks at Wolf Ammunition, and a second is the Winchester company, which produces the outstanding Xpert shotshell loads. With these two brands you have no-nonsense, standardized steel loads modestly priced at a working man's level. (Wow, shotshells you can actually afford to take into the swamp? What's next?) With some extensive work during the past several hunting seasons in which I covered budget shotshell loads, I can say that Wolf and Winchester brand shotshells of the economical sort took up a good deal of my time afield. These loads are as simple as field dirt in construction, but are made to stay dry and trouble free, and kill clean to the ranges each shot size tested was designed to handle.

Following on the heels of Wolf and Winchester, Kent Cartridge has now jumped into the lower-priced, but still effective steel shell market by offering its All Purpose 3-inch steel in 12-gauge 1¼-ounce payloads.

Shooting large quantities of these shotshells over high-quality mallard blocks resulted in darn few cripples and, in almost all cases, stone dead birds via single, well-centered shots. With many areas of the country now turning to mandate use of non-toxic shotshells for both waterfowl and upland hunting, a load like this Kent economy package is exactly what's required afield at a time, when price is something the hunter considers.

At close range, Black Cloud-killed ducks took a beating. Dead before they hit the ground, after-shot inspection revealed deep wound channels. Today, the Black Cloud lineup includes a load specifically for close-range birds, but, whichever you choose, these loads are effective, ethical loads, bar none.

WHAT HAPPENED TO THOSE SUPER TUNGSTEN LOADS?

There are, of course, non-toxic loads that are not steel. Bismuth was one of the first to depart from steel, but it was tungsten that made the largest splash when it was introduced. Hunters loved it. But where is tungsten today? Let's take a look.

If you loved tungsten shot but are having trouble finding it these days, you're not alone. Tungsten-based ammunition is fast going away. This is largely due to the Chinese holding up the commodities markets with ultra high pricing of raw tungsten. Because industrial cutting tools are based largely on tungsten metal, the Chinese with their large stores of the ore want to control the market. (Just to give you an idea, a couple quick Google searches at the time this book was being written showed that future prices for ferro tungsten are running around the $50 U.S. dollars per kilogram mark.) Thank goodness we have some alternatives that work just as well if not better than tungsten, best of all, they're not going to cost you as much.

A few years ago, Remington made a big push along this road with its HD tungsten shot line of advanced "designer" loads. Now, several years hence, everything has changed. The HD in its very costly tungsten iron product is completely out of production, having been replaced with the fastest shotshell load ever commercially developed, the Hypersonic. Remington books the velocity of this load at 1,700 fps. However, by my measurements through two different chronograph units, the loads met out a foot or two under a whopping *2,000* fps.

Winchester is now offering a new "designer " Xtended tungsten steel shot load in a No. 6 shot size. This will be a big winner among turkey hunters, but of limited use among duck and upland shooters. If you need payload density in a duck decoy load, a basic iron

(above) Kent's Fasteel seems to get faster every year. Its velocities now are downright astounding. (right) Kent has refined its high-velocity steel loads for specific species, as in the newer TealSteel load of No. 5.

(another name for steel) shot load in a budget-priced configuration will get the job done and not break the bank. Still, if money's no object, go ahead and have at it with the Xtended. As marketed by Winchester, the 12-gauge No. 6 Xtended should be a real hard hitting killer both close up and even to moderately longer ranges; tungsten, as most of us know, is generally some deadly stuff at just about *any* range you can ethically connect with a bird. But I've hands-on tested the new No. 6 Winchester Xtended and found this new offering to be nothing short of a deadly *long*-range powerhouse.

Environ-Metal, Inc., is always a company to keep an eye on in the non-toxic shot market. The folks behind the company are innovative to the core and, if it's new, you're very likely to see it first under their brand name.

When conditions get tough over the blocks, tungsten in the form of Environ-Metal's Hevi-Shot saves the day. But cost rules in this discussion, as does a definitive push for tungsten replacements from consumers. So, advancing from the first Hevi-Shot loads, Environ-Metal is now offering its Hevi-Metal non-toxic load.

Bismuth was the first non-toxic to provide an alternate to steel, but it was expensive and short-lived in popularity. Still, it worked, though there are better alternatives today.

Developed with a mixed payload of common iron shot and tungsten pellets, this load is designed to save you dollars at the ammo counter, but still provide some hard-hitting effects downrange.

The primary reason this new load was developed was to give the hunter the chance to shoot at least *some* level of Hevi-Shot waterfowl ammunition, but at a greatly reduced price. Word has it that this new load is selling for the price of the competition's premium non-toxic waterfowl ammunition. If so, this would indeed be a breakthrough for the guys who want to gravitate toward Hevi-Shot as their shot type of choice, but of can't afford to shoot a full load of the costly ore.

NEW NON-TOXIC KIDS ON THE BLOCK

There are several new entries into the iron shot market that could be major money savers down the line for both target range use and for hunters. One of these, a standard iron shot load, is from B&P, also known as Kaltron Outdoors/Baschieri & Pellagri. This firm has come out with a new, complete line of steel shot ammunition manufactured in Italy. B&P will offer 12-gauge 70mm (2¾-inch) non-toxic loads ranging from steel No. 7, No. 4, and No. 3 up through a magnum-style 76mm (3-inch) magnum in No. 4, 3, 2, and what it designates 2/0, which must be close to a No. 1 or BB pellet. I am well versed on B&P shotshell ammunition, especially its special subsonic, low-recoil ammunition

as I've applied it to my Subsonic Metro Gun System and, of late, the .724 Orion 12-gauge suppressor "can." B&P has been around for a very long time in Europe, and this ammo has won more world shooting events than any other shotshell manufacture in business today. Its new steel offerings should be something to keep an eye out for.

Another newer kid in the non-toxic ammo business is Rio Ammunition, Inc. Rio is a Spain-based company that sells massive amounts of ammunition around the globe. In 2003, for example, this company sold 550 million rounds to 80 different counties.

Some of that ammunition was non-toxic. Rio Royal steel shot loads are offered in 2¾- and 3-inch magnum lengths and cover pellet sizes ranging from BB and No. 1 down through No. 5. According to its spokesperson, the company is increasing its steel shot line by adding several high-performance loads to the mix for sale in the U.S. market; I think that says a lot about where the market for such shells is heading and why this topic is making a difference in how we define the modern shotgun and its uses. One of these new offerings will be a special, bore-safe, bismuth-type load intended for use in high-end smoothbores.

New steel shot loads are now coming from Fiocchi, in a flexible range of iron shot pellet sizes and payload weights. Like others making shotshells for this market, Fiocchi is expanding its line of waterfowl loads to fit a broad range of applications.

ROUND PELLETS—SO YESTERDAY?

Not only do the folks at Federal Cartridge and Environ-Metal, Inc., build shotshell loads using unusual pellet shapes (Black Cloud, Hevi-Shot, and Winchester Blind Side), an ultra high-velocity handloading outfit in Pine Island, Minnesota, has also hit the deck running. Developed for goose hunters, Reloading Specialties now offers its newly developed "E Shot" pellet, which has a very unique shape. The soft E Shot takes on the look and somewhat the feel of the old Bismuth brand shot, but, like Federal's High Density, it carries a banded belt around the center of the pellet. That pellet centerline belt has a broader band than Federal's Black Cloud pellets. E Shot isn't truly round, either, rather it's slightly longer than it is wide. The shot is being introduced to the shooting public first in bulk form and specifically for handloading practices. At some point, this new shot will be offered in full factory loaded ammunition, as well.

The reason for the mid-line belts we've been seeing of late on some brands of pellets is due to the manufacturing process more than anything else. In fact, most of these oddly shaped pellets are the results of different methods of turning the raw material into a shotshell pellet. Call it an accident, if you will, and, at least in some cases, these pellets, were *exactly* just that when first developed, an accident during the manufacture of other shot types. From there, ballistics engineers got hold of the odd pellets and started running tests.

It's actually long been believed by many that the use of round pellets in shotguns isn't always the best solution for every application, but there haven't been a lot of options out there with which to put the theory to test. Too, and for all the obvious reasons, you won't see this type of information in the advertisement-driven shotgun writing reviews over the broad range of national shooting and hunting publications, but the truth is that, in some cases, the best performing loads today are the results of throw-away shot "seconds" that turned premium. Belted shot is one of these, and it gets the job done just fine, as we've seen, in Black Cloud. Now let's take a look at another player I just mentioned in this realm, Winchester's Blind Side.

WINCHESTER BLIND SIDE

In terms of pellet shape changes and downrange performance, I don't believe any load on the current market can compare with Winchester's Blind Side, especially in that this shot's shape has never before been thought of as workable in a shotgun pattern. Yet it works out at the target end of things quite well.

Blind Side, in fact, isn't round at all, but, rather, a ball of iron shot that has been fabricated into a hex-sided projectile. Downrange, it shoots tight and hits hard—but, for the most part, it really makes no sense at all as to why it works as well as it does. Winchester engineers told me that because every pellet is exactly

alike, they tend to work very well as an in-flight team or swarm.

Oddly enough, as ammunition manufactures have been marching forward with all sorts of designs in the attempt to make gains in the ballistic performance of non-toxic shot, Winchester, for the most part, sat on the sidelines. That was fine. For those of us who prefer to shoot Winchester ammo, the aging, but nevertheless effective, offerings by this company have delivered fine enough downrange performance over the years. Indeed, Winchester's Supreme line of shotshell game loads in its black hulls, for instance, have been considered by many to be the benchmark in steel shot performance. I rather assume the thinking at Winchester

The Hard Stuff

Of course, all waterfowl guns need to be steel shot or tungsten-iron safe. That means their chrome bores, hard forcing cone metal and screw-in chokes, most cases. Don't shoot anything through your gun or those chokes the manufacturers say not to.

I shoot hard iron shot through lower-cost 870 replacement barrels much of the time, as I don't worry much about "corn row" damage or forcing cone erosion. I have shot thousands of rounds through the modern 870 Remingtons, 500 Mossbergs, Winchester SXPs, BPS Brownings, and an assortment of others, without any noted damage whatsoever. I worked with iron shot (steel) from the first day it was introduced and, in fact, for a good three years before it was the law of the land. In my opinion, and having seen how far we've come, the modern steel shot load and its now dedicated engineering make for one hell of a clean, effective, game taking system. For those hunters who gave up waterfowl hunting because of steel shot development, all I can say is they cut off their noses to spite their faces.

has been why mess with something that didn't need fixing?

While that approach can be fine, the fact remains that time moves on, and within the industry there is a constant battle to be and maintain the position of top dog in the waterfowl shotshell load business. And so it was that Winchester was required to make a move into the current arena of non-toxic shot development that was being led by others. To do less would mean loss of market share, and that just won't work in any advancing business, regardless the product. And so we arrive at Blind Side.

Winchester states that Blind Side enables more shot per a measured volume of space, due to the fact that the pellets are flat sided. This makes sense. The flat-sided hex-shaped shot allows the pellets to stack with more contact area between each pellet and less open space, thereby increasing the pellet count (and charge weight) that can be launched from, say, a basic 12-gauge 3-inch shotshell designed to send a maximum of 1¼-ounce payload in round shot.

Blind Side test ammunition that came to me in a No. 2 pellet size carried a 1³⁄₈-ounce payload in the 3-inch

Remington's HyperSonic is another top player in the souped-up steel loads race. The author found they worked equally well on specs and snows.

hull. That's a *stiff* payload for an iron shot load. Winchester booked the muzzle velocity at 1,400 fps, but I measured them at 1,263 fps through an Oehler Chronotech Model 33. The test barrel in this case was 22 inches long, and the choke was Improved Cylinder. A bit more barrel length and tighter choke could have pushed up the muzzle velocity a bit, but it still would have been a stretch to get that published 1,400 fps out of the shotshells I was sent for evaluation. (Note that this is the opposite of what I found with

Remington's HyperSonic steel loads, where my chronograph testing showed velocities much higher than Remington's data. You must test your loads if you really want to know how they work in *your* gun.

Winchester states that its hex shot will produce tighter pattern and put 25-percent more shot on target within normal game-killing ranges than traditional round shot will. After a stint on the static test range, I took these loads to the snow goose fields to see if this was true.

(left) Winchester's Xtended shotshells in the company's Supreme packaging is a "designer" tungsten-based load. In the No. 6 size, it's a great choice for turkey hunters, but it lacks the payload density at distance for consistent taking of ducks and upland birds at distance.

(below) Environ-Metal's Hevi-Shot load and the author's Winchester SX-3 shown with a variety of chokes. The loads are a mix of common iron and tungsten pellets, designed to save the consumer some dollars compared to all-tungsten loads.

Polywad's GreenLite load makes use of no wad what so ever, rather just a small paper cup behind the payload. However, it works. Note: This photo was taken at 25,000 frames per second. (Author photo, via the Georgia Project material)

When the first loads of GreenLite arrived for testing, I selected five 20-gauge rounds and dropped them into the bed of my pickup truck, where they would spend a week riding around our South Dakota dirt roads. What I was trying to accomplish was to get the powder to migrate into the buffer, being there was no wad between the two. After hauling these shotshells around, I shot them over my chronograph screens, where I noted no difference from test loads shot fresh from the package box—there had been no migration of propellant at all.

As far as the propellent itself was concerned, once I dissected a shell, I believed I could have been looking at Alliant Green Dot, as it did retain a small, green, flake identifier in the otherwise dark-black mix. In terms of payload in the shotshells I received for review, the 28-gauge contained a ½-ounce of No. 7 steel shot for 220 pellets in the load. The velocity indicated on the box showed 1,000 miles per hour and, as such, a run through the chronograph screens would be required to get a feet-per-second database started on this new non-toxic offering. In 20-gauge, the 2¾-inch hull contained a ¾-ounce payload of No. 7 steel shot for 240 pellets. Both 20- and 28-gauge loads are designed

But, believe me when I tell you that, knowing Jay Menefee, the president of Polywad, and his knowledge of ballistic balance and design, this guy never leaves a stone unturned, when bringing together a new product.

to maintain low recoil, to be easy on the shooter when addressing clays or small game birds. Young shooters and ladies who are just starting out will appreciate this gentler type of fodder, to be sure.

Over the chronograph screens, I recorded a string of test shots in 28-gauge that measured an average of 1,581 fps. This is a fast-moving load and, with the very small No. 7 pellets, speed is not just a good thing to have, but one *required* to bring down game birds. Shooting the 20-gauge rounds over the speed screens, the muzzle velocity was much the same as it was in the 28-gauge, with those pellet leaving the barrel at 1,567 fps on an average. In both cases, an extreme spread (ES) of shot-to-shot velocity calculated out to 28 fps for the 28-gauge, and 48 fps for the 20-gauge. This is tight, in terms of ballistics results, and every indication that the wad-less and gas seal-free loads do shoot very well in maintaining muzzle energy and velocity.

I next put the new GreenLite loads on the pattern boards. Patterns in the 20-gauge were test-fired by way of my Remington 870 Express with a Modified factory Rem Choke tube. The test distance was 30 yards for this and the 28-gauge, more appropriate than the standard 40-yard patterning distance for 12-gauges; in the sub-gauges, the No. 7 steel just can't retain enough pellet speed to do much more than wound game beyond about 35 yards maximum. At 30 yards against a 30-inch circle, the Polywad Green-Lite 20-gauge returned 97 to 100 percent in a five-round test string, for an average of 97.5 percent. The 28-gauge patterns held to almost 100 percent by way of my Franchi stack-barrel mounting a Modified choke in the upper test barrel. Five rounds indicated an aver-

age pattern of 96 percent (with a single 100-percent pattern falling out of that test group).

I was so impressed with these two loads at 30 yards that, out of curiosity, I went ahead and shot two patterns for each gauge at 40 yards. There the prints were still great looking, at 80-plus percent, but knowing the loads are just not designed for that kind of far side of the decoy spread distance, I didn't press the issue further. These new wad-less loads are designed for the hunter who cares more about a very tight, clean kill shot with a higher-end gun, versus just pushing shot up at all distances. In other words, it's about the gun and the day, versus filling the limit.

Of course, sub-gauge hunters are the minority. To that end, work is underway at Polywad to apply its wadless design to a workable 12-gauge small duck load, as well as those for general upland applications on smaller birds.

SHOTdata Results 08/14/2008	Range (YARDS)	Velocity (FPS)	Energy (FT/LBS)	Time of Flight (SECONDS)	Drop (INCHES)	Wind Def@45mph (IN/10MPH)	Lead Required (FEET)
Steel No. 7 Shot	0	1,585	5.8	0.0000	0.0	0.0	0
Standard Metro 12-gauge	5	1,311	4.0	0.0112	0.0	0.0	0.7
	10	1,106	2.8	0.0239	0.1	0.6	1.6
Pellet Weight (grains): 1.041	15	956	2.1	0.0386	0.2	1.5	2.5
Effective Standard Deviation: 0.0149	20	843	1.6	0.0555	0.5	2.8	3.7
	25	753	1.3	0.0745	0.9	4.4	4.9
Pellet Diameter: (inches): 0.100	30	683	1.1	0.0956	1.4	6.4	6.3
	35	619	0.9	0.1188	2.1	8.9	7.8
Standard Deviation: 0.0149	40	562	0.7	0.1444	3.0	12.2	9.5

Legend: Energy (ft/lbs) is per pellet, not the overall load.

Finding a (Near)-Perfect
DUCK GUN

We have now covered one massive amount of information, regarding shotguns in general and the ammunition that keeps them running. As you most likely have guessed, the waterfowl gun is a primary area of mine, one you could say commands a certain level of specialization and expertise. I've spent about 50 years of my long life gunning wet birds across the entire North American continent, not to mention South America and far northern Canada. Over that long span of time, events occurred that allowed me to gain experiences with everything from time behind the very first (and, by any measure, old) English market guns in 4-bore gauging to some 20-plus years behind a 3½-inch 10-gauge on almost every available weekend I was able to hunt. You could say I've seen the best of two worlds, those old guns and the big bores, but, more important, is how I've seen those shotguns translated into the modern, slick-handling 12-gauge duck gun of today.

With the development of these now very advanced gas and inertia systems, the semi-auto has taken off big time among both professional waterfowlers and the general public alike. Why is this the case? Because the modern auto-loader of today functions well, maintains great balance across a wide variety of models and brands and, when a flock of, say, Canada geese close to gunning range, there's a good chance that, by staying on your gun stock and following through with your shots, more then a single bird is coming to bag. Without question, when multiple targets are the opportunity, the semi-auto is tough to beat hands down.

The second-most type of waterfowl shotgun employed by hunters is the pump gun. These workhorses step up as the most dependable repeating smoothbore in use today, in large part thanks to their continued simplicity. While the gun is nothing but an auto-loader lacking the gas or blowback operating mechanism and, as such, has its loading of the chamber and ejection of spent hulls manipulated by the shooter, it holds an unquestionable edge in the area of reliability—a simpler mechanism means less to go wrong. That stated, a pump is simply the best functional action type ever developed for field use. The drawback to the gun over ducks or geese is that it requires a solid cheekweld to the stock for fast, second-round recovery. This is fine for the practiced pump-action shotgunner, but, in many cases, the shooter is required to leave the stock as they work the shucker to eject the spent hull and chamber a fresh round. The small amount of time it takes to perform that forward and backward action is just enough to enforce the need to reacquire the next target (or follow up on a poorly made first shot), and that increases the probability of a missed or wounded bird.

The third choice in wet-bird cannons are the twin-pipe systems, those being over/unders and side-by-sides. In Europe, they are considered a "gentleman's gun," kind of a reflection of the attitude those gunners have toward our American "corn shuckers" and self-stuffing guns that go afield here. This is changing a bit, however, in that the English are increasingly using pump guns, when building their well-known (well, at least over there), suppressed 12-gauge field gun systems.

Doubles are great, and I like to shoot them every now and again. As I told you early on, I was tied to a massive 10-gauge side-by-side for years back in the day, when steel shot was a rotten substitute for lead and you needed the massive 10-gauge to get much of anything up to a passing goose or duck. Following my time behind that behemoth, my first real over-the-counter shotgun was the Winchester Model 24 side-by-side. I shot that gun well for all the years between the start of high school and the end of my college education. Today, I own one 10-gauge Zabala double in a side-by-side, and a Tristar to follow that in 12-gauge. Other fine stack-barrels include a great Ruger 20-gauge and a 28-gauge Franchi, though, in general, I prefer those doubles for upland hunting and light clay target work.

With that bit of background, let's take a look at a one of the most modern waterfowl shotguns gracing retailer shelves today. Hailing from Mossberg, this is one guns that's truly changing the face of waterfowling.

Mossberg calls it the "FLEX System," and it amounts to a gun design that can be completely dismantled and reconfigured into everything from a coyote shotgun to a deer slug gun or from a duck gun to a home-defense system in less then two minutes (sometimes even 30 seconds, with a bit of practice). Mossberg unveiled this advanced shotgun at the 2012 SHOT Show, and I'm here to tell you, this is as close to a do-it-all, one-gun system as you're ever likely to find. As to exactly how it works, stay tuned, because this hot scattergun was completely checked for inclusion in this book.

Almost forever, shooters have wanted a system that could allow the ownership of one gun that fit many needs, even down to one that could accommodate an entire family of users, if necessary. Mossberg was listening to hunter requests in particular for such a rig and finally came forward with an answer.

The solution was a modular stock, fore-end, barrel, and receiver system that can be reconfigured from, say, a basic target gun to an assault setup in less then two minutes. Yes, two minutes, my friends, and that's a timed run that includes reinstalling stocks and barrels that I performed during the gun's review period with me.

The Mossberg FLEX gun is based on the tried and true Model 500 pump-action shotgun. Mossberg, in just this past year, sold the greatest number of pump guns ever recorded in modern manufacturing history. The gun company hit over a million guns built, well ahead of all other well-known pump gun makers in the USA. Now, by adding the FLEX system to the list of design developments associated with its other pump gun models, the Mossberg brand has, in effect, spread itself across the total gambit of smoothbore needs, everything from sport to military requirements.

Hunting sea ducks over the rolling seas off the coast of Maine, is a far cry from mallard hunting in timber or over ponds. These are big ducks and require some powerful loads to bring them down. They also need a gun that can take the rough ride and rougher weather—Mossberg's FLEX system makes the grade all around.

This last is an interesting twist. For a very long time, Mossberg has been a primary supplier of pump-action shotguns to many free-world governments, for use in everything from military interdictions to basic police crowd control. The FLEX has become particularly useful for this market, as it can be reconfigured to generate an exact fit for female or small-statured male officers on up to a linebacker-sized S.W.A.T. members. Of course, such flexibility also has application in the sporting field. As a FLEX, the Model 500 can now be made to fit a nine-year-old boy starting out hunting, or the biggest, tallest hunter who needs a gun long enough to ensure correct fit and handling.

The highlight of the FLEX is its ease of reconfiguration. If a gun can't be taken down with ease—and believe me, I've seen some that required a gunsmith to accomplish the task—it is of little use to someone searching for a flexible firearm. The Mossberg system keeps things simple, its design centering around a unique and protected link and lock system that makes use of a simple, turn-key design that, when in place, holds the stock to the receiver and the fore-end to the magazine tube in an iron-clad way.

Hunting sea sucks with Mossberg on Maine's ice-cold, off-shore rock islands, I went to work testing the gun's ability to hold up in some nasty shooting conditions. Going to sea by way of 20- and 22-foot deep-"V" duck boats that were designed more like small Coast Guard cutters than waterfowling transportation, the Mossberg pumps were at once subjected to concentrations of saltwater that were so dense it turned sticky before drying on your skin. I know for a fact that this was no place for your upper-crust Caesar Guerini or Perazzi double gun. I was pleased that the camo-coated working guns in our possession were just the ticket, when subjected to this kind of harsh environment.

With long chains of decoys shifted to the boat's stern in preparation for setting out and the bow rising against the sea swells, the guns got their share of bouncing around; it was less then a gentle introduction to that northern sea. We all know that the 500 pump guns have acquired a reputation over the years as solid working tools of the trade, but would the newly designed links that held buttstocks together and for-ends in place make the grade?

According to Linda Powell, my friend and Mossberg associate at sea with me, the basic design of the link system had to be created as something actually a bit less precise than you'd imagine; the first prototypes didn't want to release easily. The reworked system we were using, guns based on Mossberg's Tool-Less Locking System (TLS), allows a stock change to be completed within a half-minute. This was tested time and time again during the field review of the shotgun. Changing

The beauty of the FLEX system from Mossberg lies not only in its inherent flexibility, but also within the absolute speed at which components can be swapped out. The system has been a bona fide home run for Mossberg.

out a fore-end was a bit more work; it took me about a minute to accomplish that task.

Over decoys, the FLEX 500 isn't different from any of the fixed-stock 500. The gun is the same, fast-handling slider scattergun that has been used for years. Shooting the Environmetal, Inc., Speed Ball steel in No. 3, with guns mounting standard, Mossberg Invector-style choke tubes, produced some solid results against sea eiders at ranges exceeding 50 yards at times. About the only small issue for me was the use of that upper tang safety. I shoot a Mossberg 835 all the time on turkeys, and with devastating results, so the safety wasn't unknown to me, but, with fast-flying targets against deep cold and rough weather in late fall, I did at times find myself searching for my gun's button safety.

While hunting the salt water off Maine's coast, the gun didn't see a whole lot of takedown, but duck hunting in Mississippi, a bit later in the fall, allowed some controlled review of the gun system. The FLEX concept is not only new, but one that's just about right on the nose, regarding its time of introduction to hunters and shooters in general. Built on an affordable receiver system, hunters like myself, who tend to move across the full range of game and varmints over the course of a year, will find a massive amount of value in this gun, in that less money will need to be spent to address different applications. It's almost like finding one magic golf club that can do it all for every stroke of your 18 holes. While I haven't endorsed or singled out many individual guns in this book, the Mossberg FLEX get my vote all the way across design and development spectrums—but, at its heart, this shotgun is a duck gun all the way.

Configured for ducks, the FLEX can be a long-range guns with extra barrel length for a smooth and balanced swing, or it can be a "pit" gun, with a shorter barrel that helps a hunter seated in the confines of a narrow blind take close-in birds swinging in over the decoys. Heavyweights 10-gauge magnums and the big 3½-inch 12-gauge guns really aren't necessary for most field work when gunning over decoys and. In fact, the big 10 can slow down some shooters, when the birds get in tight to the muzzle; there's just too much gun to control the swing. These big guns are pass-shooting equipment, in most cases, or best left for specialized use on large spreads of decoys, such as massed for sea duck gunning or big water diver duck hunting. In other words, the method I advocate here is to match the gun to the task at hand. The FLEX is at its best for general duck hunting, early teal to late mallards, pintails to eiders, gadwalls to bluebills. Duck, duck, duck, bang, bang, bang, Mossberg's FLEX will keep you in limits.

AFTER THE BARREL: SHOT DISPERSION

While some folks tend to think that shotguning is simply slinging pellets into the air to, in some random fashion, hit clay birds or feathered targets, nothing could be further from the truth. In actuality, shotgunning is an art form unto itself and, as such, there are a number of complicated areas to it that, if better understood, can result in the target shooter or hunter doing a better job with their guns.

OVERBORE 12-GAUGE PAYLOADS

It can be complicated subject, but, boiled down, powder and shot are the culprits in many a pattern gone astray. I'm speaking here of a practice used today by both industry and handloaders alike. That practice is massively overloading shotshell loads with heavy payloads of shot. The end result is an "overbore" situation.

The 12-gauge (I'm emphasizing this gauge, as it's the most used gunning system), will make the best use of a load consisting of 1 1/8 ounces of shot. What that means is that the bore of this gauge, at .724-inch and as married to this payload charge, will, in general, produce the very best patterns with the least amount of barrel or choke stress. This payload will also produce the least amount of blown patterns and patterns ragged on their perimeters.

Now let's look at the powder side of things. During the grand old days of the 8-gauge and 10-gauge waterfowl cannons, a charge of about 1¼ ounces was actually considered massive, not to mention the 1½-ounce load; today we cram those payloads and more into 12-gauges without a second thought. I don't know how many of you have ever touched off an 8-bore goose gun, but I have, and I am here to tell you that it is almost a religious experience when that 1/8-pound of powder goes off. The trick to working with these big guns was as much about powder charge as it was about the pellet payload. Did those old super-bore sneak boat market hunters know something we've forgotten? I tend to think so.

If many of those mammoth market duck, goose, and fur-taking cannons used so little shot, why have we choked the 12 bore to death with overbore charges of steel shot pellets? As I have eluded already, it is a sales gimmick of sorts, as in the good old American way of bigger is always better. Right? Well not all the time. Most of the time, massive charges of shot don't add up to doing much more than pounding more holes in the sky or sending more pellets into a mud bank across the river.

Now, before the guy that gets great results from his 3½-inch 10- or 12-gauge loaded to the crimp with charges of steel shot that equal the weight of a deer slug turns on me, let me say that, yes, there are exceptions to the rule. Just as there are barrels that tend to pattern well, there are some heavy powder and shot combinations that a few guns will take a liking to. If you own one of them, my advice is don't sell it, but hunt hard and be well on the marsh and fields for many years to come. For the rest of you?

Well, here are a few facts you're going to need to face about the performance of your guns and loads.

The truth is, hunters don't take the time to pattern the loads being taken afield. For the few who do, it's a shot or two downrange at paper target, one they quite often don't have a clue about what its telling them. I hunt with some dedicated duck hunters out here in the West whom I have never seen shoot a single pattern. What these guys do is ask me if the load and choke are workable for the task at hand. If I say quite possibly, that's good enough for them, and the game goes on.

So there's my preaching, but just why is there a problem with over-boring a payload in the 12-gauge duck, goose, or heavy predator shotgun? The issue comes down to a large mass being squeezed down a too small hole. When this happens, the shot charge acts like water from a garden hose and sprays shot all over the place, or at least into clumps that can miss even well-centered targets at acceptable and general

Pattern Results — Overbore vs. Light-Bore
Remington 870 Express 12 Gauge 3½-inch

Load	Choke Type	Pattern Percentage	Notes
Remington 2¾-inch 1 1/8-ounce No. 3	Dead Ringer	84%	Uniform Dispersion
Remington 3-inch 1 1/8-ounce Sportsmen	Rem Choke Modified	78%	Uniform Dispersion
Remington Nitro Steel 3½-inch 19/16-ounce BB	Dead Ringer	90%	Tight Core
Remington Nitro Steel 3½-inch 19/16-ounce BB	Rem 40 point full	66%	Blown Core
Kent Fast Steel 3½-inch 1¼-ounce BB	Rem Choke Modified	70%	Soft open core
Wolf 3-inch 1¼-ounce BB Tungsten HD*	Safe Rem Full	78 %	Blown core
Kent Fast Steel 3-inch 1¼-ounce No. 2	Rem Choke Modified	79%	Solid Core
Federal Premium Steel 3-inch 1 1/8-ounce No. 3	Rem Choke Modified	77%	Uniform Dispersion

Note 1: * HD Remington High Density Shot.
Note 2: Suggested Reading: Smooth Bore Ballistics, 4 and 8 Bore Shotguns And Loads by Tom Armbrust, 1108 West May Ave, McHenry IL 60050

working range limits. This can also occur, even when shot payloads are a small as 1¼-ounce. Now, drive this fairly standard payload down an ultra-tight Full choke, and the end result can be major gaps in the pattern, gaps large enough to allow a duck to fly untouched through it.

This phenomenon of heavy shot charge versus heavy powder charge is something I've observed for many, many years. Way back in the late 1960s, I shot bluebills, fast movers, in north central Minnesota, with a 2¾-inch 1 1/8-ounce handload of copper-clad lead No. 5s that was moved out of the barrel by way of a heavy charge of AL 5 (Alcan powders, long discontinued). This load depended on a powder charge that was stiff, rather than a shot charge that was massive, and it worked very well. One of the worst conditions I experienced when steel shot came onto the scene was that I was forced to give up this very effective, modest priced duck killer over big water decoy sets. While some guys up on the big northern Minnesota lakes shot 10-gauge cannons, I shot my lightning fast 1 1/8-ounce payload and simply plastered ducks by the limit year after year. See, even back then, with a long out of date powder, the *shot* charge was the ticket.

CONTROLLING OVERBORE

The market is what the market is, and for hunters, that means store shelves are going to be full of heavy shot payload merchandise. So what do you do if you don't handload? There are several ways to control overbore payload conditions when using these big payloads of steel. The first is one that ties into the last chapter, and that is run them out of a choke designed to handle them. A second is to use an over-sized bore, something you'll see marketed as guns that are "backbored." Recently a good friend wrote me about his results using a steel shot-safe Full choke (.40 constriction) paired with 3½-inch 12-gauge turkey loads boxed as Winchester Xtended. That load had 1¾ ounces of No. 5 tungsten shot. Now, at $3.50 a shot, you won't find me giving this ballistic event a try anytime soon, but what's interesting was that, as shown in some patterning work, the mating of a quality super-Full choke in a back-bored barrel, this hunter *owned* the air space over head completely. Overbore situation here? Yes, but in this case the load was well controlled.

Ever wonder why the industry worked toward developing the back-bored (oversized)

barrels? It was because engineers *knew full well* that steel shot in the heavy payloads its sold in would require more room to run. Today, Mossberg, for instance, offers the .775 bore, the standard bore for a 10-gauge, in a 12-gauge 3½-inch. Browning offers the back-bored waterfowl guns in both 3½-inch and 3-inch, and Beretta's Extrema 3½-inch is also drilled larger than normal. These are just a few. But they're there because the demand for more load in turn demanded more bore room, if shooters wanted their guns pattern well. (Keep in mind, though, that the big loads in the 3 ½-inch 12-gauges and over-loaded 3-inch hulls tend to string shot column out a good deal, creating the issues inherent with those we discussed in the last chapter.)

In my work researching just this angle of shotgun load performance, I hunted extensively with single shot sizes in large steel pellets, and there is solid evidence that smaller payloads of shot can produce positive returns, both in quality patterns and also effective knockdown capabilities. During the late waterfowl season in South Dakota, I elected to give this "go light" program a try on ducks, by way of budget loads paired with a Dead Ringer of my own design. Running a small set of mallard blocks (eight) at the smooth headwaters on a stretch of a local stream, I waited out a flock of greenheads that had been visiting the hole each morning for the previous week. Chambered in my 870 Express with a Dead Ringer choke tube was a Remington 2¾-inch, 1 1/8-ounce load of No. 3s. When the first flock of puddle ducks arrived, I pulled for the edge of the flock, which held about 15 birds or so. At a strong 35 yards, my first shot connected on a feet down descending mallard that, without question, never know what hit him. That morning, I took three birds with three rounds. All shots were within a 35 to 45 yard envelope, and no a hint of a cripple was evident. My birds were all stone dead when they touched down. Need another observation? I have never seen common lead perform any better then what took place that morning on that small body of almost frozen water, and, remember, I've been shooting since well before lead became illegal for waterfowl.

During the remainder of the last month of the waterfowl season, my light payload gunning methods accounted for 28 solo birds. That means birds I shot at alone, virus other guns in the mix and possibly providing confusion about who shot what. (I did have two cripples, which were retrieved by my partners excellent Chesapeake retrievers.) Summing up the results, I'd reduced my payload substantially, saved a pile of money in the process via the use of that low budget ammo, and lost nothing in the transition.

NOTHING BUT FAST

So, we've talked about over-bores, back-boring, and heavy shot payloads. Now, if you've noticed, the marketing efforts in shotshells these days is all about speed, and that seems the next logical point in this discussion about ammunition performance.

Speed kills, right? I pose the question because, of late, speed seems to have become the law of the land, especially in terms of advancing steel shot waterfowl ammunition design. (Yes, speed has become a defining attribute in all shotgun ammo it seems, everything from competition sporting clays loads to those for upland hunting, but the biggest advancements are being witnessed in the waterfowl arena.) With this thought, I took some time and set out see if the speed thing is more of a myth than a working tool.

With the start of the South Dakota waterfowl season, the folks at Kent Cartridge saw fit to send out a couple of test packs of their new, ultra high velocity 3½-inch 12-gauge shells, moving at a reported 1,650 fps. Loaded to 1¼-ounce, I had the loads available to me in both No. 2 and BB. Now, I know for a fact that, when large steel pellets reach a velocity above 1,600 fps, strange things can start to take place downrange. But, with the exception of loads I put together for testing some years ago, I just haven't seen these kinds of payload velocities from factory rolled fodder.

In a project dealing with high-velocity shotshells during the 1980s, I built loads made up of less than a ¾-ounce shot charge packed into 3½-inch 10-gauge magnum hulls. With a possibly somewhat unstable powder charge, and with the guns locked to a machine rest, I fired them by way of a lanyard cord. Test-firing the loads on targets to 100 yards, the results were very interesting! With chamber pressure checks indicating that the loads were quite safe at about 12,000 LUP, I found that steel shot from No. 1 through F (.21-caliber) would turn on the afterburners, dealing out some deadly energy after massive starting velocities. It seemed at the time that somewhere around 1,600 to 1,700 fps was the threshold for revealing major improvements in performance. I knew I was onto something, but, because of the low pellet counts and a lack of suitable powders at the time to take that would have allowed loads of this kind to go commercial, no real interest from the industry came forth, and the project went on the backroom shelf.

Commercial ammunition or not, how did my research apply to field use? Since those initial tests back in the '80s, I've continued research of the same kind, and I've learned that very high velocity can cut the lead in front of a target and, to some degree, add more foot-pounds of killing energy to a pellet of shot, thereby giving the hunter a margin of added confidence. Eventually, I was able to sit back and watch ammunition manufactures steadily move up the horsepower in duck and goose loads, year by year, and approach that seemingly magical 1,700-plus fps pellet velocity. The big question today is simply this: With the added value of many more years behind the gun and modern chronograph equipment, are we chasing a phantom, or are these new fast-moving iron shot loads the real deal? I left the hunting grounds and turned to the computer for some answers.

AT THE KEYBOARD

Ballistic computers, love them or hate them, each and every one can help sort out some of the questions involving the real value of these new hot-shot pellet speeds. Clicking on SHOT Data System in my computer's address book, I asked my old friend Ross Metzger to light up the old ballistic PC and see what would roll out the other end, in terms of a solid value regarding pellet performance. What SHOT Data found

was that velocities were indeed holding up well, as you can see for yourself based on the fact that, at 70 yards, BB steel was still humping along at a quick 579 fps (or just under the threshold of my 600 fps working velocity rule). In other words, a pellet launched at 1,600 fps *is still a penetrating projectile at about 65 through 68 yards downrange.* As you can also see, the No. 2s, again 1,600 fps, will thump a mallard in textbook fashion to a strong 55 yards.

Based on this information, I had to ask what real gain there is with the fast loads, compared to the known and tested performance of slower moving fodder. Data would suggest that the BBs leaving a gun barrel at 1,450 fps will generate 45 fps less terminal velocity at 70 yards, when compared to the same shot initially moving at the 1,600 fps figure. So, at 40 yards, the edge really goes to the speed load, with a difference in the plus column of 62 fps. But the real-life gain here is not so much penetrating or raw kinetic energy, as it is an apparent reduction of forward allowance—your basic, good old fashion lead in front of the target. At least in theory, the new Fasteel loads from Kent Cartridge and the new Remington and Hevi-Shot lines should be easier to hit something with.

Forward allowance on a crossing duck moving at 45 mph will require an actual measured lead of 10.1 feet at 50 yards with the new hot-shot steel BBs. Continuing the comparison, shooting a slower 1,450 fps load increases that lead to 10.8 feet. That may seem like a very small .7-foot savings in lead, but, in my opinion, any gain is always a positive element when we are dealing with common iron shot pellets. This really is improvement for which we've been waiting a long time.

With the math in hand and early goose season on top of me, I had made plans for a hunt in central South Dakota and hauled along the new Kent Cartridge loads. Testing by way of my Remington 870 Express and my Dead Ringer choke, I set up with my pals on a beaver hut whose pooled waters held a few non-migrating Canada geese. (FYI, I keep talking about Dead Ringer, because I designed it to produce better downrange performance with standard steel shot ammunition, rather than the new and much more expensive "designer" type nontoxic loads. If we are going to stay alive in this business of shooting ducks and geese we need to keep standard steel shot right in the working performance loop.) With these new ultra velocity loads such as those from Kent and Remington, we have now achieved a sort of maximum velocity. Knowing that, now we need more work on effective ways to harness that increased speed and energy and improve pattern control. What do I mean by that? Super-velocity loads will often result in blown core or inner 20-inch ring patterns. Some of these holes are large enough to allow a mallard to fly through them untouched. However, test shooting on paper at 40 yard by way of the then prototype Dead Ringer choke indicated that the BBs in the new Kent Fast Steel produced patterns at roughly 78 percent, but with a very tight core that contained about 65 percent of that total payload. Had I struck an optimum combination of shotshell and choke?

As the first goose passed high and running with the wind, a few goose calls turned the large bird. As it locked onto the decoys, a crack from the Remington pump gun just about rolled the bird over in mid air at the 50-yard mark. At exactly the same time I fired, another hunter in the group touched off his shotgun, also loaded with the same Fasteel load. We did a hand check of pellet damage reviewed from both the rear and side of the bird, and was a bit surprised to find that pellet penetration didn't seem to indicate much, if any, major advantage over the slower steel shot BB pellet size loads available at that time. A broken wing and several pellets in the breast had slowed, but not killed the bird. I think we tend to call this condition down and immobile at best.

It took several weeks of additional hunting to gain enough examples of the field performance results with the Kent Fast Steel shotshell loads to get a better grip on what had happened with that first goose killed. Luckily, several friends got into a major flock of Cana-das on a cut wheat field and, with a total of 33 rounds, killed 21 larger race geese without loosing a bird. Gunning was all inside 45 yards over decoys, and good dogs were used in pairs to run down several hit but not quite dead birds. For the most part, it was a dead bird flying, when those dark geese got inside the 40 yard kill net. So you know, as these hunters had been testing a number of different loads for me over a couple seasons, I tend to trust what they told me, in terms of the bird reaction to the Kent Super Fast Steel loads. They revealed to me that the Kent high-velocity steel held its own against some of the other higher-grade loads available.

Right behind that testing with the Kent Fasteel, Remington came forward with Hypersonic steel in 12-gauge. Now, a bit later down the road, it is available in 10-gauge and 20-gauge, as well. Thanks to Kent, which got the ball rolling with ultra high-velocity steel shot, and then Remington, hunters and recreational shooters now have several other meaningful choices available in that magical 1,700 fps realm. Yes, we'd answered the question about speed and its ability to kill. It does. And, in when it comes to steel shot, that means we've come a long way since those early loads we were forced to contend with.

SHOTdata Results 05/06/2007	Range (YARDS)	Velocity (FPS)	Energy (FT/LBS)	Time of Flight (SECONDS)	Drop (INCHES)	Wind Def@45mph (IN/10MPH)	Lead Required (FEET)
Shot type: BB steel	0	1,600	34.5	0.0000	0.0	0.0	0.0
Standard Metro	10	1,296	22.6	0.0217	0.1	0.3	1.4
Pellet Weight	20	1,078	15.7	0.0473	0.4	1.5	3.1
(grains): 6.070	30	923	11.5	0.0776	1.0	3.5	5.1
Effective Standard Deviation: 0.0268	40	807	8.8	0.1126	2.0	6.3	7.4
	50	718	7.0	0.1523	3.5	9.9	10.1
Pellet Diameter (inches): 0.180	60	645	5.6	0.1965	5.7	14.6	13.0
	70	579	4.5	0.2459	8.7	20.6	16.2

SHOTdata Results 05/06/2007	Range (YARDS)	Velocity (FPS)	Energy (FT/LBS)	Time of Flight (SECONDS)	Drop (INCHES)	Wind Def@45mph (IN/10MPH)	Lead Required (FEET)
Shot type: No.2 steel	0	1,600	20.0	0.0000	0.0	0.0	0.0
Standard Metro	10	1,245	12.1	0.0222	0.1	0.3	1.5
Pellet Weight	20	1,010	8.0	0.0492	0.4	1.8	3.3
(grains): 3.513	30	849	5.6	0.0820	1.1	4.2	5.4
Effective Standard Deviation: 0.0223	40	734	4.2	0.1203	2.2	7.6	7.9
	50	644	3.2	0.1641	4.0	12.1	10.8
Pellet Diameter (inches): 0.150	60	566	2.5	0.2141	6.6	18.3	14.1

Note: A pellet of shot looses a massive amount of velocity over the first couple feet after exiting the barrel of the shotgun. The data presented here has been run as to account for the first velocity loss as close as possible to the gun muzzle. With screens placed at a three-foot intervals, the mid-point of 1½ feet is indicated in the above muzzle velocity. Kent Fast steel is listed to be moving at the muzzle at a velocity of 1,650 fps.

WIND DRIFT: YES, IT AFFECTS SHOT PATTERNS

You mostly hear rifle shooters talking about the wind and its effects on how their bullets travel from muzzle to target. But the truth of it is, your shot pattern is affected by wind, too, and you need a way to fight it, at least to some degree, though especially when winds are high.

There are several ways to go about taking a bite out of the problem of big wind problem. First of all, position yourself, if at all possible, with the wind head-on. Better yet, have the wind flowing straight down the back of your neck. This would be an advantage, say, to birds coming into your decoys.

When your hunting doesn't allow for changing your shooting position, say, a walking upland hunter, who would certainly try to work, along with his dogs, into the wind but doesn't always have that option when it's time to take the shot, I'd advise you move up in shot size. Increasing the pellet mass and having that extra weight will fight off wind drift to some degree. Added speed through using hyper-velocity loads will cut "hang time" as well. Riflemen know this term well, especially-long range shooters. The time the shot is in the air after leaving the muzzle, its hang time, will directly affect wind drift. Fast loads drift less. The new Hypersonic Remington, by example, shoots flat even when common iron shot pellets are in the mix. Why? Speed and one heck of a lot of it (1,700 to 2,000 fps at the muzzle).

I had an editor ask me why I list pellet time in seconds, regarding their flight. The answer should be obvious: less time in the wind means less time making a right or left turn downrange. For instance, some very new data from the Hypersonic 20-gauge 3-inch shells have illustrated that these loads made up of a small No. 4 steel pellet are crossing the chronograph screens at a flat-out 850 fps. That adds about *15 more killing yards* to the light 20-gauge waterfowl or upland shotgun. Bottom line, the less time the shot is in the air, the better your success rate will be if your lead is otherwise correct, especially in cases of strong winds.

Of course, hang time can also be adjusted by simply shooting at closer birds, so sometimes adjusting for the winds means being more selective in the shots you choose to make. By adjusting decreasing your allowable range in heavy crosswinds, you are cut the time the pellets fight those winds, which means they don't get pushed as far off course as they would over a longer distance in the same wind.

As a final element in the fight against wind, move to the more expensive solution and shoot high-density loads. More density means less wind drift, period. Still, take note of the table included here. Even the high priced stuff, including the almost pure tungsten (TSS) can't fight wind forever. As long range riflemen well know, everything bends to the wind—that certainly includes smoothbore shot.

Wind Table — Ballistics Research & Development

Shot Size/Type	Muzzle Velocity (FPS)	Range Wind Drift (10 MPH WIND)
TBI* No. 6 (experimental	1,450	@50 yards 10.9 inches
		@55 yards = 13.5 inches
TBI BB	???	@50 yards = 7 inches
		@70 yards = 13.7 inches
		@80 yards = 18.2 inches
TSS** No. 5	1,450	@40 yards = 4.1 inches
		@60 yards = 9.4 inches
		@90 yards = 21.6 inches
Steel No. 3	1,315	@40 yards = 8.6 inches
Steel No. 2	1,400	@40 yards = 8.0 inches
		@50 yards = 12.6 inches

* TBI Tungsten bronze-iron high-density shot. **TSS Tungsten Super Shot .19 density (comparable to lead's .11 density). Note: Table is based on a wind direction at right angles (full value) to the shooter. You can see that steel shot, regardless being a small No. 3 or a larger No. 2 pellet, is dying a quick death beyond 40 yards in a moderately stiff wind. Also note that even the new super shot types used in this example can't fight off wind deflection. Now add the fact that at a wind velocity of 30 mph all these factors will triple in measurement. In other words, if pellet drift in a 10 mph wind at 40 yards equals eight inches, it now drifts a full 24 inches in a 30 mph crossing wind. At some point, the shot drifts so badly that it is just about paralleling the crossing bird. The basic formula for wind is the following. Horizontal deflection (drift) = crosswind velocity x (time of flight to target/muzzle velocity). Note that drift will be proportional to the crosswind velocity.

A Winning Triplex Load

Lacking much, if any, reference ammo based on current testing, I turned to the big 3-inch two-ounce loads offered by EnvironnMetal, Inc., in its No. 5-6-7 triplex tungsten shot load. With the high price per shotshell, I didn't shoot many of them, rather saving a good portion of my stash for my local gobbler and duck hunts. Despite its high cost, this is one of the best loads ever designed for turkeys in particular, bar none. How good?

What I did shoot at a 30-inch circle proved very interesting indeed. At 40 yards, while an exact pattern percentage can't be measured for reasons I've already discussed, what I did see was that this round, fired from a steady bench rest via my long-range waterfowl Hevi-Shot choke installed in my 3½-inch chambered Winchester SX-3, drilled about 80 percent of the payload dead center into a 10-inch circle. The rest of the triple pellet load covered the rest of the target within just eight inches of the core pattern. Even shooting high on the target three times (for some unknown reason), the pellet payload was still all in the 30-inch circle save for five stray pellets out of hundreds. A term that best fits the performance of the loads is "crushing." While this was not a waterfowl load design, it clearly illustrates that loads of multiple pellet sizes can be devastatingly effective.

Duplex loads have been fooled with from time to time. While they've tended to be dedicated to turkey loads, Remington also made them in a BBB x No. 1 steel load for waterfowl and a No. 7½ x No. 8 load for target shooters. None lasted long and, today, you'll be hard-pressed to find more than a dusty leftover box or two on a retailer's shelf.

There once was a load I favored that I'd dubbed the "Tri-Power." It was a three-pellet offering in steel shot, one created by Federal Cartridge well before it became ATK Corp. As has been its history, Federal was searching for a better mousetrap, in this instance at a time when many steel loads were lackluster in performance. The load made it to market, but was dropped from Federal's lineup somewhere along the way. I contacted my friend and associate at Federal, Tim Brandt, and asked him any information as to why those loads were dropped, as I'd found them to be great loads for dusting off large race Canada geese over about three years of selective test shooting. According to Federal, the triple pellet loads in steel were offered over a two-year period, in the small, 10-round packs. However, hunters didn't take to them well; they were simply more interested in single pellet size loads at the time, so the load was quickly phased out of production.

This old load from Federal was once a favorite of the auhtor's. They were offered for only about two years, when lack of hunter interest (and downright skepticism) killed it off.

The Federal ballistics department indicated to me that, while these loads are no longer produced, the option is always on the table to resurrect them from the dead. In my humble opinion I don't believe the Tripower loads ever got their day in the court of hunter opinion. Shotgunners overall are a finicky bunch, and, as such, new loads take some getting used to with them.

That said, the concept of multiple pellet sizes and even pellet types hasn't fallen off the idea tree. Environ-Metal, Inc., employs the concept in its new Hevi-Shot Speed Ball load, which has a duplex load of No. 2 steel and No. 4 tungsten pellets in the same load. Hevi-Shot double also makes its Hevi-Metal loads with both small-er tungsten and larger steel pellets. Though it's still not come around to making that triplex load I liked, Federal has blended both round shot and cutter pellets of steel into the same payload in its Black Cloud ammunition for still a third example. So, how are hunters reacting to these new loads?

Reviewing several of the Internet's gun talk forums, I see piles of experts (who never use their real names) tearing apart any suggested use of a load that's different in any way from the old 1¼-ounce 3-inch 12-gauge iron (steel) shot load for any and all waterfowling and other hunting. They are truly being left behind. If the industry had not walked away from that dead center those "experts" keep proposing, we'd still be throwing rocks at ducks and with better results then those early steel shot loads were able to produce.

"Different" is always the key, and it's a word that goes right along with the "creative." That's the stuff that builds better ballistic performance for all of us to take into the field—and you must admit, the current steel shot fodder we have available to us now is a far cry from the stuff we had to start with.

I have always believed that there was a general conspiracy to do away with waterfowl hunting through the non-availability of non-toxic that could kill a duck. (Note please that I have not stated "harvest," but "kill"—we ain't messing around here.) Well, for whatever reason it didn't work out quite that way and, today, we have loads that totally outgun anything, including lead shot, and doing so at new (extended) practical and effective ranges. As for the multi-pellet shot size loads, I know for a fact that they work and work well. For instance, my subsonic shooting customers buy piles of them in custom Polywad loads, and I never get a complaint from any of them. These are tungsten No. 4x2 in a 3-inch 1 ¼-ounce subsonic/low recoil load intended for duck hunting over decoys, and a triplex big iron load in BBxTTTxFF for big geese at close range. Truly, if I know anything for sure, it is that understanding multi-pellet loads can be a day changer over the duck pond. Let me demonstrate

A little while back, with a busy fall waterfowl hunting on the calendar, I decided to take a crack at turning some of my own specialized handloads into multi-shot

Remington used to load a duplex shell of BBBx1. The author dug out an old box he still had on hand for some testing, and found it absolutely slayed big Canada honkers.

loads. My first test location was the state of Maine, for a hunt for sea eiders and old squaws with Mossberg Firearms and the brand-new Mossberg Flex shotgun system (reviewed elsewhere in this book). On that hunt, I took along my duplex creations and a different model Mossberg.

I was shooting shells holding a mix of Hevi-Metal No. 4 and Speed Ball No. 3. I had choked a Mossberg 835 with a 28-inch barrel with the Hevi-Shot High Performance waterfowl choke tube that had been supplied by Mossberg specifically for just such work, and I quickly found it to be a terminator well out to 55 yards and more. The big heavy weight and fast moving eiders were no match for the 1600-plus fps fast movers sent aloft by the Mossberg over-bored .775 barrel. This gun was clearly the best choice for the task at hand and I took my limit of big eider drakes in short order.

Moving back inland to mid-state South Dakota, I set decoys with my friend Tyson Keller, who's in marketing for the new waterfowl equipment company that goes by the name of "Banded." Tyson, as he always does, had scouted a hot location for decoying Canada's off the Missouri River. Now, armed with my Winchester SX-3 and with Tyson shooting his Beretta auto-loader, we proceeded to chamber round after round of Federal Black Cloud 3-inch No. 2s and BBs, interspersed with single rounds of Remington BBBx1, a bygone load in its original green box wrapper that I had saved over the years. During the eight minutes of shooting it took to fill our three-bird apiece limits, both the Federal advanced Black Cloud steel (with its two different shaped pellets), and the old style Remington two-size duplex loads I was chambering had done the trick. As it had been with the the sea duck hunt, again the Black Cloud's multiple pellet shapes had flat-out cut those big gray Canadas out of the sky to 55 yards, like laying wheat to the blade. As for that old green box Remington multiple pellet size loads? I think hunters have made a mistake letting them just get up off the dealers shelves and go away. If you find any of them remaining on some back road store shelf. Buy them because they work and will get the job done effectively.

SHOT STRING DYNAMICS

for just about ever, we shotgunners have been bombarded with two forms of data applied to the effectiveness of shotshell loads. The first is payload weight and the second is pattern percentage on paper based on a 40-yard range and a 30-inch circle for a target. While there is no doubt a good pattern is required to bring down game birds or break clay targets, a third area also crucial to such performance is an observation that's almost never discussed. To be sure, this is because, lacking some very expensive equipment, you're never actually going to see this phenomenon.

I'm talking about shot stringing. Shot string has been studied a great deal by a number of ballistics experts over the years and, to be sure, some extensive research has been done by the ammunition industry as a whole in this area of shotshell performance measurement. The problem with it all is that there is almost no way of coming to some exact conclusion about the behavior of shot string length for a given load, choke, or gauge. Add in the fact that the element for determining a gun/load's pattern circumference is possible only via complicated measuring systems (plus the fact that they are not, at times, very accurate), and it should be obvious that a good deal about a payload's performance as it moves downrange is largely unknown.

WHAT WE DO KNOW

What is clearly understood among the stuff that is a mystery is that shot string lengths vary greatly across different loads and different choke configurations. Over the years, experiments have been conducted, using some very basic tools, in order to get a better handle on shot stringing effects downrange. Bob Brister, for instance, a top-notch ballistics evaluator and shotgunner, did some testing by towing a large sheet of plywood on edge and mounted to a

trailer pulled behind the family station wagon. Adding sheets of paper to the plywood, he fired various rounds at the whole rig, while his wife drove past him at set distances. Bob discovered that, when hitting the moving pattern paper, the pattern print was always oval. Compare that to the normal round and centered print produced by a shot on a *static* patterning target. In essence, through his experimenting, Brister had brought to the forefront the visual evidence that not all the shot in a payload gets to the target at the same time.

In later years, the development of a large drum that held a large sheet of paper around it was built by shotshell pattern evaluators. When the drum was rotated at a uniform and high velocity by an electric motor and shot at, a pattern effect was seen that extended almost all the way round the drum. Again, clearly it could be seen that incoming shot was stringing, the pellets in the load hitting the drum at different times, i.e., over the length of the string.

In the physical world of field gunning, we see shot stringing all the time, especially when waterfowling over water. And then there are the exceptions. Back in the early 1960s, I was shooting 2¾-inch paper-cased handloads of Red Dot powder and 1⅛ ounces of No. 5 copper-plated lead shot. Using my old and trusted Winchester Model 24 side-by-side and its fixed Modified choke, this load produced one solid pile of shot on an incoming, low over the water bluebill. In effect, there was almost no stringing at all. Why there was no stringing I have not a clue and, try as I did, I was never able to duplicate the effect with other handloads.

Sea duck hunting also will produce much the same kind of information, if you're paying attention to the splash over the wave tops on those fast-moving, surf-skimming scoters. While one gun/choke will string pellets for 50 feet, the next will spatter every pellet inside a few yards or less. What I've seen in my years of shooting is that it's about the guns and chokes where the subject starts to get interesting.

When I wrote about the effects of shot stringing as we analyzed it from the research done during testing called the Georgia Project, it created quite a buzz among shotgunners. What we observed and I reported on was that more *open* chokes tended to produce shorter shot strings. "Who would have ever thought?" became the standard response to those who read my reports. Considering how long we've

Back in the early 1970s, I had several discussions with Dave Fackler, owner, at the time, of Ballistics Products, the Minnesota outfit that today offers a complete line of shotshell handloading components. The discussion was, for the most part, about the observed differences in shotshell load performance. Dave indicated at the time, and I have never forgotten the conversation, that there are loads that look dreadful on paper and yet shoot ducks like there's no tomorrow. The obvious question is "Why?"

thought the opposite to be true, what was going on?

Based on the information I can gather, I believe we were surprised by these findings because we don't measure but a small fraction of what makes a great load drop ducks and geese like so much rain. The common, two-dimensional pattern percentage evident on a 30-inch circle, the one thing most shotgunners rely on to tell them whether they have their gun/choke/load right, is only a part of the story.

Am I saying that we all need to start shooting Modified or even more open chokes? In terms of hitting a target or bird consistently, yes, that would seem to be a good starting point for all of us. Now add into the equation that we know that, because most forms of non-toxic shot are harder than common lead shot, the Modified choke seems to be the one choke that brings home the groceries. But where do we go from here? Is it really that simple? Is the Modified choke the thing that gets you closer to perfection than anything else?

The author's home-rigged mud test. While it's nearly impossible to get exact readings of what your shot is doing, due to the difficulties in maintaining the test gun's angle to the mud, this still provides more information about your shot string than a static 30-inch paper patterning target ever will.

I think it's just possible that some of the answers to that question could involve the choke constriction. It could also be the method used to control the payload upon exiting the barrel, which isn't just the task of a choke's constriction, but also wad strippers, claw tooth designs, or even the old tried and true Russian "jug" choke that once graced competition trap guns on otherwise fixed-choke barrels.

A method I often use to determine payload control is by way of a small stock pond on a rancher friend's place near my home. This pond isn't much more then a glorified mudhole, but the spring that feeds it keeps the water level about the same all year round, and even on windy days it is almost always smooth as glass. As a test of shot stringing effects from proven payload control systems, I will shoot three rounds of a given load onto the pond surface at exactly 40 yards. While I can't give you the exact muzzle/target angle to the pond surface, it is close to seven degrees.

Shooting both a Remington 887 new out of the box and my Winchester SX-3 in its 3-inch model, I selected different chokes for use with BB steel shot test loads. At the shot, I watched the pattern spread and the shot string length plainly visible on the water's surface. This may be a much as seven to 14 yards in length or as tight as a five yards. What is interesting is that *less* constricted chokes tend to look better, in terms of overall payload control.

The chart at the bottom of this page is a general measurement of payload effects, arrived at from different chokes tested at 40 yards. Even though quite rough, measurements were assessed by way of using the half-sunbaked mud at the edge of the pond. Shooting at a lasered 40 yards and through a set of stakes set exactly 30 inches apart, the shot string was recorded. A third stake was set at the location of the last pellet to make contact with the ground.

I'll admit that this is a rather rudimentary test. In conducting this evaluation, the angle of the shot into the mud surface has to be exact, as any change in angle would result in a different shot string length. But such consistency wasn't easy to maintain and, as a result, *exact* measurements were not always possible. Still, even in its imperfection, the water/mud testing serves as a nice visual indicator of the shot string as it hits an angled surface.

The ultra high-speed camera used during the Georgia Project (covered in a later chapter) to film shot in flight was without question, a much better tool than my mud setup. But considering the expense of the equipment, engineers paid, and the time spent test shooting, it's good to know that a more available medium such as my muddy bank can provide similar, useful information that can be passed onto the hunter. Try it yourself. Get off the static patterning board and make some consistently positioned shots on water, soft earth, mud, or snow and see what your gun, choke, and load are really doing in combination.

After some review, it should be apparent that the question of shot string measurement as a significant player in evaluating load performance seems to have some validity. For a fact, it's better than simply playing the old-school game of "That's how Dad did it." Add the fact that shotgunners, by their very nature, are stuck-in-the-mud thinkers when it comes to any form of change or creativity, and the development of new ideas, let alone reevaluating old materials, can be a very slow process. What this boils down to is, whether you like non-toxic shot or not, if steel shot development did one thing for us, it was to move the mindset about smoothbore performance off the dead center of where it has been for ages. We finally had to ask, could some of those concepts be all wrong? You bet they could.

The charts on the following several pages show some basic shotshell ballistics that will give the reader an idea of what steel shot, being the most problematic of the shot types, is doing after it leaves the barrel. Note that the shot sizes in the examples on page 81 are smaller than what we've discussed so far, and so are best applied to light game or clay targets and, as such, are not the most appropriate for extended range hunting use.

The second set of raw ballistic measurements, shown on page 82, are those of Speed Ball by Hevi-Shot. This is a single-size duplex load of both tungsten iron and steel shot. It is an example of the very flexible nature toward which current direction factory loads have been turning, regarding load design.

THE STACY PROJECT— TESTING SMALLER SHOT SIZES

The Stacy Project was named after an airfield and small town local to the Minneapolis-Saint Paul, Minnesota, metro areas. This test area was loaned to me on off days, (meaning no flights coming in). The strip measured a distance of 3,000 yards, counting the rough landing area, and, as such, it was a safe

Choke Type	Approximate Pattern Width	Approximate Pattern Length
Carlson's Black Cloud	30 inches	4½ yards
Remington Decoy (.006 constriction)	33 inches	3 yards*
Dead Ringer **	30 inches	4 yards
Rem Choke Modified	32 inches	3½ yards
Trulock Browning Invector Plus Black Cloud	30 inches	4¾ yards
Undertaker Decoy	32 inches	3 yards

Legend: * The bulk of Remington "Decoy" choked load was inside seven feet. ** Dead Ringer is an author-developed research and test choke. Test guns: Remington M887, .724 bore diameter (standard); Winchester SX-3, 3-inch chamber back-bored (non-standard). Ammunition: Wolf 12-gauge 3-inch No. 2 steel 1¼ ounces.

If you really want to see what your pattern's doing, you must get off the static pattern board. Shoot across water and mud, instead, to get the real view.

SHOTdata Results 08/17/2009 Shot type: No.5 steel	Range (YARDS)	Velocity (FPS)	Energy (FT/LBS)	Time of Flight (SECONDS)	Drop (INCHES)	Wind Def@45mph (FEET)	Lead Required (FEET)
Pellet Weight (grains): 1.799	0	1504	9.0	0.0000	0.0	0.0	0
Effective Standard Deviation: 0.0178	10	1118	5.0	0.0242	0.1	0.5	1.6
	20	886	3.1	0.0548	0.5	2.3	3.6
Pellet Diameter (inches): 0.120	30	735	2.2	0.0924	1.3	5.3	6.1
Standard Deviation: 0.0178	40	624	1.6	0.1370	2.8	9.7	9.0

Note: Steel shot trajectory calculated for nominal 1,400 fps muzzle velocity at three feet from muzzle and for a Modified choke.

SHOTdata Results 08/17/2009 Shot type: No.6 steel	Range (YARDS)	Velocity (FPS)	Energy (FT/LBS)	Time of Flight (SECONDS)	Drop (INCHES)	Wind Def@45mph (FEET)	Lead Required (FEET)
Pellet Weight (grains): 1.385	0	1,512	7.0	0.0000	0.0	0.0	0.0
Effective Standard Deviation: 0.0164	10	1,096	3.7	0.0245	0.1	0.5	1.6
	20	856	2.3	0.0559	0.5	2.5	3.7
Pellet Diameter (inches): 0.110	30	704	1.5	0.0950	1.4	5.8	6.3
Standard Deviation: 0.0164	40	589	1.1	0.1420	3.0	10.9	9.4

Note: Steel shot trajectory calculated for nominal 1,400 fps muzzle velocity at three feet from muzzle and for a Modified choke.

SHOTdata Results 08/17/2009 Shot type: No.7 steel	Range (YARDS)	Velocity (FPS)	Energy (FT/LBS)	Time of Flight (SECONDS)	Drop (INCHES)	Wind Def@45mph (FEET)	Lead Required (FEET)
Pellet Weight (grains): 1.041	0	1,520	5.3	0.0000	0.0	0.0	0.0
Effective Standard Deviation: 0.0149	10	1,071	2.7	0.0247	0.1	0.6	1.6
	20	823	1.6	0.0573	0.5	2.8	3.8
Pellet Diameter (inches): 0.100	30	669	1.0	0.0982	1.5	6.4	6.5
Standard Deviation: 0.0149	40	551	0.7	0.1480	3.2	12.3	9.8

Note: Steel shot trajectory calculated for nominal 1,400 fps muzzle velocity at three feet from muzzle and for a Modified choke.

SHOTdata Results 06/18/2012	Range (YARDS)	Velocity (FPS)	Energy (FT/LBS)	Time of Flight (SECONDS)	Drop (INCHES)	Wind Def@45mph (FEET)	Lead Required (FEET)
Shot type: Ballistics Speed Ball No. 2	0	1,668	23.8	0.0000	0.0	0.0	0
	10	1,367	16.0	0.0207	0.1	0.2	1.4
Tungsten Pellet Weight (grains): 3.850	20	1,142	11.1	0.0449	0.3	1.3	3.0
	30	980	8.2	0.0735	0.9	3.2	4.9
Effective Standard Deviation: 0.0289	40	859	6.3	0.1064	1.8	5.9	7.0
	50	764	5.0	0.1437	3.2	9.3	9.5
Tungsten Pellet Diameter (inches): 0.138	60	690	4.1	0.1852	5.1	13.3	12.2
	70	624	3.3	0.2310	7.8	18.6	15.2
Standard Deviation: 0.0289	80	565	2.7	0.2818	11.3	25.2	18.6

Note: Since the exact composition of the tungsten shot is unknown and diameter data is limited the following is a best guess as to the trajectory expected.

SHOTdata Results 06/18/2012	Range (YARDS)	Velocity (FPS)	Energy (FT/LBS)	Time of Flight (SECONDS)	Drop (INCHES)	Wind Def@45mph (FEET)	Lead Required (FEET)
Shot type: B Steel (Sample of 3 pellets)	0	1,668	31.5	0.0000	0.0	0.0	0
	10	1,329	20.0	0.0210	0.1	0.3	1.4
Pellet Weight (grains): 5.100	20	1,089	13.4	0.0462	0.4	1.6	3.1
	30	922	9.6	0.0764	0.9	3.7	5.0
Effective Standard Deviation: 0.0252	40	800	7.3	0.1116	1.9	6.7	7.4
	50	709	5.7	0.1517	3.4	10.6	10.0
Pellet Diameter (inches): 0.170	60	631	4.5	0.1967	5.6	15.5	13.0
Standard Deviation: 0.0252	70	563	3.6	0.2473	8.7	22.1	16.3

backstop for long-range shotgun performance testing. The test setup worked this way: I would take a weekend and drive up to the airfield/range with pattern paper and a number of previously killed waterfowl, upland birds, or fur bearers (raccoon, badger, or coyote), along with various handloaded shotshells of both non-toxic shot and conventional lead pellets in both 12- and 10-gauge. The dead fowl and mammals would be rehydrated (water added by injection to the tissue), then positioned on a target frame and re-shot at various ranges. (While this will seem a bit grizzly to some of you, I promise, it's nothing compared to the things and methods of the studies done by other agencies whose work I've reviewed.)

The second element involved in the testing would be the use of a chronograph to measure the exact speed of an incoming pellet as it made contact with the test subject. The subject would be covered with a lightweight, soft paper cover and, after the test firing, hits would be measured and recorded when aligned with the photo screens of the chronograph, which was fully armored for protection. Every contact hit would then be measured for penetration by way of a steel rod pushed through the paper surface material and into the wound channel. The results were interesting, and I was able to construct tables showing the exact range at which pellets of different types and sizes were still lethal over ranges of 30 to 100-plus yards.

Now for the real kicker. When measured for penetration, it was found that, at a given range appropriate for the shot size being used, the "rule of thumb," the velocity minimum standard of 600 fps we'd always assumed was correct was actually *a dead-on match* to the depth required for a pellet to reach a game animal's vitals! The testing system had worked, and I now had a very clear barometer from which I could build everything from loads for night shooting gray fox to advanced, ultra long-range waterfowl ammunition.

With the raw numbers in hand and a big pile of recorded data dealing with precise, real-time speed of both lead and steel shot at the target point, the next element of the project was turned over to my lifelong associate Ross Metzger of SHOT-data Systems, of New Brighton, Minnesota. Ross took my numbers and, over the course of several weeks, developed the complete and first time ever ballistic tables dealing with smooth-bore shot performance at just about any range it could be measured. When we looked at those numbers for the first time, we knew for sure what it took to kill a goose, duck, or whatever game at any range you wanted to plug into the system. Even better, if a load didn't measure up, it was thrown out of the list and replaced with a load that could deliver the mail.

In a matter of months, I was getting calls from all sorts of ballisticians and old-time gun writers. With all that interest being generated, I was sure I was on the right track to a better understanding of shotshell ballistics. In the process, I had started to make some new friends and associates in the business of manufacturing shotshell ammunition. Best of all, as non-toxic shot had erupted into a full-blown cause *du jour* in sport hunting at the time, my timing could not have been any better. (Or as my "psychic" wife, Colleen, often says, "There are no accidents.")

(Note: If you have taken the time to review any and all of my data presented in this book, know that it has, first of all, come from SHOTdata

Understanding Duplex Load Ballistics

It has always been my thought, when shooting different pellet sizes in the same load, the larger and heavier pellets will tend to break the air ahead of the smaller shot and thereby "draft" the small shot and hold it within the air stream of the big pellets. I have actually observed shot pellets, filmed at 25,000 frames per second, run directly behind one and another. When the lead pellet is overtaken by another pellet of the same size pellet, the now advancing pellet penetrates deeper when reaching the mass of ballistic material. Also, the smaller pellet would most likely not overtake the bigger one and, as such, simply maintains a clean, level path to the target. I know this sounds a bit abstract, but, in this business, because we can't really take a ride down the barrel in a shotshell.

Taking the concept to task, there are only two places that can tell the whole story of a duplex load, and that is on the static test range against pattern boards and in the field during real time events. It was on a section of South Dakota prairie that my portable pattern standards that got the call. Shooting my Winchester SX-3 3½-inch waterfowl 12-gauge paired with an Environ-Metal's long-range choke tube at 40 yards, the pattern results were as follows.

First, shooting Environ-Metal special Hevi-Shot "Magnum Blend," a multiple pellet load consisting of Nos. 5, 6, and 7 tungsten loaded to a two-ounce payload at 1,200 fps, the massive 3-inch round turned the pattern board surface into something that looked like black pepper had been dumped on the surface This crusher tungsten load is primarily a turkey load, but, rest assured, on waterfowl it is also a devastating tool (if you can afford the price of pure tungsten based shotshell loads).

Patterns were not recorded by percentage points, as each load will contains a somewhat different pellet count, but, observing the inner 20-inch core versus the outer 10 inches of ring on the full 30-inch circle showed the load was looking quite deadly for potential waterfowl use. What I searched for were breakdowns in the patterns, such as obvious holes and areas where pellets strung across the pattern to leave a section wide open for a bird to then fly through.

The dense core patterns I saw with these Hevi-Shot loads mean a whole lot of shot is staying on track and not turning into fliers. Density also says that, at the range tested, the load will be good for some additional range, in that those core pellets have not yet moved very far off the point of muzzle alignment.

Still, there is the element of shot string that, without any question in my mind, exists and changes with different chokes and loads. I have run numerous test loads across my Oehler Chronotech Model 33 and found enough velocity differences in small to large multi-shot loads to convince me that, indeed, the payload is lining out over a long shot string downrange. While there is always an element of conjecture, when interpreting both data and physical results, I do believe my conclusions allow me to be comfortable with them.

Systems, and, second, that system stops sending back information at or about the 600 fps mark. Now you know why. That's the threshold of a given pellet's performance based on what the Stacy Project revealed, as well as other contributing data of the time that had been generated by this researcher. When you read the data, there is no way you can't come away from this material with a better understanding of how your shotgun works downrange.)

CHRONOGRAPHING BASICS

For me, using the chronograph, an electronic machine that measures the speed of moving objects through air, started about 35 years ago. In those days, it was quite common among ballistic types to chronograph rifle and pistol bullets in flight. But, when it came to chronographing shotgun strings, the art form was so young that, in most cases, gun writers believed it was not only impossible to do, but also that if any information was gained by trying to record shotshell pellets in flight, that data would be less then trustworthy and mostly useless.

With that encouraging bit of knowledge in my back pocket, I headed out to the old Stacy airfield I had permission to use, and there, for the next three years, worked at perfecting the art of measuring not only shotshell pellets in flight from the muzzle of a smoothbore, but also downrange flight speeds. At first, my tests were so meager in terms of success that I didn't share my results with anyone. I was shooting by way of some old hand-me-down equipment that required me to shoot through a very small three-inch window at whatever range I was testing. Then, using a table I'd been developing, I turned around a bunch of raw numbers to find the exact velocity of my recorded pellet speed. If I don't get deep into how I came up with what I did and how I did it at this point, it's because it would take almost every page in the book to even begin to explain it. Regardless, the more I failed, the harder I worked.

My real break came when Doc Oehler, inventor of the Oehler Chronotech velocity recording system, came along. Doc had designed a system that was user-friendly and returned far more information than anything I had seen up to that time, even in commercial production. Today, the Oehler Chronotech system is used by our industry's ammunition manufacturers when bringing new commercial loads together, as well as the U.S. Army when testing anti-tank rounds or main gun tank rounds for downrange and muzzle velocities. With that kind of company, you could say that the Oehler system, as used by the common shooter, brings them into some very exclusive company.

MEASURING MUZZLE VELOCITIES

Whether Oehler's or that of another maker, any chronograph system will include directions to get it up and running. Beyond that, one of the elements

about its use you'll need to keep in mind is that you don't want to press the muzzle of your shotgun directly over or close to the first velocity recording screen. To advance the muzzle too far forward will result in error recordings; the muzzle flash will cause

The author set up on the bench for chronograph work.

the chronograph to react incorrectly to the exact speed of the shot that has passed through the first and second photocell eyes. So, keep your shotgun muzzle at least three feet back of the first screen face. This won't give you the *exact* muzzle velocity, as shot falls off in speed very quickly at the muzzle, but it is a very positive indicator of just how your loads are doing, in terms of uniformity and peek velocities.

Another thing to know is that you may find that the velocities you're recording don't match the load speed printed on the manufacture's box. That is because today's manufactures usually run data from a single run or lot of components and call it good for

general review. You, of course, will always know the exact velocities at which your given shotshells are leaving the gun.

MEASURING DOWNRANGE VELOCITY

When applying a chronograph to downrange shot cloud velocity measurement, you have to remember to armor (protect) the system, in order to keep stray pellets from damaging the unit's recording screens. Regardless the chronograph make, the screens must be shot across, in order to produce the start and stop times of the shot string, which return the velocity in feet per second measurements.

The author setting up his muzzle velocity screens (top and left), and armoring his downrange screens (opposite page). When setting up your muzzle velocity screens, they have to be a little bit out in front of your muzzle, otherwise the photocells of the chronograph register the muzzle blast and produce inaccurate readings.

Part of the solution to this will be removing the overhead sunscreen filters, which you'd normally keep on for single projectile shooting and for shooting during high overhead sun. (Oehler screens can be used "de-horned," as such, for testing with low sun angles at early morning or evening or on a cloudy day, when the overhead screens are unnecessary). If your sun filter screens can't be removed, you'll need to find another model. Beyond that, armor specific to the photocells is required. Thankfully, this is something that's easy to do.

To protect my chronograph's photocells, I use steel railroad tie plates, eight inches by eight inches, set at an angle of 35 degrees against the incoming side of the photocells. This armor will stop a 180-grain .30-06 bullet at 100 yards downrange. To date, no smoothbore shot of any type has even moved these plates of 5/8-inch heavy cast steel. My steel plates are supported by taping them to a 2x4-inch pine rail/ramp that acts to also retain the photocells and which is also armored with 3/8-inch aluminum. That aluminum is also plated, though for lighter duty work, such as fine lead shot at medium ranges (40 yards).

A word of caution here: Always remember to protect the chronograph unit by digging into the ground or using heavy wood or steel plates around the chronograph cables. Any downrange exposure to incoming shot will result in damage that will require new cables, as splicing them is not an option. As to the chronograph computer system itself, move it well away form the impact area. In the case of the Oehler unit, it's separate from the screen system and can be "bunkered in" or set behind an armored screen.

DO YOU NEED TO CHRONOGRAPH YOUR LOADS?

No, but it's a nice thing to do when you're trying to gain the very best out of your loads. Too, handloads can change, even with the use of different propellant lot numbers—change to a different hull, and your pet load can come unglued. Chronographing can work as your personal detective agency and allow you to build close-to-perfect ammunition off the handloading bench plus, at times, I have found problems that would have otherwise gone unchecked if chronograph testing had not been employed.

SHOTGUN CHOKES
The Key to Patterning Proficiency

Shotshells are changing fast. The current trends are for more velocity, better base components (materials inside the shotshell), and improved priming and propellant energy generation. In effect, the modern shotshell is just that, quite a development.

Right along with the new direction in shotshell load development has come better payload delivery. I'm talking about the choke on the shotgun's muzzle. With the advent of faster loads have come choke tubes that are able to send them further downrange as

You're going to need to experiment, not just with your load, but with the chokes you run them through. Especially with today's super-fast non-toxic loads, the need for tight chokes has fallen by the wayside, but to find where between Skeet and Modified your loads work best in your gun, you're going to have to sample both ends of the merchandise.

still solidly effective payloads. I realize some readers aren't all that interested in shooting to ranges that exceed a reasonable decoy gunning distance or blocking rooster pheasants on cornfield ends to 70 yards, but there are more than a few pass shooters and competition clay shooters out there, as well as other unique gunning scenarios (i.e., self-defense) that do require better downrange ballistics from a given load.

I can remember the day when everyone was saying that the then-new non-toxic shot was pure junk. Well, that thinking went the way of the buffalo, didn't it? Today, some are saying our tungsten-based non-toxic loads and ever many iron loads are almost too good and shoot too far. I guess some folks are just never happy. Regardless, part of the success of these long-range loads is, in fact, due to the modern choke tube.

Because aftermarket chokes make up the bulk of the designated long-range and performance chokes marketed to consumers, I selected several to see just how effective they are with these advanced non-toxic loads, compared to some more standard grades of shotshell ammunition. Using the standard 30-inch patterning circle placed to a distance of 40 yards, test shooting was conducted and the patterns assessed for percentage points, core density, and pellet spread uniformity. Here's what I found.

One of Browning's dedicated waterfowling chokes, the extended portion made to look like a goose band. Cute, eh?

THE TEST SETUP

My test gun for this experiment was my Winchester Super X-3 12-gauge with an Invector Plus choke tube set. This particular gun has the 3-inch upland chamber. As a test base load, I selected Kent Cartridge's 12-gauge 3-inch, 1 1/8-ounce No. 1 steel shot at 1,560 fps, and Hevi-Metal 3-inch 1 1/4-ounce BB at 1,500 fps for use with each choke tube being compared (it should be obvious that, if the chokes weren't balanced by way of the same test gun and shotshell, my results would otherwise be completely invalid). I selected these two loads, one, because the Environ-Metal Hevi-Metal load is an example of a blend of steel and lower-grade tungsten in a budget-friendly shotshell, while the Kent loads have gained a reputation as an effective but cost-cutting alternative to higher-dollar ammunition. The Kent shell is also able to retain some fast pellet speeds downrange ballistics. As a side note, I also chose both these loads based on work I'd already done with them through my own Dead Ringer choke. I knew these loads could shoot very well, which dispelled any skepticism from the start that there could be problems with the ammo. Why didn't I elect to test Winchester Xtended or Hevi-Shot tungsten iron? Well, what would be the gain there? Most hunters are and will be shooting budget loads as time marches on, more so than they ever will the high-dollar loads. Best to find out what the cheaper ones do then through today's chokes.

the payload to travel a good distance away from the muzzle), I elected to press the turkey choke to the test. This tube is Hevi-Shot (tungsten) safe and, as such, can also take on any hard steel shot. To my way of thinking, if it's good on long-range turkeys, why not as a pass-shooting or other specialized field gunning tool, as well one for use on ringneck roosters? Different targets yes, but the same goal.

As a side note here, and one generally *not* discussed in print, this choke design, according to my sources, was first built by someone who was not a Hevi-Shot engineers. The original intent was the same—long-range performance—but the material originally selected for the choke was not up to standards and, as such, the chokes failed on a regular basis. When Environ-Metal picked up the design, a change in materials made for a tube of much higher strength. In my opinion, it has become one of the best long-range tubes available to date, bar none. I have had readers call me or e-mail me and request my thoughts on a well-designed choke and gun combination, and my first choice in these matters has been the Hevi-Shot long-range tube with a Winchester Super X-3 behind it. I rest my case.

ENVIRON-METAL HEVI-SHOT AND STEEL SHOT CHOKE

Environ-Metal, Inc., the maker of Hevi-Shot, has turned to designing and marketing its own choke tube. This tube makes use of a ring system (three, to be exact, much like my own Dead Ringer design), and the tube has a constriction of .671, with parallel, slit-shaped porting added to aid in payload control. Built in both waterfowl and turkey variations (certainly also applicable to any other situation that requires

Environ-Metal Hevi-Shot/Steel Choke Pattern Results

Load	Range (YARDS)	Pattern Percentage (THREE-SHOT AVG)	Notes
Kent No. 1 steel	40	83%	Workable core
Hevi-Metal BB	40	94%	Dense core

FLAMBEAU FOWL MAX CHOKE

Built as a heavy choke with massive parallel section extensions, this tube makes use of some straight-line porting, as well as small, round ports. With a tube constriction of .710, it makes for a good balance between a tight tube and gas relief, providing the ability to reduce payload stress and vibration prior to the load exiting the muzzle.

Flambeau Fowl Max Choke Pattern Results

Load	Range (YARDS)	Pattern Percentage (THREE-SHOT AVG)	Notes
Kent No. 1 steel	40	81%	Workable core
Hevi-Metal BB	40	88%	Workable core

CARLSON'S LONG RANGE X-FULL CHOKE

Just about the time I was wrapping up this material, the folks at Carlson's sent a set of three tubes for my Winchester Super X-3 that included an X-Full long-range waterfowl special payload control choke. I was about to head for Minnesota, for an extended fishing and hunting trip, including a hunt for crows over decoys with my old partners at Buffalo Ridge hunting camp, when the chokes got to me. I asked my hunting pal Todd Gifford to push some decoys back a bit on

our fresh-cut hayfield so as to get at 50- and 60-yard birds with some soft-shooting Winchester Xtended one-ounce No. 6 steel general purpose loads. The Carlson's choke sent payload after payload of the small pellets at distant crows with devastating results. Todd was shooting a stiff 2¾-inch 1¼-ounce No. 6 lead load at the black bandits and, after seeing the buzz-saw effect, of the Winchester Xpert with that Carlson's choke tube, he, too, went with that combination in his Beretta on the very next incoming bunch of black-feathered devils. Let's just say, lots of crows bit the dust that day.

Selecting two chokes from my test and evaluation box that will henceforth be called "X" and "Y," I found that it was possible to obtain some very different and *less* effective results on the pattern board with these tubes, both of which were so-called "long-range high-performance" choke tubes. Shooting the first sample "X" choke with the ultra high-velocity ammunition produced the results you see on the next page.

Carlson's Long Range X-Full Choke Pattern Results

Load	Range (YARDS)	Pattern Percentage (THREE-SHOT AVG)	Notes
Kent No. 1 steel	40	79%	Good cor
Hevi-Metal BB	40	83%	Solid prin
Win. No. 6 steel Xpert	40	92%	Buzz-saw

Judging by its construction, sample "Y" did actually seem to be a choke designed with long-range work in mind. The tube used porting, and its internal geometry was set up for "ultra tight, extended-range patterns," according to the manufacture's own words. However, like the similar "X" choke, this number just didn't roll out the best performance.

So what went wrong? Why such poor performance with chokes claimed to be specifically designed for the just the kind of shooting I was testing? The fact is that *nothing* went wrong with the choke test, but several choke tubes didn't like my selection in waterfowl ammunition. I see this all the time, and what this should say to you, loud and clear, is *don't assume anything about the choke tube in your hands!* You must put your loads and chokes on paper, because relying on the "Best-Ever!" shout-out on a choke tube's packaging can get you nowhere.

Because the selected test loads were ultra high-velocity types, the type of load we are seeing more and more of all the time, the design of some of these tubes just couldn't keep the pellet load balanced and on target center. An unbalanced load and speed can return blown patterns—and that's exactly what happened in the case of "X" and "Y."

By my count, only three chokes out of the group I tested could be considered to be high performing with these loads. Does that mean that the "X" and "Y" chokes are worthless? No, not at all. But my results do suggest that, if one of those chokes was one I was going to take afield regularly, I should be looking at different load options, including those of slower velocity, different brand, or different shot size. Like I said, you can't assume anything about your choke, gun, and load—you must put it on paper and see what it really does.

Mystery Choke "X" Pattern Results

Load	Range (YARDS)	Pattern Percentage (THREE-SHOT AVG)	Notes
Kent No. 1 steel	40	68%	Blown core
Hevi-Metal BB	40	63%	Blown core

Mystery Choke "Y" Pattern Results

Load	Range (YARDS)	Pattern Percentage (THREE-SHOT AVG)	Notes
Kent No. 1 steel	40	60%	Weak core
Hevi-Metal BB	40	58%	Blown core

At left, a Hevi-Shot choke shown against the printing surface of a spent wad. This is one of the best long-range chokes offered today. Below, two extended Carlson's chokes made for the author and his frequent testing.

While this review is not about stroking anyone in particular, in terms of brand names, the folks at Environ-Metal, Inc., Carlson's Chokes, and Flambeau/Fowl Max seemed to have gotten it right. But also recall that the Browning barrel used on the Winchester Super X-3 is back-bored to a diameter of .742, rather than the industry 12-gauge standard .724. Could that have made a difference in my testing? Well, perfecting patterning can get right down to air temperature, humidity levels and just pure luck sometimes, so the answer is yes, over-boring or back-boring a barrel can change the outcome of a pattern.

In the end, fixing an issue means patterning your loads each and every time you change ammunition, guns, or chokes. I'm willing to bet that two-thirds of the shotgunners out there today don't pattern much of anything. These same shooters buy very expensive chokes, simply assuming they work just fine. But the truth is, looks and cost don't equate to great performance. Do what you have to on the patterning board—do it!—but then stick with the choke or three that work well with a wide range of loads. Alternately, find a choke that performs well with just a few selected loads and use that combination of choke and loads all the time. I know professionals who follow this second choice, for the most part shooting the same shotshell and choke all the time—and so goes the philosophy of if it ain't broke, don't fix it.

From left to right: a Mossberg extended X-Factor Turkey choke; Hevi-Shot's ported extended turkey tube with a .662 constriction; an extended and ported number from Carlson's; and an extended Improved Cylinder Duck-Decoy choke from Briley. And this is just a tiny sampling of what's out there!

10-GAUGE vs. 12-GAUGE MAGNUM
Is There a Clear Winner?

CHAPTER TEN

The author with a couple giant Canadas taken by way of one of his favorite 10-gauge scatterguns. He has hopes this gauge will see new life as modern steel shot continues to improve.

ike caliber measurements in rifle barrels, the gauge size in a shotgun will dictate, at least to some degree, how best to use a specific smoothbore. In some cases, shooters become disappointed with a shotgun's performance, when, in reality, it's because the wrong gauge and load were selected for the task at hand. Gauge selection affects range (distance to the target) and terminal performance. Shoot too light

a gun and load and ballistics will start to fall apart quickly.

It's easy enough to find much information on field loads for pheasants or the best recommendation for a rabbit target on a sporting clays course. What I'd like to tackle here is what you don't see much material on, the 10-gauge and what many erroneously consider to be its equal, the 3½-inch 12-gauge magnum.

THE 10-GAUGE

The big bun with a big hole in the muzzle is still the shotgun the top of the ballistics food chain, and though its popularity has ebbed and flowed over the decades, today it has a firm place among sportsmen, specifically waterfowl, with a cadre of turkey hunters who also prefer its extra reach. But before we get to those applications, I have to say that to go without understanding the dynamics of the 10-gauge and its guns will lead to your failure in getting the best performance out of not only them, but many *other* shotgun gauges and types.

The 10-gauge magnum has seen a recent readjustment in its position of favor, due in part to the 2012 and 2013 elimination of many high-performance 3½-inch 12-gauge loads that have been a mainstay for years now among long-range pass shooters and hunters of very large waterfowl (Canada geese in the *B.c. maxima* subspecies—known colloquially as giant Canadas—turkeys, and Sandhill cranes, to name a couple prime examples.) I've long been a fan of this round, and it's not new to me in any way. As I've told you before, I cut my teeth on the big gun well back in the early 1970s. In those days, decoys were few and far between. Most hunting for big waterfowl, and even a pile of duck hunting, was done from shallow water passage points or along higher elevation ridgelines and road ditches close to refuge systems. At that time, the 10-gauge was the long-range king. Getting hold of one was almost mandatory, if you wanted to stay in the game of pass shooting and maintain a suitable amount of field success.

When steel shot came into the picture as a mandatory waterfowl load, a lot of hunters were caught off guard: there simply *weren't* any non-toxic 10-gauge loads. I was lucky, doing what I do, and many of my colleagues and I set to work building our own iron ball loads. We bought ball bearings in bulk, annealing them in a ceramics kiln to a dead-soft state, then loading them by way of a charge of SR 4756, a Remington SP 10-gauge wad, a handmade liner of rolled aluminum roofer flashing (for bore protection), then a shot payload of 34 FFF (.21-caliber) iron balls. All this was packed in a buffer of the breakfast cereal Cream of Wheat (obviously, in its dry, uncooked state), set to a "B" card, 4-inch, uncrimped 10-gauge hull (four inches was the length of an uncrimped 10-gauge paper hull), primed with a Federal No. 209 (that one being

Another successful Canada goose hunt for the author, this one courtesy of the Remington SP-10 10-gauge. Brezny hopes this gun and others like it will be making a comeback in the years to come.

the hot primer of the day), and then taken into the field to drive game wardens nuts. The guys in green uniforms thought for sure that, when that 70-yard-high Canada dropped out of the sky, we had done the deed with the recently outlawed lead shot. We could almost count on red lights and speeding green state or fed pickup trucks coming our way on each and every hunt.

In some cases back then, hunters held record shots on big geese and other birds shot at distances that exceeded 100 yards, thanks to those super big-bore guns of the day. I know firsthand, as I was a refuge ditch rat who lived along fence lines, right along with many old friends and acquaintances, for better then a decade. That was where I learned to shoot a shotgun well at long range, and also to load new and different types of shotshell ammunition from scratch. (As an aside, if you don't load ammunition of all types, you're doomed to know very little about the craft in the long run.)

I must admit that, for many years, the 10-gauge guns in my possession around the era of mainline steel shot introductions didn't see much, if any, work afield. The industry race for advanced non-toxic loads was running at full speed for 12-gauge rounds, so there was little time to dwell on those old super-gauge guns that were just about being outshot at every turn by advanced loads in the 3½-inch 12-gauge.

Well, that was then and this is now and, if you look closely, the 10-gauge never went away in the hands of pass shooters and critter control experts. Notice I have indicated "experts." That is because, when your paycheck depends on success, you tend to stay with what gets the job done. With steel shot returned as the primary shot type in use today, due to the reduction of designer loads in tungsten shot and the introduction of high-performance steel, I believe the big 10-gauge gun is going to again find a new home among gunners who want more range and more energy on target.

In some hands, and as predator hunters have always known, the 10-gauge never went out of services. Last year, crossing the winter landscape of eastern South Dakota with some of my friends from Avery Outdoors and Banded Gear, we came across seven-foot snow drifts filling miles of open ditches that were the entry and exit points Canada geese were using, as they fed on blown-out sections of cut grain cops or, in some cases, standing corn that was now barely sticking out of the drifts. Many goose hunters were packing some very heavy ordnance: 10-gauge doubles, pumps, and autoloaders. These pass gunners needed all the ballistic assistance they could get from a smoothbore firearm. While a decoying Canada can be taken with ease by even a 20-gauge loaded with a heavy charge of powder and No. 2 iron shot over decoys, the passing goose in open country is a completely different story. To have a chance at them, hunters clad in white camo crouched and laid out in their snow forts and hollowed-out foxholes to blend into the landscape. The phone line-high Canadas, as well as some of their

brethren drifting in from quite a bit higher, never had any idea what lay in wait below them. *This* was work for the big 10-gauge.

That hunt last year reminded me of my early years of refuge rat goose hunting at Rochester, Minnesota, where we took on the giant Canadas in just the very same way. You couldn't know this, but we gun writers spend hours of computer time processing essays on the subject of decoy gunning for all types of waterfowl. What's left out all too often are the stories and information about the pass shooters who hunt from government blinds set up by the game and fish folks, both federal and state. Then there are the freelance hunters who roll across the goose range, spotting, stalking, then gunning birds going to and coming from feeding areas.

Lest you think these are just memories of a time gone by, the bottom line is that even well into the today's age of American waterfowling, complete with all its bells and whistles, the pass shooter is still alive and well with the 10-gauge, and that gun is still fully entrenched as an integral part of the total equation. While 200 full-body decoys are nice, as is owning 4X4 off-road rigs to haul gear and quality layout blinds, the fact is that everyone can't afford to waterfowl hunt that way. So these big guns and pass-shooting methods tend to even out the playing field among sportsmen. It makes many wonder why companies have discontinued so many 10-gauge guns (most recently, Remington and its SP-10), but still make the very best high-performance 3½-inch goose loads in 10-gauge. Truth is, there are more than just a handful of 10-gauge guns already out there in the hands of sportsmen, and keeping them buying ammo for them comes down to performance. That .775 super-bore in today's premium loads can deliver the mail—at least when it's shot by hunters who know how to use it.

WHY A 10-GAUGE INSTEAD OF THE 3½-INCH 12-GAUGE?

Many 12-gauge shooters wonder what's so special about a 10-gauge waterfowl gun? First, as I've already explained, this round is able to launch massive payloads of non-toxic shot at high velocity. Of course, you'll say, "Yes, but so can the 3½-inch 12-gauge." Okay, true, but while the biggest 12-gauge round can do just that, what it can't do is maintain payload *control,* due to its very long shot column and comparatively smaller bore size. The largest 12-gauge also has a felt recoil level that would knock over a horse. Because 10-gauge guns weigh anywhere from eight to 13 pounds, they eat up recoil fast. The unique Remington SP-10 and Browning Gold, for example, are nearly recoil-free, due to their outstanding gas systems.

I've shot the SP-10 for more than 25 years, and heck, they can bury me with it, for all I care. Several weeks prior to writing these lines, by way of comparison, I was hunting with the new Browning A-5

3½-inch 12-gauge packed with Winchester Blind Side 3½-inch super magnums. In a span of seven rounds, I had pounded my shoulders straight through the backside of my layout blind, sending its hinge pins flying in all directions. Recoil delivered by the big gun and load had actually wrecked the blind's frame-locking arrangement. It had also done a job on me. Now, I'll admit, the 3½-inch 12 is a great turkey or coyote killer at one shot, but all day long in a goose or duck blind? Nope, not my cup of coffee. Find me my SP-10, please.

Patterns out of a 10-gauge are almost always outstanding. Add the developments in ammunition (listed below), and payload control is nothing but the best. With flight speeds from 1,350 to 1,700 fps, steel and other metallurgy fired through a 10-gauge move like lighting.

During the past several years, I have given dedicated field time to my favorite 10-gauge gun and, in fact, recently purchased an old favorite, the tried and true Richland side-by-side 10-gauge, with 32-inch, super-Full "goose extermination" chokes. This cannon produces some hard-hitting patterns, due to its payload and speed, the combination of which are effective beyond ranges most hunters would consider taking a shot. As a decoy gun, it is an unmitigated murder weapon; naturally, it is king on the pass-shooting fields. This gun and its loads are a performance combination very hard to beat, regardless what you might take afield in a 12-gauge. About the only gun I have ever fired that flat-out surpasses the 10 is an English market hunter's 4-bore; in a 5-inch chambered gun, it was beyond description to touch off.

With Remington having discontinued its SP-10 (the website still shows a listing for them, but Remington's people assure me it's gone from current production), Browning's BPS and Auto Gold 10-gauges are about all that's left in the American marketplace, if you want a new 10. The old stack-barrel Richlands and varied side-by-sides from a variety of Spanish makers, once fairly available, are drying up fast. If you are in the market and find a clean one at a good price, my advice is to buy it fast.

When writing this review, my son-in-law Scott went to work back in Minnesota, where he located two 10-gauge guns, one of which he sent to me. He kept the other for himself, but he really didn't understand the gun's possibilities, until he took one to the range and touched off a few rounds on pattern boards at 60 yards. He was sold, and now there are two more long forcing cone Spanish super guns in the family. Even better, according to what I've been seeing, the cost of feeding a 10-gauge factory ammo is only about four dollar a box of 25 rounds higher then that of 3-inch 12-gauge shells. What a deal!

Finding a 10-Gauge

If I've peaked your interest in a 10-gauge, and I hope I have, you're going to have to do a little searching to find both guns and loads. I've done some of the research for you, and here's what I've found, both new and used for the gun side, based across several states scoured over the last three years.

The author with a now-discontinued Remington SP-10, preparing for some testing with Remington's Hypersonic shot loads.

Available 10-Gauge Guns

- Remington SP-10, semi-auto, new; three-shot waterfowl and turkey models available

- Richland over/under and side-by-sides, used

- Armsport Model 2700 over/under, used

- American Arms WT over/under, used

- Ithaca Mag 10 pump-action, used

- Browning Gold semi-auto, new

- Browning BPS pump-action, new

- Assorted Spanish double guns, used

Current 10-Gauge Loads, 3½-inch Magnum

- Winchester Supreme, $1^3/_8$ ounces; No. 2, BB, BBB

- Winchester Super X, $1^5/_8$ ounces; No. 4, BBB, T

- Remington Hypersonic Steel, 1½ ounces; BB, BBB (1,700 fps)

- Remington Nitro Steel, 1¾ ounces; No. 2, BB, BBB, T

- Remington Sportsmen, $1^3/_8$ ounces; No. 2, BB

- Remington HD, 1¾ ounces; No. 4, 2, BB

- Federal Cartridge Speed Shok, 1½ ounces; No. 2, BB, BBB, T

- Federal Cartridge Black Cloud, $1^5/_8$ ounces; No. 2, BB

- Environ-Metal, Inc., Hevi-Shot (Hevi-Metal), 1¾ ounces; No. 4, 3, 2, BB, BBB

12-GAUGE FIREPOWER

It was an early morning in late March, and the first flights of big, mature snow geese were moving up well into the middle of South Dakota. My partner Scott Butz, of Real Wings Decoys, had set aside a large quantity of Hevi-Shot's new Speed Ball ammunition; this would be one of the first runs against snows for the new line of ammunition offered by Environ-Metal, Inc., the Hevi-Shot people. Scott had Hevi-Shot as a sponsor for his TV shows and field events and, as such, it was his job to feature the new ammunition. The Speed Ball wasn't only new, it was and is a cost cutter. Compared to similar loads of the high-priced tungsten iron shot that, in the past few years, has hit $36 to $46 for a box of 10. *That's nearly $5 a shot!* With Speed Ball being a duplex load made up of a blend of steel and a smaller shot size in tungsten iron, its cost has been better held in check.

The author with some of the results of Hevi-Shot's Speed Ball ammunition. Not many ducks are going to survive this kind of core pattern, if the shooter's doing their job.

On a cut cornfield that morning, we had 12-gauge 3-inch magnum 1¼-ounce Speed Ball loads of No. 2 tungsten combined with a charge of BB (.177-inch) steel. This ammo had demonstrated an ability to hold 80-percent patterns much of the time through my Winchester Super X3 and Scott's test guns of a Browning Maxus and an A-5, both waterfowl specials. Some of the first birds in slid wide of the hole we'd created in the decoy spread to draw them in closer, but, when we turned loose the new double-charged tungsten/iron loads, three birds out of three came crashing into the deck, generating a cloud of dust when they hit the ground. If there was anything out of the ordinary, it was that both Scott and I were sending our final rounds at that third bird as it slipped further out of the decoy spread. The range that bird was downed at? About 55 yards and change.

The chance to use Speed Ball surfaced once again that fall, in Maine, and the targets were sea eider. If you don't know a lot about these very large birds (about the size of snow geese), to be sure, they are a substantially hard target for any waterfowl load tested against them. Eiders often fly very low, just a few feet off the water, as they skim the decoy lines. This makes for interesting shooting, because you'll have a visual on almost every shot, in terms of pattern spread and the exact point of shot impact on the surface of the water. It's kind of like watching old war footage of

Japanese Zeros coming at American flattops, with some destroyer turning loose every gun on its deck against the aircraft. Over the course of several days, and with four or five hunters taking part in the shooting, the 12-gauge 3-inch 1¼-ounce Speed Ball, this time gunned through Benelli semi-autos, held its own well. If sea eider, a bird that can dive several hundred feet below the surface of the sea, are wounded, they are almost always lost—we lost only two birds over the entire hunt. Not a bad count at all, consider all the limits of birds we took home.

While the spring snow goose hunt with Scott Butz was the major event of that early conservation order goose season, and while the Maine sea duck hunt had been a decided success, more action was to come down the pike. First, my friend Tyson Keller, out of Pierre, South Dakota, after opening a new company with friends to create a "banded" line of clothing for waterfowling, had finally found some time to actually get into the field. About the same time, in early October, Federal sent out two flats of 250 rounds each of Black Cloud No. 2 and BB. The loads were 12-gauge 1¼-ounce 3-inch magnums. The interesting thing with those loads was that not only did they perform as expected for Tyson and me, when we put them on big

A cut corn field provided ample opportunity for the author and friends to give the 1 ¼-ounce Speed Ball BB loading an honest go—and to great success. These birds came down so hard, they raised clouds of dust when they hit the ground.

Canada geese over the Missouri river bottoms, that test ran through a total of 500 rounds (via several dozen hunters) and accounted for just over 470 giant Canadas. The cripple rate was not even noteworthy, and total loss was clearly acceptable for as many hunters as were present, given the sheer volume of birds harvested. With those kind of numbers in mind, I think it's fair to say that the modern 12-gauge non-toxics have completely come of age.

TEXAS PROVING GROUNDS

My second significant test with Black Cloud in 12-gauge came on the Texas Gulf Coast and its wintering redheads and pintails. This time the ammo we would work with would be that meant for close-range work. Unfortunately, what we didn't know was that the birds trading off the water wouldn't pay a great deal of attention to the decoys much of the time. That meant one thing: pass shoot (or go home with full ammo belts and no ducks).

When birds move from one freshwater hole on the coast to another, they fly at or close to 70 yards up. That meant we were just about out of luck with the close-range loads, save for a cache of No. 2 goose shot we'd hauled aboard our blow boats for potential use on the salt marsh flats. We were armed with 12-gauge 3½-inch Benelli Super Black Eagles choked Modified. Black Cloud and its deadly sabot shot container doesn't require tight chokes and, in fact, will perform better with a more open choice. My friend Joe Coogan, Brand Marketing Manager at Benelli, was the first to turn a big redhead inside out at a very long range—with his SBE *20-gauge*. Of all the things, *sub-gauge* Black Cloud loads! And it wasn't even a fluke! On the next pass, Joe dumped a second bird, and then a gadwall became the third duck down. Joe was connecting on ducks *nearly 70 yards out*, all with a Black Cloud 3-inch 20-gauge.

Though armed "only" with our 12-gauge Super Black Eagles, the rest of our team and Black Cloud didn't do too bad at all. Within an hour, we had limited in both redheads and other miscellaneous ducks. Yes, lots of hunters take limits of ducks. So why was this hunt all so special? Because even though the early testing of Black Cloud had produced great results, we could plainly see that the current production ammunition had only gotten better.

I know that Federal is constantly working to improve loads with new powders and components. Evidence of this is the introduction of 12-gauge 3-inch Snow Goose Black Cloud. This special load is faster and uses large shot to reach out and get the job done on those particular birds. That Federal pays the same attention to its "regular" Black Cloud loads seems obvious. Too, at various times, I have had the company of Federal engineers on some of my industry hunts, and I am here to tell you that, at those times, I shut by mouth and pay attention to what they say. That's included the info I've learned about Black Cloud. It's a

The author's good friend, Tyson Keller, shown here with a hunting buddy, is one of the best goose hunters he knows, devoting hours to scouting. His expertise gets put to good use when the author has new loads and guns to test.

Just Us Local Boys

Some of you who've just read about the Black Cloud test that ran through 500 rounds and accounted for nearly as many geese killed will wonder at such numbers. I think it's important to explain how this hunt went down, less there be some misunderstanding.

The hunters we worked with for this hunt and ammo testing were, for the most part, local South Dakota boys who have been raised with a shotgun in their hands, nearly straight from the crib. I can attest to the fact that some of these hunters are the best shots on feathers I have ever seen, period. Tyson Keller is among them, and he is, without question, one of the best goose hunters on the river. He will work days to set up a hunt through his scouting of a region, and, when he marks the calendar with an "X," unfailingly the day will work out. Because of the skill these hunters have, when I have required assistance in gun load reviews or ballistics information gathering like this, everything falls into place. To be sure, thanks to them, I got an eyeful of Black Cloud performance and its ability to take out big geese with ease, even at solid pass-gunning ranges.

Brand Marketing Manager at Benelli, Joe Coogan, and one of his company's Super Black Eagle's he used with Black Cloud ammunition to slay some ducks—in 20-gauge!

As good as Black Cloud is, and as much as he likes the 10-gauge for big birds, the author found that the ultra-fast Hypersonic Steel in 12-gauge from Remington takes high-up snows with ease.

design monster, and few if any younger hunters today can understand just how complicated it is to get it up and working correctly. We hunters and researchers in ballistics worked very hard, years ago, to build loads that could did what Black Cloud is capable of doing. By comparison, we failed, even though we had 10-gauge loads back in the day that moved ultra-light payloads at 1,700 fps—but the truth is, we never even got close to what Federal Cartridge's Black Cloud can produce in energy and penetration.

Clearly, I'm a fan of Black Cloud in 12-gauge, but there's one more nontoxic 12-gauge load that needs reckoning with, the long-range fodder that is Remington's HyperSonic Steel. HyperSonic is the fastest factory production shotshell load ever developed. Tested by me, as I previously noted, this round topped 2,000 fps on occasion, even though the book velocity as stated by Remington is 1,700 fps. That's quick, my friends, fast enough to send even lightweight steel high enough to snag many a passing snow goose with ease.

Hunting Lake Benton spring snows in Minnesota, during the first year the loads were out, produced excellent results, and those birds were not at all decoy friendly. Since then, I have tested them on everything from night-hunted raccoon to ringneck pheasants blocked and flushed at cornfield ends. I've found the HyperSonic outguns many lead loads of old, when used back to back on upland game, and geese don't stand a chance against them, if the hunter can put the pattern on the target. I also like the fact that, in 2013, Remington introduced a brand new 20-gauge 3-inch in HyperSonic that is under testing by me at this time. Early results indicate that this sub-gauge offering, much like Federal's Black Cloud, will completely outgun any 12-gauge 2¾-inch non-toxic shell in terms of retained velocity downrange and raw, game-killing energy.

What all of these loads have in common is that they have been recently developed, use state of the art ballistic science applied to both the 10-gauge and 12-gauge (and, even now, the 3-inch 20-gauge), and are deadly effective. For the past several years, I have pressed all of these varied loads to work on many types of warm targets, with phenomenal results. Because of that, my confidence level is always high, when I decide to take one of these loads afield. Yours will be, too (even you can't decide between the 10 and 12).

Oh, Those Other Gauges

The 16-gauge shotgun started to die a slow death about the time the 20-gauge 3-inch magnum surfaced. Eventually, the 20-gauge flat-out took over the 16-gauge shotgun. Still, some shotgunners can't seem to get that fact straight in their minds, so, every now and again, one of these guns will be seen in the pheasant fields of South Dakota, those guns paired with a weak handload or old factory fodder; truth is, these days there just isn't much 16-gauge product on the store shelves that can be applied in the pheasant fields. When I see a hunter with such a gun and ammo combo, I try and get a heavy 12-gauge shooter to be right at the 16-gauge guy's side, because ringneck roosters with some shot in them by way of the Sweet 16 will invariability try to slip away into deep edge cover, eventually to become food for the fox instead of the two-legged hunter.

In its day, the 16-gauge was a solid winner. We hunted with double guns in 16 for a long time. But, as the 20-gauge 3-inch began to walk all over the 16, the load offerings for the latter began to dry up, and no one made upgrades to what was there. As a result, the 16s just can't cut it against the big-league, high-performance offerings from 20-gauge on through the 10.

Right along with the woes of the 16-gauge, you must fit in discussion of 28-gauge and even .410-bore ammunition. As it is with the 16-gauge, there just isn't a lot of high-quality game loads, if any. Shooting a 28-gauge on waterfowl, for example, is nothing short of a stunt in my mind. Sure, you can drop a duck if it's in almost in the blind with you, but, for the most part, the gauge offerings are completely ineffective at normal game-taking range limits.

It should be obvious that the gauge selected by the shooter is going to reveal either the good or poor performance characteristics of the selected bore size. What should also be obvious is that the 12-gauge is by far the most accepted gauge in use today, and it is followed by the 20-gauge in both 2¾- and 3-inch fodder. This is because of both the available firearms options and the massively wide range of loads the hunter can choose to take afield at any given time—and one case where following the crowd is the right thing to do.

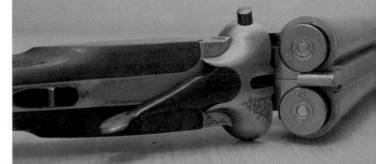

CHAPTER ELEVEN

UPLAND SHOTS, GROUND POUNDERS and MORE MODERN LOADS

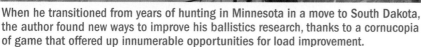
When he transitioned from years of hunting in Minnesota in a move to South Dakota, the author found new ways to improve his ballistics research, thanks to a cornucopia of game that offered up innumerable opportunities for load improvement.

Up to this point, a good deal of my attention has pressed the reader towards loads primarily designed for waterfowl use. I guess that's because, for a very long time, I worked heavily with the industry, editors, and publications in that area of load development. It was the new age of non-toxics and, as such, the assumption in those early days was that waterfowling was on a slow path to its

death unless we got something into the air that could killed ducks and geese cleanly. In the area of upland game, turkeys, and fur bearers, much of my attention had been devoted to ammunition development for these pastimes during my years hunting in Minnesota, where I'd focused my attention on game farms, eastern turkey haunts, and the northern grouse woods. But, when I relocated over a decade ago to South Dakota, everything was completely turned upside down. I was planted smack into the middle of an upland hunters paradise, and with that came the flow of both knowledge and experience given off by ringneck roosters, sharptail grouse, never-ending turkey hunts, and doves by the millions each fall. As a result, my ballistics background research took a massive jump forward into these other realms of sport shotgun shooting.

UPLAND SHOTGUNS AND LOADS

Faced with moving away from carrying heavy, long-barreled magnums across miles of open prairie or sections of cut cornfields, my attention turned to both lighter-weight 12-gauges and the 3-inch 20-gauge magnum as my new tools for pheasants and sharptails. My thinking on the subject directed me straight

to point, balance well in the hands of a guy with an average build, and both come with an ample number of choke tubes to produce positive payload control of upland loads downrange.

As I took those guns afield, it became clear to me that the advances in the development of lead shot ammunition designed for upland hunting has benefited greatly from the research of the past 30 years in the non-toxic shotshell department. For example, we now know that when targets are big geese, turkeys, or coyotes, the 20-gauge commandeers loads and chokes that can make those hunts successful. That didn't used to be the case. But let's get more specific for a minute and look in detail at a light 20-gauge meeting these challenges with these advanced lead loads.

If you've been paying attention of late, you've surely noticed that more industry energy is being directed toward the 20-gauge shotgun, in terms of advanced

Miles and miles of pheasant country are not the place for big, heavy, long-barreled shotguns. Thanks to the author's decade in the rooster fields, though, we now have better loads for lighter guns and gauges.

away to a weight reduction on the 12-gauge and, so, the Remington 870 in a 26-inch barreled model came up for consideration. That choice worked out well, but then I also got to participate in several industry hunts for ringnecks in Iowa and North Dakota, with stack-barrel 20-gauge guns from Beretta and Ruger. It didn't take long to get hooked hard on the 20-gauge. In fact, I ended up owning a Ruger Red Label, as well as a second, backup 20-gauge 870 in the 26-inch barreled configuration. The 20-gauge Remington was a lower priced Express version and, between that one and the Red Label, I'd hit on a good combination for sharptails and roosters. The lightweight 20-gauge guns are fast

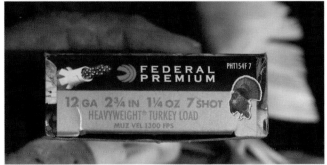

Yes, this is a turkey load in No. 7. A few years ago, requesting such a thing at a gun shop would have had the counter guy looking at you like you were crazy, but not today.

Turkey camp South Dakota style. Plentiful birds over the years have allowed the author and friends ample opportunity to test out new and improved gobbler loads in both smaller gauges and smaller shot sizes.

loads for big game, turkeys, and waterfowl. With these advancements come the ability for this gauge to also take up a good deal of the upland field work that used to be reserved for the big, meaty 12-gauge.

While the 20-gauge has always been regarded as a light and fast-handling shotgun by both upland hunters and clay target shooters, the current trend seems to be moving toward building sweet little 20s into something that can actually *rival* a 12. Now, before you 12-gauge guys go off half-cocked, be advised that I just write the facts as they roll out the muzzle. Good, bad, or indifferent, the 20-gauge is the way the game is being played now. In fact, in some circles, the 12-bore had better be ready to move over, because the wave of advanced ballistics indicates that far more can be done with this sub-gauge offering than has been previously thought. New powders, plastics, and shot material have all contributed to the upward movement in the world of the 20-gauge.

This past fall, my home state of South Dakota decided to allow non-residents a chance to take on our wild turkey population. Bird numbers were way up and, as such, some additional hunting pressure wouldn't pose a problem with the general bird population. With a phone call from Tim Brandt, ammunition marketing guru at Federal, the local wheels started turning to get Tim and his sidekick in development, Melissa Juneski, the chance to lay a very new 20-gauge turkey load on a couple of our big Black Hills toms. While fall hunting is not the calling adventure of the spring hunts, most of the time it is a very interesting time afield, with ample numbers of turkeys in the western part of the state.

The load we were destined to experiment with was a 3-inch 20-gauge load consisting of a new FliteControl wad and Federal's trademarked Heavyweight shot, in this case in a No. 4 pellet. Given that this shot material retains a density number of .18, nothing in the industry even comes close to this stuff, in terms of retained energy, velocity, and pure knockdown power. Loaded at 1½ ounces in the 20-gauge, on paper, this load looked like it should outgun a 12-gauge lead shot load hands down in a turkey shoot-off. We were about to find out.

On the day Tim and Melissa arrived at my home in the hills, the weather was clear and a bit cool, perfect turkey hunting conditions. Within an hour, I had both of them down on 40-yard backyard shooting range, where I'd set up turkey head/neck targets developed by Champion, along with a box of the prototype 20-gauge shotshells. Shooting Benelli autoloaders and Modified chokes—FliteControl wads do not take well to super Full chokes, as the wads tend to develop their own choking via a special sabot-like design—at 40 yards, this new load put 43 pellets in the appropriate area, and those Champion turkey targets are not some unrealistic, over-blown design.

Years ago, when I was developing duplex 3½-inch

A Turkey-Slayer Bar None

In my state of South Dakota, I tend to shoot several guns that are very turkey-specialized. They mount full 12-gauge suppressors (silencers), scopes, 21-inch barrels that make use of ultra-tight turkey chokes (and which also tend to be barrels that can be quickly swapped out to quickly accommodate some other shotgunning task). For instance, I have one Remington Model 1100 in a custom-built turkey model that was rebuilt by a barrel company that makes a barrel that's worth twice the price of the whole gun when it was new. Why? Performance, and little else. If a gun will not shoot tight patterns as a turkey gun, it's not going to be a turkey gun in my camp. This should be your primary goal, too.

My suppressed 1100 aside—not everybody has access to or wants to shoot a suppressed shotgun—I set out to find an example as a state-of-the-art turkey gun. With all due diligence, the Winchester SXP pump gun came to the forefront. It is a truly solid example of what the modern, specialized turkey gun is all about.

When the Winchester brand moved to Browning Arms a few years back, Browning went to work developing a brand-new Winchester auto-loader known today as the Super X3 (SX3). But that left a void in Winchester's product lineup, specifically, a working-grade pump-action shotgun. Browning's BPS held its own for that brand, but the Winchester brand was without a modern slide-action shotgun. So Browning/Winchester's new owners turned to the development of a pump gun designed around the very smooth shooting and successful SX3 gas semi-auto. While the SXP slide-action is no Belgium-built SX3 auto (and I own enough of them to tell the difference), the pump is a fair match against the semi-auto's stock design, enough to give a field shotgunner a very workable option in action types, while also gaining a solid, functional, new design.

The gun sent to me from Browning for this book review was brand new, though it came with only a single Invector-Plus ultra-tight .60 choke. The basic shotgun was sound and solid, and it sparked my interest in that it pointed almost like the SX3 gas gun, but with a shorter barrel. It used the same furniture on the buttstock and

The author with a 40-yard turkey target. If it had had feathers, it'd been dead.

fore-end. The test gun I was sent was dressed in a full Mossy Oak camo coat.

Packing a stiff load of Hevi-13 turkey shot (moly-coated and buffered) in a 3-inch hull, I headed off to the local hills in search of a gobbler. A few patterns on paper had indicated that this load, paired with the gun's tight choke was quite capable of planting 70 percent of its payload in No. 5 tungsten shot within a 20-inch core pattern at 40 yards.

It took four days of calling the rocky ridges of my northern hills before I located a willing tom. I finally managed to coax the big bird into range and, with the gun's TruGlo sights set on the big guy's neck, one blast of tungsten-iron sent Mr. Gobbler sprawling.

I attribute much of that hunt's success to the gun's good balance; it makes for a great static sitting position gun. That's absolutely something you should look for in a specialized turkey gun, and there are other inherent features you need to look for, too. First, the barrels are always a bit shorter. A turkey shotgun's sights are also an important element; remember, the vast majority of the time you're aiming, as you would with a rifle. Still, if there's a primary focal point in the development of today's turkey gun, it's in the choke design. The choke is key to performance on the narrow target that is the head and neck of a turkey, and lacking a good sight system, you might as well just be shooting your average duck gun.

10-gauge loads, the very best I could generate with them—a 1-ounce-by-1-ounce mix of No. 4 and No. 6 copper-plated lead shot—was 40 pellets in the head/neck at 40 yards. I'll say it again: It took a *2-ounce 10-gauge payload of shot* (sent downrange by way of a Remington SP-10 choked super-tight Full) to match the results of Federal's hot-shooting 20-gauge 3-inch 1½-ounce No. 4 load at 1,100 fps. Yes, turkey loads in the high-density tungsten pellets have come a very long way in the past several years, but the 10-gauge comparison is still a valid comparison to the Federal 20-gauge load we were testing.

With pattern work completed, it was time to get into the pickup truck and give my guests a quick tour of the area. After covering some 30 miles of prime turkey country, I told my two hunters it was time to get saddled up.

Setting up on a small field I knew would act as a

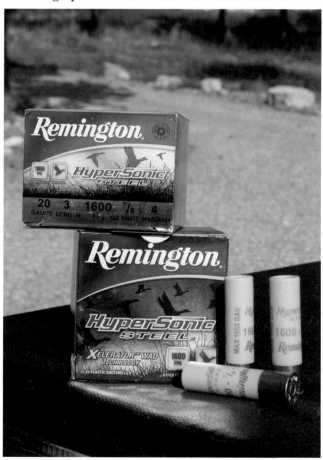

draw point for flocks of birds moving to roost toward evening, I placed both hunters in positions to cover the main shooting lanes. Fall birds will respond to calling, but, in most cases, they won't move too far off their established routes to and from roosting areas. I set up Melissa to cover a grass flat, giving her a wide open shoot-

Remington's 20-gauge Hypersonic load. Like similar offerings from other big ammo companies, these souped-up sub-gauge loads are proving their own and providing great field alternatives to heavy, traditional 12-gauges.

Beyond the Bead: Turkey Sighting Systems

The updated turkey gun has many features that make it so, and its sights are one of them. This is due, for the most part, to the advanced level of turkey shotshell ammunition today.

Turkey guns were once relegated to suitable use at 40 yards or less. Today, that's changed wholly. More and more hunters are taking longer-range birds. I am not about to get into a discussion regarding what is ethical or not, regarding extended range. The fact remains that range, both allowable and practical, is increasing. This is so much a fact that here in the American West, my state and others allow rifles as turkey guns, while some of my associates have been taking scattergun birds at the ranges I used to prefer to use my .221 Fireball or .22 Hornet. The truth is, today's turkey guns, ammo, chokes, and sights far exceed the expectations we had about this sport as little as a decade ago.

Of course, if you're going to shoot a shotgun beyond the 40-yard standard that used to be, you're going to need to upgrade your sights. Sight systems I like very much—and have found to be effective against the 167 gobblers to date I have dusted off in a span of 45 years of turkey chasing in almost as many states—boils down to an uncomplicated, low magnification, lightweight scope or the red dot kinds offered by companies like TruGlo. TruGlo, in fact, has been a huge help to me, when setting up turkey guns for testing and evaluation on hunts. I've also used the very basic fiber optic "iron" sight systems all the way up to the TruGlo red dot, multi-reticle, dual-colored unit that's about 2¾ inches long as it stands on a Weaver-style mounting rail. I also like the newer HUD (heads-up display) sights, which really aid in putting ultra-tight patterns on a bird's head and neck. With any of these tools, used depending on my turkey habitat and terrain and the type of load I'm running, I can do about everything necessary it takes to be successful.

To be sure, there are other tools that can up the success of your turkey hunt. My personal turkey gunning systems make use of the HUD sight, night lights for varmint work after dark via the same shotgun, laser sights for backup night work (defense or varmints), and full suppressors for stealth applications (which can also apply to turkey hunting, especially in suburban settings where noise and neighbors are a concern). While this may sound like it's a bit much, remember that I, just as you should, started with the gun, and today's over-the-counter shotguns set up for turkey hunting today will fit almost any gobbler hunter's needs. Take a look, read the reviews, and try a few out. There really is a wealth of fine turkey guns to choose from.

ing lane, while Tim got to work eye-balling a sharp ridgeline that rose up about 85 feet directly in front of him.

Within an hour, the first birds, a pair of gobblers, walked right in front of Melissa. Unfortunately, before she could react to the situation, a pair of roaming, wild-eyed cattle dogs also showed up and split the pair, which headed uphill and out in front of Tim. I was pressed against some heavy brush cover, watching the situation as it played out through my field glasses.

As the birds came back together up on the ridgeline, they picked a fight. For a minute, I could see Tim, a first-time turkey hunter, come unglued, but then he gathered his wits and began an old-fashioned Arkansas belly crawl on the pair, moving an inch at a time up the steep hill.

Leaving my cover location and moving up below Tim, I saw him wave me up to his position. I knew he was a little nervous and needing some help, so I moved up near to him. Reaching a depression in the terrain, I motioned for Tim to rise up and take the shot. One gobbler had split to the left of the other and presented a clear shot. Like it had been written, Tim pulled up, sitting straight as a good willow stick, and his Benelli spit thunder, sending that massive shot charge of Heavyweight shot at the big bird. The bird went down, *hard*, and Tim had dusted off his very first gobbler, right in my backyard of the Black Hills of South Dakota. His bird was ranged at 48 yards, which, by most turkey hunting standards, is a somewhat extended shot for a larger firearm, let alone a 20-gauge.

A day later, it was my turn to loose a load of 20-gauge Heavyweight on a good Hills bird I'd caught off-guard along another ridgeline. This bird, like Tim's, took the load of shot and died in its tracks. (Unfortunately, though I set up Melissa on a flock of more than 30 birds, that flock didn't have a tom or even a decent jake. Neither she nor I like to shoot hens or their kids, so she declined to pull the trigger on our short hunt.) Anyway you look at it, the prototype 20-gauge got the green light from this turkey hunter.

That super 20-gauge load from Federal is just one example of the advances being made in the lead shotshell arena. But just what are the elements that make up a pellet's ability to kill its subject cleanly? It sounds like something that should have an easy answer; a pellet hits something hard and, with velocity, penetrates and takes out the subject right? Well, not so fast. The dynamics of what goes on when you fire that ball of iron, tungsten, copper, or lead have a wide range of performance characteristics.

First, you have to understand some basic physics. Anything that has a round shape and is expected to fly straight and retain velocity is facing a very tall order. Round balls just don't do well in this department, but, for better or worse, round is the shot shape we hunters use, for the most part. You have to wonder why, sometimes. Round balls were so bad during early firearms development that, as soon as inventors could figure it

EXPERIMENTAL
MAG - SHOK TURKEY
20GA, 3IN 1 1/2OZ @ 1100FPS
HEAVYWEIGHT - 6

MAG·SHOK

out, rifling replaced the musket smoothbore. Rifling, of course, caused a single conical bullet to rotate and maintain its velocity and energy well downrange. That's not really possible with a payload of multiple little spheres. So, what *do* we know about shot in flight and how do we get the most out of it?

When round steel balls that are sent downrange at pre-killed and mounted test waterfowl, or even just at common clay blocks, we learn that not all shot sizes are created equal. Truthfully, some pellet sizes are just more *efficient* then others. For example, ever wonder why that teal just gets crushed with a load of No. 3 steel, but a mallard hit by the same load tends to end up as a long retrieve for your dog? It's because those No. 3s in iron (steel) shot are better *balanced* when used against the more fragile teal, versus their tendency to merely slap the feathers of a big greenhead.

When I write of load "balance," what I'm talking about is the correlation between the frontal area of a pellet (size) and its velocity versus its weight. Steel shot's lack of density is also a critical factor, in terms of its effectiveness against warm targets. Say the pellet has a large frontal area, but is light in weight. If the balance between the two is well off the mark, penetration reduction will be the end product. An example of this is the old and now outdated F shot (.21-caliber) that was loaded by both Federal and Winchester some years ago. While F was a good pellet size for use on

big geese if the velocity could be held up, it didn't penetrate anywhere near as well as T shot (.20-caliber) did. Why? Because T steel retains the best of both worlds, in terms of frontal contact mass and weight of the individual pellet.

During the Stacy Project I told you about, I found that, when shot against pre-killed giant Canada geese that I mounted breast forward on a target backer at 55 yards, the smaller T shot actually out-penetrated the larger F shot *by a full third*. With its larger frontal area, the F shot faded fast, as it worked its way into the tissue of the goose body. Conclusion: the best shot size for all geese in general is T steel, if you want to maximize performance characteristics.

Of course, shotgunning isn't limited to goose hunting. What about the best duck shot size? Here again, testing at 45 yards illustrated that, based on pre-killed mallard re-shooting, a pellet of No. 2 steel will outperform most others, in terms of inflicting damage and generating deep penetration, thus the conclusion is that the frontal area of a No. 2 steel shot pellet is *balanced* quite well against its weight. But back to the upland discussion we started this chapter with and how other loads are evolving from our recent knowledge of big-bird non-toxic loads.

A box of the prototype 20-gauge Mag-Shok turkey loads from Federal. The author found its affects on big toms to be devastating.

Heavy or Light,
You're the One to Make it Work

As waterfowl hunters take more birds and become better acquainted with steel shot ammunition, we generally find some gravitation towards shot sizes No. 2 and BB. In fact, BB steel has proven to be rather a catchall, a shot size that gets the job done across a wide spectrum of birds. The problem is, if we have a small payload of such a shot size, those large pellets don't always fill out a pattern well. And some people want a smaller payload, because of reduced recoil, lower cost, etc.

Just the other day, I was called by one of my readers, and this very discussion came up during a general conversation about choke tubes and the best way to control a pattern. This reader had been an advocate of 3½-inch 12-gauge loads for a very long time, largely because he figured he was getting a denser pattern, even with big shot sizes. But what he'd found by doing some patterning board work was that the good old 3-inch magnums in 1¼-ounce BB payloads were doing a very solid job on targets well out to the far end of decoy gunning ranges.

How did he make that happen? Simple, he worked hard to match his choke tube to the given load (in his case, the budget Kent Cartridge Fasteel No. 2 and BB loads. As the reader said to me, this is what you do, "when you're on your own."

Shot Size Measured Performance

Pellet Size	Muzzle Velocity (FPS)	Distance (YARDS)	Terminal (@ Target) Velocity (FPS)	Energy (FT/LBS)
No. 2	1,325	50	588	2.70
No. 1	1,348	50	617	3.61
BB	1,339	50	659	5.85
T	1,349	50	734	13.26

Note: T steel has a 75 fps increased advantage over BB steel at 50 yards, and a kinetic energy advantage of 7.41 ft-lbs. However, energy does not increase proportionally to pellet size in the case of BB versus T shot size. For instance, No. 1 steel measures .16-inch. Its velocity gain over No. 2 steel at 50 yards is 29 fps, but, with a frontal area just .02 larger than No. 2, it is less effective in penetrating. Even when muzzle velocity is modified, the basic performance rule of No. 2s and T steel tend to hold up quite well.

Author 12-Gauge Steel Load Recommendations

Federal Premium Ultra Shok Waterfowl 3-inch 1¼-ounce, No. 2 and T

Kent Fasteel 3½-inch 1 9/16-ounce No. 2

Kent All Purpose 3-inch 1¼-ounce No. 2.(Outstanding duck load with proper chokes)

Winchester Super X Super Steel 3-inch 1¼-ounce No. 2 and T.

Remington Nitro steel 3-inch 1 3/8-ounce T and 1¼-ounce No. 2.

Wolf 3-inch 1¼-ounce No. 2.

Nothing here is set in stone, but is, rather, based on observable outcomes when applying various shot sizes on game birds in the field. The short form is that you won't go very far off base by selecting No. 2 steel for ducks and pheasants, and the big, bad, steel T for larger birds. BB steel and even the BBB are also right in the mix, if they are either priced right or specifically selected. Regardless, to my way of thinking when you have an option, always shoot large shot.

Cornfields and ringnecks ("ditch chickens," as we call 'em), can tell a major story, when it comes to load design today. Increased pellet mass and added velocity has taken hold among nearly all the guys I know who hunt pheasants in our big Missouri Breaks, in South Dakota. Enter Remington's new Hypersonic steel, whose box proclaims its load of No. 2 steel moves at a whopping 1,700 fps. That's impressive, but my chronograph recordings say it's closer to *2,000* fps.

The autumn of 2011 was test time for the Hypersonic on upland birds. I did what I usually do and took a full case of Remington Hypersonic 12-gauge 3-inch 1¼-ounce No. 2 and passed them out to four of my associates to use for the opening week of ringnecks in South Dakota. Hunting along with our little Dakota group were shooters from Minnesota, who were packing the traditional 2¾-inch and some 3-inch No. 5 copper-plated lead shot. Once the hunt got under way, it was obvious the Hypersonic was not only holding its own, but making serious advances over the lead shot rounds. In short, the ultra fast-moving No. 2s were *devastating* up to and including 70-plus yards, the distance at which our field end block-

As good as the Hypersonic steel is on waterfowl, it's just as deadly when a group of South Dakota hunters pushes a cornfield full of ringneck pheasants. That's the way to get your limits done in a hurry!

Remington's Hypersonic 12-gauge in the No. 2 shot is a spectacular pheasant load and a great replacement for the old No. 5 lead shot rounds hunters have shot for decades, especially when an area mandates non-toxic shot.

ers were taking shots. Today, some three years later, Hypersonic is still requested by my local hunting partners far and above any lead shot load taken afield. And, with changes such as are going on now—for instance, at this writing, California is about to go all non-toxic regardless what or where you're hunting—Hypersonic is right in the driver's seat to meet those challenges head on.

Just as it is with Remington's Hypersonic, Winchester's Blind Side line has advanced non-toxic loads to a place hunters want to shoot them. This is especially true when the loads are tailored to be game specific, as in this Super Pheasant load.

Is something like Hypersonic in No. 2 a "super load?" I think so. When taking a quick look at the basic makeup of the this shotshell, we can see that it's right out of the twenty-first century playbook. First, tube priming is a major part of this shell's ignition design, and this is revolutionary by any standard. Yes, tube priming has been around since the nineteenth century, but, because of the complexities involved in building up the tube priming system from the primer hole itself, cost was a significant factor in preventing it becoming a component standard (not to mention the fact that tooling has always stood in the way of any advancement in production). Remington worked through these problems by utilizing part of the overall propellant charge within the tube and designing the tube itself as part of the wad. This one-step production makes for priming ignition that produces ultra high velocities from relatively small amounts of propellant. (Other uses for the priming tube can be found in anti-aircraft ammunition, so I think it's fitting that bird loads are following that development; again, the military takes the lead in civilian load design.)

The second major element in this new load are the velocities achieved both at the muzzle and downrange. Due again to the priming system and propellant type, which are closer to that of a rifle-like fueling materials, this load gets up and moves beyond anything known in factory shotgun ammunition in the past. Remember, Remington states that the velocity off the gate is 1,700 fps. But, again, my chronograph readings showed, 2,000 fps; recordings taken four feet from the muzzle have returned 1,800 fps or better. This is *significant*. Shot loses velocity very rapidly after leaving the barrel, something actually compounded by the fact that the faster it's moving, the greater the loss over a single foot of distance.

Other ballistics labs that have run chronograph recordings of the new loads have come up with the same readings I have. In fact, my old friend Tom Armbrust at Ballistic Research, in McHenry, Illinois, has run hundreds of shots, and they come in at about a five feet-per-second difference in measured velocity from my conclusions. No matter how you cut the deal, this stuff is quick—quick enough to start a product development revolution within the sporting arms industry.

BIG WARM TARGETS CANADA

Alberta, Canada, in September, can have some nice weather—and then there are the days the gods decide to hand out wind and rain to a group of researchers testing both the new Hypersonic loads and Remington's just released auto-loading Versa Max. Shooting over full-body decoys, but in small sets of 25 blocks, the gunning was unlike anything I had done before in Canada. We had ample selections of both mallards and pintails early in the morning, and all sizes of geese visiting the spread a bit later. This provided great flexibility in terms of target samples, but, as we'd hoped, again by way of the No. 2 shot in a 1¼-ounce payload, there were very few birds that left the kill zone alive. This load, as previously illustrated, has an extended range of 65 to 70 yards on smaller waterfowl, and a solid 65 yards on big geese. With dense patterns produced through a standard Modified choke (though a new design by Remington for the Versa Max 12-gauge back-bored barrel), the cripple rate stood at less than four percent over the entire hunt; at times, we had a flat-out zero in the losses column.

Hypersonic shotshells are hard-hitting loads—these are not your daddy's shotshells. At the time of static range testing, my partner Ed Donnigan, a gun expert at Cabela's in Rapid City, South Dakota, aided me in getting the velocity recordings from the chronograph screens and putting down some patterns on paper. Shooting Remington's 887 pump gun with a tight, .62 choke, the fast-moving Hypersonics produced almost 100-percent 40-yard patterns, with ultra-tight 20-inch cores every time. Switching to a Modified choke expanded the core pattern a bit, but still held the overall pattern to a solid 75 or 80 percent inside the 30-inch paper pattern circle. There were no blown core patterns, something that can often be expected with extreme velocity. I attribute this to the design of the Remington Xelerator wad. The wad petals (four) are left uncut at their mid-points and, as such, slow a bit in opening. (These wads are pure junk when you can recover them, the net effect of the unbelievable muzzle velocity the shotshell generates.)

In time, and not so very far away I think, we could see an advanced military application from the Remington technology and, for sure, additional load development in the sporting area of smoothbore gunning, everything from upland ringneck rooster killers, coyote gunning tools, and general purpose wackum-and-stackum loads. To be sure, a whole lot of folks in the industry have to be taking a hard look at Remington's newest shotshell developments—as a load researcher of more than 30 years, I can tell you this new development has gotten *my* full attention. Plus, with a price tag of about $23 for 25 rounds, it's a round that's affordable to use in the blinds and cornfields and, as such, should make things interesting when it comes to the direction in non-toxic shotshells that are accepted by both the sporting industry and its consumers. If there is one major problem surfacing with Hypersonic ammunition, it is that not enough of today's hunters understand exactly what this kind of advancement represents. That's a shame, because between Federal's Black Cloud wad system and the Hypersonic Remington wad designs, hunters are looking at the two single most important developments in modern smoothbore shotgun, bar none. Of course, you're reading the book, so you can now count yourself among the wiser.

Making Your Own

With the development of both subsonic shotshell ammunition and other low-recoil types, the handloader can match many of these newer loads by working with a chronograph system. By keeping muzzle velocites at or close to 950 fps, recoil is greatly reduced, energy is maintained at a high level to 40 yards, and the sound is better controlled.

When I get calls from customers using my Metro Gun System who want to load their own low-sound/low-recoil ammunition, the first thing I ask them is if they own a chronograph. Without one, you'll be fishing for the best load possible. This is particularly true if you're looking to create training loads, where you need enough steam on them to produce positive results (i.e., broken clay targets), but not so much that the new shooter develops a flinch. The chronograph can match the load to the gun and shooter, by giving the handloader the correct amount of velocity to get the job done, but without running to excess.

Owning and using a chronograph is a worthwhile tool to have. While your loading data says one thing, the chronograph may tell you something very different—and that kind of information is what gives you the opportunity to tailor your loads. I'll even say the use of a home-based chronograph has changed the way reloading data and factory load data is presented today in that it keeps everyone honest.

THE SLUG EVOLVED
Big Game and the Shotgun

Living in the American West today, I don't get to see much use of the shotgun as a big-game hunting tool. The required gunning ranges in my neck of the woods are very long, critters large and, for the most part, a rancher or cowboy on a horse or in a pickup truck wouldn't have much of an idea how to even make use of a scattergun when stalking a sheep, mule deer, or elk in the Big Horn Mountains. Be that as it may, the fact is that more than half the United States are mandated the use of the shotgun (with slugs) for their big-game seasons, so, were it not for the shotgun, many areas of big-game hunting

across the country would otherwise be null and void. As such, the technologies involved in both guns and loads for slug hunting has grown considerably since this combination was last truly popular, back in the 1960s.

In the 1970s, I was involved in a number of projects that were begun because of the movement toward highly accurate saboted shotgun slugs (BRI slugs) that distanced themselves from the old, standard, Foster-style slug of the day. While BRI was developing the first saboted slug design, a design based closely on military developments in tank projectile rounds, another outfit called Hastings was bringing together the first-of-its-kind, rifled 12-gauge slug gun barrel that the company called the "Paradox." Bob Rott, the brains behind the barrel design, was breaking through the age-old barriers surrounding performance with smoothbore shotgun slug throwers (or, as they were known in my area, "pumpkin ball slingers"). Much as you'd expect from such a moniker, the slug guns of that era weren't able to hit much of anything past, say, 30 to 50 yards (and I'm being kind when I extend that range to 50). The two things the 12-gauge slug *did* have going for it were that it was a heavy projectile at one ounce or better, and it was hurled fast enough to generate some massive killing energy at its accepted short ranges. Bob Rott solved the accuracy problem; even today, the Hasting's Paradox, sold under that name but owned by a completely different front company, is still considered among slug target shooters and long-range shotgun guys as the very best in the business. Nothing has ever outgunned the Paradox, and I doubt anything will, given the production cost of trying to R&D something better.

As for sabot development? Well, that touches upon the tip of an iceberg that is still cold and very large today. Sabot bullets being about the same as those fired from a .50-caliber muzzleloader are common in contemporary slug ammunition, and all of them are propelled by driving bands on the bullet or encased in that ever-lovin' sabot systems (sabots being the No. 1 system in play today, when very good accuracy is required).

Slug development sure hasn't hit the top of the ballistics development scale, as we push solidly into the twenty-first century, but one of the latest and greatest designs I have had the opportunity to use in the field is in the 20-gauge department. This gun system defies all previous development, but has been slow to evolve because, in my opinion, it got sidetracked and pushed around by the big guys in the industry who didn't want to see a "wildcat" ultra high-velocity slug outgun the rest of the field.

What am I talking about? Let me put it to you this way: This is possibly the world's most powerful shotgun slug. With a muzzle velocity that drives a 410-grain saboted slug at 2,000-plus fps and delivers a kinetic energy figure at 200 yards of 1,006 ft-lbs, nothing else of its ilk in current production can come close to this Hastings/Hagn rifled shotgun and slug system. Developed in 2007, it was supposed to see production as a "super gun," when and paired with the Hastings 3½-inch 20-gauge ammunition.

Whitetail deer hunters across the slug gunning zones of the USA almost had a new way to move up the performance of a rifled shotgun, almost, that is, until the financial markets crash of 2009. Bob Rott, the brains behind the development of the Hastings 20-gauge 3½-inch slug loads, had enlisted the design help of Richard Knoster, who has worked in the development of slug ammunition around the shooting industry for some time and holds a number of patents covering both slugs and sabot payload control systems. Knoster retained a special contained-and-ride-along sabot slug system that allowed the whole payload, including the sabot, to stay with the slug until it made target contact. With a design such as that, the slug container (sabot) can hold anything from a pure lead deer hunter's projectile to a copper-composite specialty projectile for use on very large game like buffalo or elk. In other words, the Knoster slug system is very flexible, and it upgrades the 3½-inch 20-gauge rifled slug guns designed by Bob Rott at Hastings many times over. Then the crash happened and things got shelved.

So just what started all this redesigning of the 20-gauge slug gun in the first place, and where does it stand now? That story begins with Bob Rott and his years in the military, which included a special assignment, in Korea, as a specialist of the big .50-caliber BMG machine guns. After the war, Bob gained an interest in guns overall, going on to build the company that became known as Hastings, a company devoted to accuracy-driven shotgun barrels and chokes. At the same time, Bob also became a self-educated student of the big English Nitro Express rifles used in Africa for very large or dangerous game. As a result, Hastings Paradox barrels for 12-gauge rifle slug shooting were the first ever offered on the sporting market to those hunters; one model of this design even retained special dangerous-game open sights.

What all this told me was that even way back in the 1980s, Bob Rott was entertaining the idea of offering up a very special rifled shotgun design to the shooting world. By studying the works of Frank De Haas and his reviews in the work *A Potpourri of Single Shot Rifles and Actions*, as well as the works of some others, Bob was able to formulate a direction when thinking about how to achieve his goal of designing a Hastings single-shot rifled *shotgun*. After reviewing massive amounts of data across all the gauge offerings, Rott decided that it was actually the 20-gauge that offered the best options, when considering an advanced 3½-inch shotshell. It would be of a completely new design, one that would carry a very heavy slug at very high velocity. This was to be finalized as the Hastings 3½-inch 20-gauge Super Magnum.

For the most part, this 410-grain sabot and slug came very close to the performance of the .45-70 Government metallic cartridge round, and even the .450/400 Nitro Express! For example, the .45-70 will develop 1,880 fps at the muzzle, shooting a Winchester 300-grain Partition Gold bullet, while the 410-grain Knoster sabot/slug leaves the Hastings/Hagn 20 gauge at an even 2,000 fps At 200 yards, the .45-70 has slowed to 1,292 fps, while the 20-gauge sabot pill is coming across the line at 1,051 fps. This is a small 241 fps difference, but the 20-gauge is still delivering 1,006 ft-lbs of energy, which is a slight 106 ft-lb drop over the .45-70

The author with an admirable slug group. While, over the years, shotgun slugs and sabot design improvement have received a fraction of the attention devoted to other shotshells, there have been some improvements, such as the wildcat 3½-inch 20-gauge Hastings/Hagn slug.

As the bullet/slug design makes use of a discarding sabot, the actual projectile at .60-caliber retains a working weight of 350-grains of soft lead. Yet the sabot retainer, weighting in at 60 grains, is able to hold the two together as a complete package. Over the course of the past several years, I have taken seven adult whitetail bucks with this sabot design, as used in both the 20-gauge and the 12-gauge Hastings Laser Accurate slug ammunition. Not one animal was lost, nor even tracked much beyond 25 yards when shot with a well-centered vitals hit. At times, the sabot unit followed the lead slug into the wound channel, exited the critter, and was found on the ground after the fact. On other occasions, I found the sabot embedded deep within the animal's body, sometimes even jammed against the spine or shoulder bone. This is the only projectile design I have ever tested that actually made use of the sabot as well as the slug, in terms of the total projectile developing a wound channel.

When designing a gun for the 3½-inch 20-gauge round, Rott turned to Canadian gun maker Martin Hagn. Hagn was himself a student of the single-shot rifle and shotgun and retained a solid understanding of them. The rifle Bob Rott had built is a one of a kind and completely handmade by Hagn. It served as the test bed for the new 20-gauge cartridge and turned heads on design teams for several rifle makers.

Hastings went on to offer special rebarreled (Paradox-rifled) hinge guns, in the fall of 2007. For my money, I wanted one in a traditional Sharps configuration. Being a standard 20-gauge bore (with no other gauge offering) and using a saboted lead slug, this gun is legal in all 50 states. That meant some of those Iowa boys now had a gun that would compete with the muzzleloaders that have been steadily increasing range and projectile energy levels in recent years. Several years ago, for instance, at a range in Pasa Park, Illinois, I shot the then-new .50-caliber Knight turn-bolt Long Range Hunter muzzleloader on a 200-yard range and never missed the eight-inch steel plate. That's something well beyond what my old Hawken .50-caliber cap-and-ball shooter would do (that gun was accurate to about 50 yards, way back when), or, for that matter, my first smoothbore 12-gauge 870 Wingmaster, which missed more deer than it ever hit. By comparison, of the Knoster slug system you could say that it is close to if not right at perfection, when reviewing its game taking ability. Even if the .615-caliber slug fails to open a minimum amount, it will still be driving a half-inch hole through a deer's body.

When the first test gun got to me for evaluation, the South Dakota deer season had just closed, so I headed for the Buffalo Gap grasslands and a range out on the prairie that allowed me to push the new slug gun and loads on some three-quarters life-sized deer targets I'd drawn up quickly on large sheets of butcher paper. Starting with my improvised Case-Gard plastic benchrest at 100 yards, I first got comfortable with the

Government. I'm here to tell you, no whitetail would ever know the difference between being hit by the 300-grain .45-70 and the 410-grain 20-gauge .615-inch/.60-plus-caliber projectile. The main difference there would be that the Hastings 3½-inch 20-gauge was and still is legal in all shotgun slug zones across the country, while the .45-70 in a rifle is not.

By increasing the 20-gauge 3-inch hull to 3½ inches, Knoster and load developer Tom Armbrust were able to increase the powder charge. They then added additional special wadding that acts to absorb setback during firing. This, in turn, reduces chamber pressure enough to keep it in line with current 3½-inch shotshell SAAMI standards. (This new super slug will only generate 13,000 psi in the 20-gauge chamber. Today, this same effect is produced by Hevi-Shot in its Speed Ball 12-gauge waterfowl ammunition).

The Hastings 20-gauge Super Magnum possesses a .615-caliber slug backed by a sabot that stays with it all the way to (and often right on through) the intended target. A deer killer? Oh, yeah.

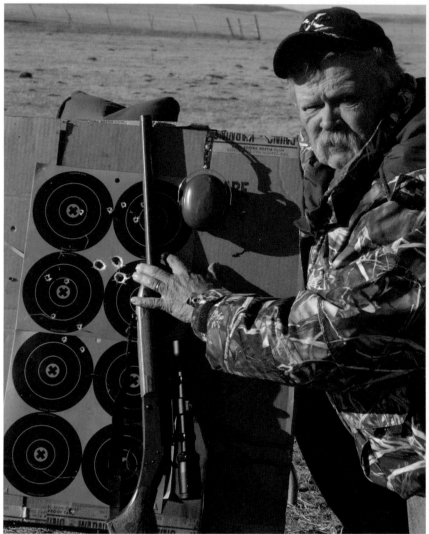

gun by shooting at an eight-inch Caldwell Insta-View target. With the Hastings/Hagn .615-caliber (20-gauge) resting over a Caldwell bag, I proceeded to shoot a nice 1½-inch three-shot group. Recoil was not light, but it was quite manageable, in fact, no more than a 12-gauge 3-inch slugger shot from a benchrest.

Moving out to 175 yards, my next two shots took out both eyes of the deer drawn on my butcher paper targets, and a third shot went into the target's spine. Three rounds downrange and a "dead deer" with every shot. I managed to next throw two wild shots off target center, but each would still have resulted in a deer slowed down enough to allow a second, finishing shot. With that, I was satisfied with the gun's accuracy for the time being, but there was more in store for it.

Arriving back home, I found my phone ringing off the hook. John Anderson, my editor from *The Varmint Hunter Magazine* was on the other end, asking me if I could be 200 miles east of the Black Hills at Pierre, South Dakota, by late afternoon? John's publisher had lined up a buffalo hunt on the Triple U Ranch (605-567-3624; www.tripleuranch.com), for the next morning, and we both saw this impromptu event as a chance to get the new Hastings slug on a real-world hard target. It seemed that John had had a discussion with Janet Hansen, his magazine's CEO at the time. Her husband just happened to work as a pilot flying fence for the Triple U, a 58,000-acre buffalo operation known for its role in the movie *Dances With Wolves*. All the hunting scenes were filmed there, as was the Fort Sedgwick footage and many other scenes used in that famous film. Thanks in part to the movie, buffalo hunters from all over the world come to the Triple U Ranch and, now, thanks to Janet's husband, I was being offered the chance to try the Hastings super gun on one of the toughest big-game animals out there.

Successfully and quickly killing buffaloes is difficult, because the kill zone is a small area located at the back of the animal's ear and two inches below that point in the neck area. Miss that by even an inch and you have a wounded critter that can run up to 25 miles before stopping. Many a hunter over the years at the Triple U has mistaken his big gun's energy as a substitute for accurate shooting, making for a long and stressful chase. I was told about all this, as I headed for the target range on the ranch with my guide and fire control director, B.J. Humble. B.J. was an old hand at taking down buffalo, as shooting them is the standard method employed when only a few animals are required for making meat. This is where we came in. The order was for nine adult buffalo, and they were to be dry cows. These animals would weigh in at 900 to 1,000 pounds and would generally be at seven years of age and, so, no longer producing calves. With the seven-year drought in western South Dakota, keeping younger breeding stock at the forefront was one way to keep the Triple U buffalo ranch alive and healthy.

B.J. indicated that I had to pass a 100-yard accuracy test with whatever I was about to shoot; losing that

valuable meat to a bad shot was, understandably, just not acceptable. But, when B.J. set eyes on the 3½-inch 20-gauge shotshell I was loading into the gun's breech at the benchrest, I could see he was less than impressed.

"Is that a shotgun?" was the first thing out of the guide's mouth.

"Yep, and it's going to get the job done," I answered.

At 100 yards, fighting a stiff, 40 mph crosswind from the snowstorm that was now blowing in, my first two bullets were almost on top of each other, but a full nine inches to the right of target center. With a check of the target, B.J. nodded his head in approval, and indicated he would try and get me straight up- or downwind of a buffalo, given the amount of drift I was experiencing in the gale-force snowstorm that was, by now, coming on strong (B.J. still checked his own rifle for backup). What the guide didn't know was that *I* knew the shotshell's ballistics. If I could get the big slug in the right place, the rest of this story would take care of itself—or at least I was hoping it would all go that way.

After covering some miles of open prairie in almost whiteout conditions, I spotted shapes in the distance. From my vantage, they resembled large trees on a hilltop. They weren't. They were buffalo, and even in the 40 to 50 mph winds, these magnificent critters were moving into the wind and feeding like it was a bright summer day. That's when I knew why the American Indian had a deep respect for *Tatanka*.

B.J. circled the herd, while John Anderson sat in the back seat of the Ford 150 4x4 holding my backup .45-70 Government Sharps. I had not shot the Sharps at the range, but B.J. had figured out I knew my own rifle. I, of course, was hoping I wouldn't need anything in the backup category, when I touched of the Hastings/Hagn .60-caliber slug gun.

"We have a nice seven-year-old cow picked out for you, L.P.," yelled B.J. over the truck engine and blowing wind. "She's in this herd, but we have to locate her and keep her in sight." B.J. had indicated that we were only going to shoot preselected cows, and this made it tough for a novice buffalo hunter like myself, as all of them looked a whole lot alike. Finally, B.J. spotted the cow we wanted.

She was very large, close to 1,000 pounds, and she had a set of horns that not only were massive, but made a curl to the rear, as if they were being bent by the wind. I locked in my focus on her, but it was hard to keep her in view. She would drift between other buffalo, getting lost to me before reemerging somewhere else within the mass of moving animals. I was wondering when I'd find a clear moment to shoot, when she showed at the front of the herd, then crossed directly in front of our truck. She was moving toward a shallow draw as she walked, and B.J. quickly told to me that she would stop before dropping down into a bigger depression. When she stopped, it would give me a moment to get off a fast shot.

The author with the first buffalo he dropped. In a raging blizzard. With a 20-gauge slug.

Jumping out of the truck, I ran a few yards to the side and dropped into my shooting sticks. Searching through the Burris 2-7x slug scope, I was pleased to see the buffalo walk into my sight picture. I knew the required shot and moved the crosshairs of the scope across the right ear and down about two inches into the neck area.

At the shot, which to me was initially only a distant *thump* in the howling wind, I caught the sound of the slug slapping hard against a very solid object. The old girl went down in her tracks, never taking a single step forward. She was stone dead in an instant. B.J. whooped, and John cracked me on the back. "Dead-on perfect shot, L.P.!" yelled John. I turned to look at B.J., who was grinning widely, though with a slight look of astonishment on his face.

Between the three of us, we dropped five more buffalo with the Hastings/Hagn slug gun that day. John shot his personal trophy with a very nice 70-yard, one-shot, dead-in-its-tracks kill, while B.J. nailed a running cow in the eye at about 50 yards crossing. I dropped two more big cows at distances between 55 and 75 yards. Not a single animal ever knew what hit it. There was no tracking, no wounded critters. Without a doubt, the Hastings/Hagn 3½-inch 20-gauge, coupled with the Knoster-designed saboted slug, had passed the acid test on some very tough big game. I figure that, when a gun like the Hastings/Hagn can drop buffalo as clean as can be, there's no deer that stands so much as a remote chance against it. In fact, I fully intend to hunt elk, as well as head for bear country, with total confidence in this modern slug gunning system.

SHOTdata Results 01/27/2007	Range (YARDS)	Velocity (FPS)	Energy (FT/LBS)	Time of Flight (SECONDS)	Drop (INCHES)	Wind Def @30 mph (FEET)	????	Impact LOS (INCHES)
Shot Type: Hastings 20-gauge slug	0	2,000	3,641.2	0.0000	0.0	0.0	0.0	-1.5
	25	1,838	3,075.2	0.0397	0.3	0.4	1.7	0.4
Slug Weight (grains): 410	50	1,685	2,585.4	0.0823	1.2	1.3	3.6	1.6
Effective Ballistic Coefficient: 0.1150	75	1,543	2,167.9	0.1289	2.9	2.9	5.7	2.0
	100	1,413	1,817.1	0.1798	5.6	5.2	7.9	1.6
Zero Range, yards: 125	125	1,296	1,530.0	0.2353	9.3	8.4	10.4	-0.0
	150	1,197	1,303.9	0.2956	14.4	12.4	13.0	-2.9
Standard Ballistic Coefficient: 0.1150	175	1,116	1,133.8	0.3607	20.9	17.3	15.9	-7.3
	200	1,053	1,008.7	0.4300	29.3	22.9	18.9	-13.5

SHOTdata Results 01/27/2007	Range (YARDS)	Velocity (FPS)	Energy (FT/LBS)	Time of Flight (SECONDS)	Drop (INCHES)	Wind Def @30 mph (FEET)	???????	Impact (INCHES)
Shot Type: Hastings 20-gauge slug	0	2,000	3,641.2	0.0000	0.0	0.0	0.0	-1.5
	50	1,685	2,585.4	0.0823	1.2	1.3	3.6	2.5
Effective Ballistic Coefficient: 0.1150	100	1,413	1,817.1	0.1798	5.6	5.2	7.9	3.5
	150	1,197	1,303.9	0.2956	14.4	12.4	13.0	-0.0
Standard Ballistic Coefficient: 0.1150	200	1,053	1,008.7	0.4300	29.3	22.9	18.9	-9.7
	250	960	839.6	0.5796	52.0	36.0	25.5	-27.1
	300	893	725.2	0.7419	83.6	51.4	32.6	-53.4

Note: Ballistics data here was generated by SHOTdata System, New Brighten, Minnesota, and Ross Metzger, the engineer I have worked with closely for better then 40 years. At first, Ross didn't believe what the 3½-inch 20-gauge gun could do, but, after running the hard data through his ballistic programs, he became a true believer in short order. The first question here is, has this shotgun been turned into a rifle of sorts? I say no, because this gun, while being deadly accurate and retaining heavy-rifle (.458 Magnum) energies, still won't push a slug much beyond standard slug ranges, in terms of downrange drift. Testing I have done over the years on shotgun slugs recovered from powder snow has indicated that 20-gauge, 12-gauge, and 10-gauge slug guns can all send their projectiles up to 800 yards (with the proper indirect fire angle, an artillery shot, you could say). What this Hastings system will do is give the slug shooter an edge by way of a refined shooting system that retains the balance, look, and feel of a real rifle, but while maintaining the general characteristics of a shotgun's baseline ballistics.

The added length of Knoster-designed 20-gauge super magnum slug gets high marks in the penetration category.

It is my thinking that the review in these pages clearly shows that creative thinking when it comes to slug improvements. The 3½-inch 20-gauge illustrates the massive, nearly limitless extension in ballistics achievement that the shotgun slug has going for it. The chamber pressures may well be low at a max of 11,000 psi, but the creative element associated with using the large hull's interior makes up for the low burn pressure in the engine room. When I ran the Stacy Project on small shot penetration, I also did some extensive work with rifled shotgun slugs. What I found, working with slug recovering from fresh snow, was that I was able to send slugs downrange at about a 14 degree angle and obtain a maximum range of 980 yards. (As for finding them in the snow? Well, I had a very special golden retriever named Feather that could smell them out for me. You can't make that kind of stuff up, my friends!) I have also worked with culling operations on whitetail deer, using several new slug designs by the major manufactures, and I've recorded information produced by bear hunters who elected to use the 12-gauge with either sabot or Foster-style slugs when hunting from trees over bait sites. In each case, the data confirms that, when accurately shooting 350-grain to 500-grain projectiles at warm targets, all the advantage is on the hunter's side, when accuracy can be maintained.

LOW-RECOIL AND SUBSONIC SHOTGUN SLUGS

For as long as shotgunners have been launching slugs of lead at deer, bear, or whatever represented the next intended dinner for the table, there have been issues surrounding the subject of recoil and muzzle blast. Despite advancements in shotgun development and the Foster slug losing favor to saboted bullets, the recoil problem hasn't gone away. The bone-jarring punishment associated with shotgun slug loads just has not been reduced very much—until now.

Of late, several different companies have taken a hard look at the recoil and noise problems associated with shotgun slug ammunition and are finely doing something about reducing it. As a technical shooting development writer in ballistics and designer of a gun barrel and suppressor system (called the .724 Orion) that uses subsonic, low-recoil ammunition in loads ranging from common lead shot bird loads to heavy waterfowl shotshells, embarking on a study of subsonic slug designs was a natural progression for me. In terms of increasing the effectiveness of both my own special barrels (my Metro Gun System), as well as those used on conventional smoothbore or rifled shotguns, the low-recoil and reduced muzzle blast slug loads can offer many rewards.

What got me thinking about the development of low-recoil and subsonic slug loads was the introduction of a slug designed by Polyshok, Inc. This slug wasn't intended much for sportsmen, but rather for air defense pilots who wanted to count on it to dust off hijackers in flight, with little or no damage to the aircraft and passengers. Polyshok slugs make use of a one-ounce fragmentation projectile that, when making contact with a target, breaks apart into three separate projectiles and cuts three wound channels into that target, but does not exit the target and to cause damage beyond it.

During 2002, I tested these slugs on a number of static targets, including deer carcasses and coyotes (both on hunts and in re-shot, previously killed animals), and found them to be very effective as one-shot-stop projectiles. At the same time, the slug produced almost no recoil and projected a very low decibel (Db) rate.

About the same time my testing was underway, an associate who, to this day, continues to work on other low-sound-/-recoil fragmentation systems, started work on what could be regarded as a new direction in slug load ballistics. In that case, he was working on a slug design where the velocity was very low, down to 850 fps. This ultra low-velocity round creates virtually no recoil and, when used with something like my Metro Gun system, creates the report of a .22 LR (Db 72). Yet it dropped deer cleanly, when they were hit in the neck or the shot was centered in the vitals. In fact, over a two-year development period, those prototype slugs were applied to a state agency deer culling operation and found to get the job done and without wounding animals, which, in a suburban neighborhood, would cause all the headaches you might imagine.

Adding the data from the cull hunts to my testing data of the Polyshok loads, I was able to get a very clear view of where this kind of shotgun slug load development was headed. Here's what I concluded.

Low-velocity slugs can work well, if the design of the slug itself was one that balanced with its velocity. It can also be a winner if it is matched to both rifled and smoothbore shotguns. The latter hadn't been considered at first, but I found the consideration to be an important one. While we all understand that a rifled barrel can be more accurate, if the slug is of a fragmenting design as exists in the Polyshok creation (called the Quick-Shok slug), it actually can't take the stress of a rifled bore and, so, instead, must be used in a smoothbore pipe exclusively. With that fact calculated into my learning curve, I turned my attention to solid projectiles and, as happens so many times in this business, the commercial answers came jumping out of the woodwork.

I guess it was early in 2003 that I became aware that my partner company in the Metro Gun System was about to launch into the slug development and marketing business. Hastings, then working out of Clay Center, Kansas, and under direction from Bob Rott, was deeply involved in a project being carried out by Richard Knoster, a ballistics design guy who had worked with a number of companies prior to hooking up with Hastings. Knoster had developed a heavy 1¼-ounce slug and was loading it not only as a full-house, high-velocity load, but also as a low-velocity, very low-recoil load.

Save for the fact that my gun barrels were being marketed through Hastings, I really had no interest in the slug end of the company. Still, I did like the idea that the folks there were directing one of their slug designs into the low-recoil, reduced-noise market. But then my interest really increased, after I learned a bit about the Knoster slug system as loaded by Polywad, Inc., out of Macon, Georgia, at the time.

Knoster was using a 1¼-ounce chunk of lead that employs a nose section designed like a pie plate tacked onto a cylinder-shaped stem section. The nose measures .649-inch and has a depth of .282-inch. Add the stem section that measures .560-inch in length and has a diameter of .500-inch, and you have a stiff, resisting nose section being pushed by an equally resistant tube of lead that, along with the rest of the projectile, is stuffed into a hard plastic sabot. This is no ordinary sabot. When fired, the entire unit stays together (very much like the 20-gauge load reviewed at the start of this chapter), until it gains an inch or so of penetration in its target. The lead projectile continues on deeper, leaving the plastic pod behind. With a design like this, but working at a lower velocity, the slug makes good use of all the remaining energy at the target, its terminal energy.

When data started to come in regarding kills with the Knoster slow, low-recoil slugs, it got my attention. My fear involved in building something like this has been that such low velocities would produce wounds, rather than kill quickly and humanely. But no such wounding had occurred. The kill data indicated, quite clearly, that this projectile, even at low velocity, killed cleanly and quickly when used at appropriate ranges (inside 50 yards). As for the reduced recoil, I interviewed 11- and 12-year-old youngsters who were first-time deer hunters using the Hastings low recoil slugs. They came away from their sighting in and hunts without fear, without pain, and, best of all, they actually enjoyed shooting, even when the gun was big and heavy.

In terms of accuracy, the low-recoil slugs by Hastings hold their own. When shot in rifled pipes, they tend to produce tight groups, under two inches, to 50 yards. In smoothbore guns, they hold to three-inch groups. Either way, it's good vital area accuracy. Recoil is almost nonexistent in the Metro Gun System extended quiet barrel guns, and it's very tolerable in slug guns mounting standard 21-inch barrels; the Hastings low-recoil/low-sound slugs drop about 60 percent off the normal recoil from a standard slug gun, and reduce sound by about 20 percent.

WHAT'S THE FUTURE FOR SLUGS?

What the future holds for acceptance and application of low-recoiling and, in some cases, low-noise slug ammo, only time will tell. If shooters catch on that they can shoot slugs and not get beat up in the process, close-range woodland hunters may readily adopt to these less abusive loads. Too, there is certainly a market for these rounds where state agencies need to perform deer and other critter culling and need to do it with low environmental-impact ammunition.

A very strong market in this latter direction has, in fact, developed. Government hunters like to keep the noise down, if they want maintain peace in the neighborhood and get the hunt completed at the same time. Commercial hunters, police, military, animal control specialists, and even the USDA also have a strong need

for quiet shooting systems, to be sure, and I know this for a fact, as many departments shoot my sound suppression systems with effective results.

When it comes to the slugs you're probably most familiar with, here's where the market stands.

The popular BRI sabot slugs are available in Winchester ammunition, though you have to remember that all sabot slugs are best used with a fully rifled barrel or, at least, a rifled choke. What I call "bullet slugs," which make use of .50-caliber muzzleloader bullets, are also common and can be obtained from nearly all slug manufactures. Again, these are saboted rounds and require a rifled barrel or choke tube.

Soft slugs, such as are used in the old Fosters, are best used with a smoothbore. However, when indicated by the manufacture, a few of these slug designs can be used both ways. Be sure to read the labels when you buy slug ammunition, as the variations in applications are many.

When continuing my review for this book of both the general-purpose and advanced, high-performance slug loads available, I have to say that, while there's not a ton that's new, the entire industry does seem to be putting its best foot forward. Everyone knows that the future of big-game hunting in many areas of the U.S. rests with the shotgun slugs. The use of the sabot-contained slug leads the pack in new design development, and loads like the Federal Cartridge 300-grain 12-gauge Trophy Copper Sabot Slug shot out of a well-made rifled barrel at 2,000 fps will print dead-on accuracy to 100 or more yards. Step down to the 3-inch 20-gauge and, again, Federal's Trophy Copper 275-grain slug, which leaves the smaller bore at 1,900 fps, you still have a formidable flying object for connecting with whitetail deer, bear, or for addressing the current craze of hog shooting.

In conventional slugs, the Federal TruBall is among one of the most accurate smoothbore slugs in use today. I personally know the man who invented TruBall and, without question, you can be advised that darn little in new product engineering developments gets by this guy. It also says much that Federal picked up the design and rolled it into its product line.

As a second example of the rifle bullet being used in a sabot-sustained slug system, the Hornady Superperformance line offers the new 300-grain Monoflex Slug, a poly-tipped bullet in copper cladding that's mounted in a sabot casing. These loads are not unlike the .50-caliber bullets shot through the modern muzzleloaders, but have the obvious advantage of being fixed breach-loaded rounds.

A final example of current slug development is Winchester coming forward with a ball slug (Foster design) called the Razorback, and it is being marketed to the growing crowd of wild hog hunters. This slug makes use of the three-section segmented projectiles that, for the most part, was developed by the same

Continued on page 132

Remington's Managed Recoil Slugs

I think a note here is necessary about low-sound rounds and a misconception about muzzle noise I hear talked about frequently. Lots of folks think that suppressed "can" systems or chokes designed for reducing noise and muzzle blast are intended to be silent. Well, that's only in the movies, my friends. When a real projectile hit air at the end of a muzzle, it makes a cracking sound. Can't get around that, so, while live loads can be suppressed to some degree, they can never be totally silent. Therefor, don't expect low-sound, low-recoil ammo to be just like it is in the movies. It won't, and that's the fact of the matter.

Hastings isn't the only player in shotgun slug advancement. Remington not long ago introduced a one-ounce Foster slug that has a muzzle velocity of 1,000 fps. Remington dubbed this new load its "Managed-Recoil Slugger" and says this gentler, quieter slug will build confidence in both shooters new to the sport and old-timers who don't want to be kicked around anymore by a 400-plus-grain slug. Shooting the new Remington round in an 870 Express mounting a 21-inch barrel and open sights, I drilled groups under 1½ inches at 50 yards. Longer shots weren't attempted, because these lower velocity loads are best used only within this 50-yard range; with a Foster slug, if you push it too far downrange, the energy falls off, accuracy suffers, and wounded game can be the end result.

In terms of felt recoil, the Remington slugs produced manageable recoil, but not anything I'd consider completely controlled. Turning to my Metro Gun System, which has a track record of taming higher recoiling loads, I sent a series of shot downrange with the Metro barrel extension attached. I found a further reduction in recoil and, to a lesser extent, muzzle blast. However, when it comes to sound reduction, these slugs don't take any awards or make many friends.

Given that, what real value are these lower energy slugs? Well, I've outfitted many hunters with both quiet guns and loads, hunters who'd had to give up hunting due to heart conditions complicated by recoil, as well as others having hearing loss problems significant enough to keep them away from any rifle or shotgun. In both cases, the hunters are back hunting (and quite happy, I must add). And isn't that enough?

SHOTdata Systems
Shot Type: Hastings Laser Slug 12-gauge blunt-nose sabot
Slug Weight: 1 1/4-ounce; 570-grain
Muzzle Velocity: 1,000 fps

Range (YARDS)	Velocity (FPS)	Energy (FT/LBS)	Wind Def @10 mph (INCHES)
0	1,000	1,256	0
25	870	959	1.0
50	761	732	4.2
75	665	560	9.5

SHOTdata Systems
Shot Type: Remington Managed Recoil Slugger 12-gauge Foster
Slug Weight: 1 ounce
Muzzle Velocity: 1,000 fps
Ballistic Coefficient: (C1)=0.128

Range (YARDS)	Velocity (FPS)	Energy (FT/LBS)	Wind Def @10 mph (INCHES)
0	1,000	???	0
5	983	938	N/A
25	941	860	N/A
50	898	763	N/A
60	882	755	N/A

Notes: The computer generated Optical Game Program indicated that these slugs will bring down a 208-pound deer to 50 yards, given a vitals hit. Actual field results confirm that data.
There is no data available for Polyshok's fragmenting slug, as it's currently classified information by that company and intended for military and police use only.

folks who invented TruBall a number of years ago. These 1⅛-ounce projectiles leave the muzzle at 1,600 fps and, like the Quik-Shok loads I previously illustrated, separate into three equal parts, thereby increasing the kill footprint against large game, including wild pigs. (A personnel note here: I've hunted hogs extensively from Texas to Australia, and I have to say these animals ain't as tough as the slick ad agencies for ammunition companies seem to promote. We've dusted significant numbers of them with standard double-aught buckshot loads at close range when night hunting with short-barreled, coach-style 12-gauges.)

WHAT'S IN STORE FOR NEW SLUG GUNS?

Reviewing the basic shotgun as it's turned into a slug gun isn't difficult. For almost ever, the slug gun, at least up until the 1980s, wasn't much more then a duck gun pulling double duty as a deer killer. Some police units carried Winchester Model 12s or 97s, Ithaca 37s, or Remington 870s with cut-down barrels, but big-game hunters made use of the standard bird gun with the common bead front sight. But aside from military and police use, which will be covered in another chapter, changes in sporting slug guns only got rolling when Hastings introduced the Paradox, followed by some independent custom gun makers building basic, short-barrel guns (either as Paradox rifled or as smoothbores) on the 870 Wingmaster by

"freezing" the barrel to the receiver and adding first a custom trigger, and then a receiver scope mount. Then came the cantilever scope mount, and, finally, there was a major shift in slug gun design. The cantilever Weaver rail mounted to the barrel, instead of the receiver, and extended back over the receiver. Scopes could be mounted to the rail so that they would be in proper alignment to the shooter's cheek weld on the stock and their natural eye position. When the barrel shifted any degree at all, the scope, of course, moved with the barrel, making shooter corrections quickly identifiable and easily acquired.

The strange part to this clever arrangement was that it was slow to catch on among the manufactures. Eventually, Remington and Mossberg were two of the first major U.S. gun companies to adopt the cantilever and, today, it is very common among most commercially made shotguns set up for slug shooting—that is, if the barrel is a quick-change system and not one threaded onto or permanently affixed to the receiver (Ithaca's Model 37 Slug, by example).

If you're searching for an accurate slug gun, by all means consider the barrel equipped with the cantilever scope mount. By keeping in mind that more than half the United States uses slug guns for sporting purposes, it's never a good idea to ever count the pumpkin thrower out—and, to be sure, advanced development in accurate slug shooting systems isn't about to grind to a halt anytime soon.

CHAPTER THIRTEEN

THE VARMINT/ PREDATOR SHOTGUN

I t was not quite 3:30 a.m., when our pickup rolled to a stop just above the shallow creek bed that ran through miles of oak woods and farm fields, in central Minnesota. With a full moon above and harvested corn on both sides of the road, anything that moved became an easy target by way of my 3-9x Redfield scope mounted on the Remington 870 12-gauge's 21-inch barreled receiver.

Without saying a word, my partner Jim Korzenowski dropped down on the east side of the bridge culvert, as I moved to cover the west end of the opening. This was a common method we used for flushing out rac-

coons that often slide into these protected areas as the occasional vehicle approached. With the stream bank rich in crayfish and other sorts of food, this was a very popular place for raccoons to congregate at night.

Jim had no sooner reached the waterline, when a 30-plus-pound raccoon came rolling past me and headed into the cut cornfield rows at a lope. I pushed the crosshairs, barely visible save for two dull, almost silver lines, across the critter's front half and touched off a round of No. 4 buckshot. The 41-pellet load of Winchester SuperX buffered buck sent a trail of fire into the night air, turning the view in my scope a deep orange-yellow for just enough time to blind me from seeing the solid hit on my intended target.

Jim joined me and we advanced onto the cornfield, only to be confronted by a head-on charging and wounded raccoon that was determined to get a piece of us before he bought the farm. Point-blank, I cranked a second round out of the gun, without using the sights, but lining up the barrel as best as I could. Jim followed up at the same time with a blast from his 870 Wingmaster, sending a second charge of buckshot toward the mass of snarling fur. I don't know whose shot found its mark, but the raccoon drove into the soft earth at the shots, rolling end over end to a dead stop. Our task for the moment was completed, and the first raccoon of the night was up for skinning and the drying stretcher.

Our next stop was a large landfill that usually yielded far more skunks then raccoons, but it was an area where, if a fresh load of pizzas or some such delicacy had been dropped the previous day, the night feeding bandits would show up every so often. This was night scope time. For me, that meant my Tasco Night Vision NS 200, a unit more than capable of separating one type of varmint from another.

It didn't take any time at all before the first movement was observed. Night scope up, the optics indicated a skunk was making its way towards a pile of who knows what. Time to re-chamber, this time with No. 2 or BB lead to knock off the second critter in the game bird egg-eater category. *Crack-thud*, and our 12-gauges turned loose layers of shot against the waddling skunk, sending it spinning, dead.

Almost an hour passed before we saw movement again. This time raccoons were on the target list, with no less then three approaching the landfill containing the best of the deep dish leftovers from the nearby town. My Tasco night scope indicated a large raccoon was leading the group, followed by a good sized but smaller partner and a third raccoon that most likely was a juvenile, judging by its overall size. Jim turned loose buckshot on the lead animal and I picked up on the second target. At the shots, the third animal made a quick exit, leaving no chance to acquire a second sight picture, but the pair that had been to the front were history. With the night now almost spent and several good fox and coyote stands looming on the timetable for predawn calling, the raccoons were hauled onto the truck bed, and another successful night of bandit hunting was embedded in memory.

Raccoon hunting by predator hunters or general varmint takers is very different from hunting over hounds. I have spent many a night following the baying sound of my partner's leopard curs or blue tick hounds, at last finding the dogs with a 'coon treed on a high oak limb. Then, by way of a spotlight (legal in Minnesota, at the time) and a light-caliber rifle (.22 LR) the critter was taken for its fur. While prices even then were not as good as they'd used to be, it was just possible that a young fellow could still make a bit of fold-ing money by hunting the ringtailed bandits. A nice bonus was that, with the reduction in trapping over the past decade, the raccoon had exploded in population, finding them in workable habitat was quite easy much of the time.

Today, if you don't take to the idea of stomping around in the dark while trying to put a shot into 30 pounds of upset, tooth-slashing critter, using electronic "food" calling tapes or a young raccoon in distress call by Johnny Stewart can bring an upset adult into your kill net quickly, in the right type of country. Searching for good sign is always important and, of course, you should hunt areas where raccoons like to feed. This past year, while hunting pre-dawn calling stands, I jumped 11 different raccoons by pure chance! I was calling in food-rich river bottoms in each case, something that added to the likelihood these critters would be about in significant numbers.

In terms of an effective gunning setup for the kind of work I've just talked about, I elect to use my Remington 870 Super Magnum with a 3½-inch chamber and a 21-inch turkey-style barrel. This shotgun

Stinky Fish and High Times

Let me tell you about the time we used freezer-burned northern pike to bait varmints in the middle of a deep swamp deer camp, in northern Minnesota.

Placing the fish along the edge of a black willow swamp, then forting up in treestands after dark, things got really nuts, really fast. Our first visitors were skunks that stunk up everything by way of a trigger-happy hunter who went crazy with a Browning A5 3-inch 12-gauge. Getting past that mess, our second visitor was nothing other then a black bear wanting his share of the booty. Of course, he got just that, being a bear. About 2:00 a.m., the first of many raccoons showed up, feeding time it was, and the shotgunner in the stand well away from the main stash of fish got most of the action. That started things rolling and, by first light, we had dusted off seven fat raccoons, welcome in those days, because they brought a fair piece of cash that paid for our food and gas during almost a week of deep, northern Minnesota varmint hunting.

retains a factory-installed Remington Spec-Ops camo stock, with pistol grip of static position shooting and an AR-style, six-position, telescoping buttstock. Generally, I use Tru-Glo iron sights; when day turns to dusk and I'm hunting coyotes in sagebrush or heavy timber, these open sights are just fine. However, when hunting and calling on open riverbanks or prairie in low light, I pull off that close-range day barrel and slap on a Remington cantilever rail-mounted 20-inch number. This second barrel mounts s Simmons 3.5-6x scope with a diamond reticle (heavy lines) for night work, the Insight Model M-2 mini-light, and a red laser. This small but very effective setup can be used in total darkness, and the red laser can be very effective in low light, late evening situations.

I use this setup because this gun, coupled with several barrels, including the Hastings Paradox, a heavy target bull barrel, and a Metro Gun Raven "quiet gun" (a suppressed .724 Orion), has shot almost everything less than super big game. Even with that stated, though, for bears in a dangerous situation, I would still rely on this gun 100 percent of the time. All of this demonstrates that shotguns have become incredibly flexible gunning platforms, platforms that are moving away from traditional designs and, as such, are gaining popularity with all sorts of new shooters, and that includes those fresh to varmint hunting.

Shooting a contract job for a farmer a few years ago with the 870 Super Mag setup and a Raven suppressor from Metro Gun Systems, I cleaned out 23 gray foxes, eleven opossums, a coyote, and four skunks that had been raiding his hen house and generally tearing up the place. All warm targets were night gunned over bait at close range (inside 40 yards) with the aid of night optics and the M-2 Insight target acquisition systems. I'm not the only one going about such hunting with such guns. In terms of new shotgun develop-

ment, these days can best be described as the time of the "ground gun." What's a ground gun? Shotguns dedicated to shooting "ground critters," such as coyotes, foxes, turkeys, and such, as well as those pesky varmints raiding the hen house. Let's take a look at these specialty shotguns and what they can do.

What a coyote hunter wants in a shotgun is one that allows flexible use of sights, including scopes, red dot optics, ACOG, infrared night optics, and open iron sights. The gun needs to be shorter than a bird gun, so it can be packed into a stand as a second gun of opportunity or used from a ground hide in deep cover where a more maneuverable gun would be appreciated. Of course, many hunters want shotguns that wear camo patterns or can be easily handpainted from a dull gray or black to a series of earth or green foliage colors.

One of the major changes of late is the offering of the new AR-15 type buttstocks on such varmint-specialized shotguns. Naturally, carrying a broom-handled grip and an extendable buttstock is far from practical when it comes

Federal's Heavyweight Coyote in the 3-inch BB load paired with a tight, long-range choke is a surefire combination.

Mossberg makes a shotgun for just about anything you might want to do with a shotgun, including hunting coyotes, and it does it without breaking the bank.

to flying targets, but, in the ground game, watch out, because the tactical-type shotgun is designed for solid holding on an incoming red fox or prairie wolf. As several examples of this new age in scatter gun design, we can look at Remington Arms, Winchester, and Mossberg, all in the middle price range and gravitated toward by many, get-it-done coyote callers. Let's take a look at a few of these.

The Winchester SXP is a gun offered in just about every configuration possible to meet the needs of just about any smoothbore shooter. This gun is not only a flexible option for varmint hunters to consider, it's priced right—you really don't need to sell your firstborn to buy one.

The author and a coyote he easily took with his Mossberg 835 Turkey Special loaded with Federal Heavyweight shot. This song dog went down hard at 55 yards.

When you're calling for predators, you never know what might show up. This hunter was set up with a rifle for coyotes, but, with a shotgun for backup, he was ready when this bobcat wandered in a little too close to his dying rabbit call.

Cats are some of the wariest quarry out there. Hunters of such fur-bearing critters are thankful that so many dedicated shotguns for their pursuit are available in a multitude of camouflage patterns.

Winchester sent one of the Marine Defender versions for evaluation expressly for this book and, over the course of several months, the gun was hauled around in a pickup truck and a big, heavy, 4x4 John Deere 8960, while I roamed the roads and hills on the lookout for badgers, woodchucks, porcupines, and skunks during the corn harvest. It also bounced around in the scabbard in my rough-water fishing boat, and the Winchester served as a backup gun for brush country coyote calling in the thick river bottoms and sagebrush flats of western South Dakota.

Mossberg is another maker front and center in ground gun territory, with the well-established 835 Ulti-Mag. I have owned several of these guns and, today, shoot the camo-coated thumbhole variant. The Mossberg is a special shotgun, in that it carries the massive 3½-inch 12-gauge chamber that was developed by the company in a partnership with Federal Cartridge years ago. Back then, some indicated the new length would just not work. Today most know it's top of the pile, in terms of effective downrange energy transfer, regardless of the target. I like this "super gun" concept, because I can carry 3-inch tungsten-iron shot or move up to 3½-inch BB lead for close-in brush shooting situations. For me, the 835 really is a do it all gun.

Speaking of loads for ground guns, those on the market today approach varmints as specialty targets. These loads have changed a great deal from those No. 4 buckshot rounds we threw at everything years ago. Today, tungsten-iron shot has replaced lead and is a much better product ballistically. With a density level well above lead, tungsten can hold its velocity, and that translates to more effective killing energy. Federal Heavyweight Coyote, for instance, in its 3-inch hull, makes use

Winchester's Xtended shotshells in coyote-appropriate loads certainly do the job, but these are tungsten-based loads and fast going the way of the rotary telephone.

of tungsten high-density BB shot. With a 1½-ounce payload moving out of the muzzle at 1,350 fps, these rounds are top of the order when taking on fur. Remington-built HD, if you can still find it, and Winchester's Xtended rounds are also tungsten-iron.

TACTICS FOR SMOOTHBORE VARMINTS

At the onset of this chapter, I described a hunting situation I've been in time and time again: the quick-handling scattergun, a dirt road, low light conditions—and the opportunity to hit something once in a while. Shotguns for such situations are not long-range tools; ground-pounding fur targets is best left to close-range tactics, to be sure. When shotgun hunting with-

out the backup of a rifle or a partner carrying one, the best advice is get into a position where the predator can't see you until you see it, and then it's *on,* up close and personal.

That said, you have to know that the tungsten-iron loads designed for coyotes and other larger varmints can and do push their energy quite far downrange. The table on the next page demonstrates what I'm talking about. Note that the effective energy that has been used as a base for measurement throughout this book reaches the end of its effective limits ballistically at the 90- to 100-yard mark. No, there's nothing short-range about that (though it only matters if you can hold the patterns together at those ranges). So, the 90-yard fig-

The author and a patterning board shot with Remington's HD ammo at 55 yards. The coyote that faces this will not make it out alive.

ure is a stretch as far as the pattern holding together, but the use of an ultra long-range choke will successfully drive this type of shot to at least 70 yards. What I'm getting at is that t varmint hunting with a shotgun isn't a long-range proposition, relatively speaking, the guns and loads are.

I have been involved in hunting varmints by way of a scattergun almost forever, it seems. When the industry sends out prototype loads, I often take up a

position along one of our local waterways at night or late evening, while other times I drive ranch roads in search of opportunity. Either way, ballistics associated with many modern shotshell loads today have been so positive that, at times, almost everything I send downrange tends to work out just fine. The bottom line here is that shotguns and today's dedicated, specialized ammunition make for some outstanding varmint control systems.

Shot Data Results 02/22/2008	Range (YARDS)	Velocity (FPS)	Energy (FT/LBS)	Time of Flight (SECONDS)	Drop (INCHES)	Wind Def @45 mph (FEET)	Lead Required (FEET)
Shot Type: Coyote .20-caliber tungsten buckshot	0	1,400	52.1	0.0000	0.0	0.0	0.0
	10	1,231	40.3	0.0237	0.1	0.1	1.6
Pellet Weight (grains): 11.970	20	1,098	32.0	0.0496	0.4	0.9	3.3
	30	991	26.1	0.0785	1.1	2.2	5.2
Effective Standard Deviation: 0.0422	40	902	21.6	0.1104	2.0	4.0	7.3
	50	829	18.3	0.1452	3.5	6.3	9.6
Pellet Diameter: (inches): 0.2014 equivalent	60	766	15.6	0.1830	5.4	9.1	12.1
	70	714	13.5	0.2237	7.9	12.4	14.8
Standard Deviation: 0.0422	80	667	11.8	0.2673	11.0	16.3	17.6
	90	622	10.3	0.3140	14.9	21.1	20.7
	100	581	9.0	0.3640	19.8	26.8	24.0

Silent Stealth Shotgunning

Today, with the development of subsonic ammunition and subsonic suppression systems and silencers (www.metrogun.com), the world of quiet shotgunning is coming into its own, and it's one that's completely applicable to varmint control and several other shooting situations.

Having developing my own brand of silent gun system, which have been commercially offered to the American shooter for better then 14 years to date, I can say that, by shooting in a total stealth mode of operation, I have been able to hunt areas that previously were bowhunt-only spots and gain the acceptance of everyone from apple grove farmers trying to hold off raccoons, to dairy farmers who can't stand the thought of a gun shot near their dairy cattle, but are overrun with everything from barn rats to crows. I've also seen the Metro Gun suppression system become a dream gun for Texas crow hunters; there are even clubs in the Lone Star State that require the use of them or you can't shoot with the group. Crows are easily sent off a calling location when gunfire erupts. Subsonic, quiet gun tools (silencers) allow the hunters to get lead on the targets without a second wave of high-altitude, black-winged marauders getting a warning about the surprise set up for them.

At one point, when in the development phase of Metro Gun, I was given a task. It involved hulking down in a storm drain on a gun club range that was infested with coyotes. I was sent to eradicate, at night, several of those coyotes, which were burrowing into the backstop on the 600-yard rifle range. The club didn't want any excess noise,

as it was close to a town, and also because my assigned shooting hours were being controlled by the city fathers. I hunted that range for almost three weeks and fired a dozen subsonic rounds through that drain run. The shotshells I used were a product of my own creation and made up with handloaded tungsten-iron buckshot, but with the silencer, I never got a single complaint from the nearby residents.

That was just one example. The following account gives a detailed illustration of exactly how the scattergun, even in its full-house stealth mode, can do a job where others can't be considered.

It was mid-day on a weekend when my phone rang. On the other end of the line was an old friend, Dean Yokum. Dean had found himself directly in the downwind path of a forest fire that had been raging out of control for several days. Even with the help of smoke jumpers from around the country, little progress had been made against the walls of fire that had already consumed several farms and homes and was now threatening several whole communities.

With the fire bearing down, Dean's property had become overrun with critters of all sorts and, as such, he asked me if I was willing to take a crack at bringing the local fox population under some kind of manageable control. In normal times, I hunted

The "can" part of the author's Metro Gun shotgun suppressor creation. It is a wonderful tool for dozens of applications where noise-reduction is a benefit to getting the job done.

Silent Stealth Shotgunning

the area around Dean's place, because the fox population always seemed to always hold up well. But now the fire had pushed many more critters than usual into the area and locals were observing them putting some damage to local duck and chicken populations retained by commercial poultry farmers in the area. Even some borderline anti-hunting types had taken up arms and were trying to dust off a few of the canine critters, but without much luck. I told Dean I was willing to set up on his place and see what I could do to help.

Dean's farm was about four miles from the point at which the fire had switched to a parallel direction from his farm, so he was not in danger of a burnout in his immediate area. That also made it possible to start right away and get in some calling time. To my advantage, it wasn't just the foxes, but all the critters that, thanks to

the fire, seemed to be a bit out of balance and seeking new ground. Too, with the deep winter coming on soon, the foxes would likely be eager to come running to the dying rabbit call.

Because I hunt full time and write between field experiences, I elected to call on Dean's farm during both weekday early morning hours and evenings. This would reduce the suburban noise level, as his farm was nearly in a major metropolitan area. With vehicles running as close as 200 yards down a major highway, and even hobby farm tractors filling the air with the rapping sound of their small gas engines, I had to select my calling times with care.

Dean had told me that he'd contacted his neighbors on both sides about the critter eradication, which gave me a free run of about 25 acres to work with. This may

Some of the author's friends after a successful crow shoot with Metro-equipped noise-reduced shotguns.

sound very small to a western-style caller, but, since he was surrounded by city, this was kind of like setting up in the middle of town, so having this amount of land to move around in and search out the best wind or varmint approach points was pure gold in such a human-saturated urban area.

The small section, of course, wasn't good for many stands, even when using some very short-range mouth calls like my rabbit calls and a new duel dominant coyote/subordinate pup call. However, set up I did and, as a result, my first attempt was a complete failure. Nothing but someone's yellow Lab came to my rabbit call, though at least he hit it at a dead run. (That actually ended up being pretty funny. When the Lab reached my location, he was confronted with a mass of talking leaves, as I was dressed in a leaf pattern Scentguard camo outfit. When I spoke to the dog, he turned tail in complete terror and headed for parts unknown. I tell ya, the stand was worth the effort, just watching that dog take off running in mortal fear of a talking tree!)

On day two, I turned the plan around and started my calling runs nearly at sunset. Still wasn't right. The road noise from people coming in from the big city and returning home to their starter castles in the woods, as well as some brush cutting by a guy about 200 yards away, completely messed up that attempt. I was beginning to wonder if I had any chance at all of successfully working this possibly productive, but difficult area. But then the winds died down. That's when I noticed the smoke from the fire zone was all about, and it became obvious that, if I had any chance at taking an urban fox from this fire situation, it would be soon or never. I came up with a plan, one that involved a long night of calling on stand and the use of bait.

Bait would do two things. First, it would distract the critter from the sounds of traffic and people talking in the distance. Second, by using it strategically, I could possibly pull in my target to within a dead-sure scattergun range (clearly, rifle work was out of the question).

Since I had just wrapped up a fall turkey hunt only days before and had kept the boned-out carcass of a good size jake, I decided to use that for bait. That night, I received a call from Dean. He told me he'd observed a

red fox come through about first light that morning, and all the suet from his low level bird feeders had been cleaned out. *Great!* I thought. This meant that at least one active critter was working the area. I also now had a full moon overhead, so me, my shotgun, and night vision unit, coupled with a Game Ear, headed for Dean's and a long night of watching and calling over my pile of turkey bones.

While Minnesota does not allow the use of artificial lights when hunting fox at night, I was allowed to use my Tasco Level II night vision system, and because farm buildings within about 200 yards of me were using the usual all-night halogen lamps, I had enough light to get clear target identification. I also had a Simmons Pro Diamond 1.5-5x scope mounted on my 12-gauge Remington 870 Express, so I was in the driver's seat for maintaining a clear target picture. The last thing I wanted to do was roll a local dog or another domestic critter that came into my bait site. Not the way to stay on good terms with the locals.

In the load department, I'd elected to shoot a 2¾-inch No. 2 non-toxic Hevi-Shot 1³/₈-ounce handload I'd developed for just such work. I'd dusted off a gray fox with the load several weeks earlier and found it to be solid fox anchoring round. Using the new (at the time) Alliant Steel powder, I was able to hold up velocity well and keep pressures at a very workable, if not comfortable recoil level. As a backup load, I retained a Polywad 1¼-ounce 2¾-inch No. 2 Hevi-Shot factory load that, before this show was over, would see a workout, as well. The Polywad load was pushed by 27 grains of Hodgdon Longshot and the pellets had been hand selected for their exactness in size and weight. Along with a quality poly buffer, these were, in effect, high-tech turkey loads, and I felt secure knowing that the Polywad creations had gone into my shooting bag and into the darkness on that first night gunning over bait.

Forted up against a pine tree surrounded by several other long limbed conifers, I was in a position that would give me a clear and very safe shot within a 45- to 50-yard kill net. Starting with a short dying rabbit run by way of a Burnham Brothers Texas Mimi Blaster, I then sat back and started what I anticipated would be a

This is the beginning of a great fox and coyote setup. Hevi-Shot's Dead Coyote load paired with the Dead Coyote choke made by Carlson.

nights it's just good to be in the woods, I thought.

After that night, the weather remained on the warm side and there was no chance of snow in the forecast, so I kept up my night stands at Dean's farm. Unfortunately my time in the field was about to get complicated, as the local deer season was just about to get underway, and the gut piles and occasional wounded deer would start to provide substantial food for roving foxes and coyotes. That meant calling them in wasn't a serious option, so I decided to fold up my bag of tricks and hunt deer for the next several weeks. Dean had told me he'd

long wait. With about 20 minutes off the clock, I again turned loose a short, subdued run on the Texas mouth call. Several minutes more passed and two white-faced opossums came slipping in, sniffing for the carcass of the jake. *Wrong move*, I said to myself, and turned loose a short yelp from the call, which resulted in a pair of hairless tails in my sights heading back into the black woods as fast as they could cover ground.

Two more hours passed, with nothing but a doe and her fawn walking through my kill zone. Then, like a switched-on light, everything transitioned to an exhilarating pace, and my first young red fox came into view. It was 45 yards off to one side of the bait, but, with the wind blowing directly into his path of travel, it was only a matter of seconds before he hit the scent line.

I put the scope's reticle on his neck, following him along until he hit the hot spot. About the only thing that would've saved his bacon at that point would have been a failure of my shotgun to fire. But that didn't happen and, as the red dog hit the magic 32-yard straight away mark I'd picked and came to a stop, he died almost instantly in a swarm of nickel-tungsten pellets. *Some*

provide as much bait on a regular basis as possible, and while that would certainly have helped the cause, a sudden heavy snowstorm and falling temperatures drove Minnesota into one of the worst winters we had seen for many a year. Nothing visited the baits. With 50 inches of deep snow, foxes and coyotes simply wouldn't move far away from den areas in search of food; it just takes too much precious energy, so staying close to their homes and mousing or eating less inviting morsels, however small, is the way for them to survive.

After deer hunting, on full moon nights, I did hit other areas around the burn fringe, but the burn-off was getting hard to locate with the land all white in the deep sleep of our sub-zero Minnesota winter. Working some canine calls in heavy grass swamps along the now frozen waterways did produce a couple of gray foxes, as well as a slightly wounded song dog that came running in almost up my back. That, of course, gave me no sight picture, and the departing 'yote passed through the thick black willow cover into the night. Calling had gone south to be sure. Time for new digs, new adventures with other shotguns.

CHAPTER FOURTEEN

EVOLUTION OF THE TURKEY GUN

’ve talked a lot about shot sizes, shot dynamics, and chokes for waterfowling and general-purpose upland hunting. But there's another realm that deserves its own attention to detail, and that's America's wild turkey, for, with the development of shotguns designed specifically for their hunting have also come advancements in their loads and chokes.

If I had to select one single element that has made the greatest contribution to the modern, high-perfor-

mance turkey-taking system, it would have to be the introduction of tungsten-based shotshells. Because of its extreme density, payloads of small tungsten shot can be sent a long way off and still maintain hard hitting velocities when they meet the target. While initially developed for the waterfowl hunter, the idea that tungsten shot could greatly increase both range and energy associated with shooting turkeys, hogs, and coyotes, soon took hold.

America's wild turkeys, from Easterns to Rios, Osceolas to Merriam's, are a near-obsession with camo-clad hunters. So powerful is the call in the spring that the firearms and ammunition industry has devoted whole segments of product lines toward taking that gobbler from field to table.

Even in the area of lead shot loads designed for the modern turkey and varmint hunter, we're seeing the use of new powders, wads, and some quality hard shot that, like the advanced tungsten shot product, will increase downrange performance. But regardless the choice of tungsten or lead, and even with all the advances with both, the question still arises, what shot size is best when applied to the game animal class that includes a trophy gobbler, incoming coyote, or hog?

Tungsten shot can be used in a far smaller pellet size than lead, due to its density and ability to hold energy downrange against targets like turkeys. For instance, a No. 7½ tungsten pellet will hit as hard as a No. 4 lead pellet. Of course, the benefit of going with a smaller shot size in the tungsten means that any payload's pellet count is increased, certainly a benefit, too.

With the benefits of tungsten come, as we've discussed, increased cost, so it won't be for everyone. So what should you go with if lead is your choice? I suggest a No. 5 pellet in plated lead, as it will tend to maintain its round shape better as it travels through a tightly constricted turkey choke. Those No. 5s will retain good energy to 45 or so yards and also produce good penetration on the bird. Yes, you can go smaller in shot size. A No. 6 pellet can be great, and you get an increased pellet count, but you'll need to hold for shots inside of 35 yards. Remember, as a pellet's size gets smaller, it gets lighter in weight and, as such, will lose

The head and neck are where it's at, when it comes to clean, ethical turkey kills. You want a minimum of 20 pellets in that kill zone to effect that, and the only way to know if you've got it is to put your gun, choke, and load on paper.

a Winchester AA Featherlite 1$\frac{1}{8}$-ounce of No. 8 lead shot. Talk about a small package doing a big job! The gobbler walked inside of 25 yards, and the swarm of fine No. 8s, even at low velocity, killed him thoroughly. (FYI, I was shooting a suppressed 870 of my own design, and the light load was necessary for sound reduction in a tight "urban" gunning space.) Was this a "typical" turkey load? Not at all. Did it get the job done? Yup, but I had to know its limitations to make it work.

Back for a moment to tungsten shot and normal applications and ranges. To my way of thinking, because all you need do is check the zero of a turkey gun on a turkey head/neck pattern once in a great while, even the very high-priced tungsten loads aren't the budget consideration that are tungsten-based waterfowl loads, which are bought and shot in much higher quantities. And that's a good thing, because tungsten turkey loads are so good, that having a gobbler hang up out of range is kind of a thing of the past when you've got them in your gun.

I have taken eight birds with a 10-round box of Winchester Xtended, which holds tungsten-based shot. It would be hard to argue against the price of $2.75 a round with that kind of success rate. Still, if the tungsten price tag still sticks in your throat, by all means stay with the best lead load possible. Winchester Supreme, Federal Premium, and Remington Nitro Turkey loads are top of the line in lead shot turkey fodder. I know some of you are dedicated to lead, it's what you've always used, and you're determined to keep right on using it. However, and as has been said often in this book, you have to know that the elimination of lead

energy faster. Sure you can get more pellets of No. 6 shot into a 1$\frac{3}{8}$-ounce 12-gauge load, but it will still die a fast death in terms of effective longer range. Remember, balance is key. Starting to see the differences in trade-offs between lead and tungsten?

What I'm trying to demonstrate is that your load/ choke combo, no matter what it is, has its limitations. For instance, just a few weeks prior to writing these lines, I dusted off a big, 25-pound gobbler here in the Black Hills, by way of a suppressed 12-gauge that shot

shot for legal use has happened and will go on happening in many areas of the country that hold trophy gobblers, big coyotes, and other warm targets that a scattergun works well against.

TURKEY CHOKES THAT WORK

Assuming you're about to shoot modern high-performance lead shot or tungsten shot loads, the next step in your plan is the selection of your turkey payload delivery system. It's your gun's choke I'm talking about here. Today, almost everyone who is anyone makes a turkey tube, but not every tube is created equal, nor is every gun barrel these chokes accommodate. The short form here is that you need a choke that tends to do at least some of the workload (stress elements) outside the primary barrel, i.e., you want an extended tube. Companies like Briley, Carlson's Chokes, Truglo, Undertaker, and Primos, to name a few, are some that can meet those kinds of needs.

Briley builds many of the chokes that go by other brand names. The guys at this company are top gun, and I have used them for some of my own custom designs. Carlson's Chokes are also high quality. The thing I like about them is that the company works with state-of-the-art diagnostic equipment, when developing new chokes. While some turkey tubes don't permit the use of tungsten-based material because it is so very hard, Carlson's extended tubes, even in tight turkey choke constrictions, allow all current shot production types to be used. Another one I like is the Jelly Head choke from, Primos, a manufacture of a wide range of chokes, game calls, and other related equipment. Like many others, it is extended and drawn tight in the .600 constriction range, for maximum performance.

Today, it is important to hunters that a choke tube delivers very dense patterns at long ranges. In almost all cases, a tight tube constriction is what you're searching for to accommodate those distances. That means a tube constriction—the "choke"—of at least .550 through .650. Move much out of that constriction range toward a more open choke, and you're back to an upland or waterfowl choke and will get just those kinds of performance results—and that's definitely not what you want when you're aiming for the narrow kill zone of a turkey's head and neck. For successfully and quickly taking big American toms, a nice looking, uniform, 30 inch paper pattern will not do the trick; you'll simply up the chances for a wounded bird. Instead, what you want for turkey killing is a nice, tight, 15- or 20-inch core pattern that holds 75 percent or better of the total payload. Remember, you want to take his head off at 40 yards and break his neck at 50, if that's the shot available.

When searching for a new choke tube for your gun, ask questions, use the Internet, and check with other hunters about their experiences with various products. More importantly, and by all means, when you bring a gun and choke together with a turkey load, please

Buffered Turkey Loads—Thumbs Up

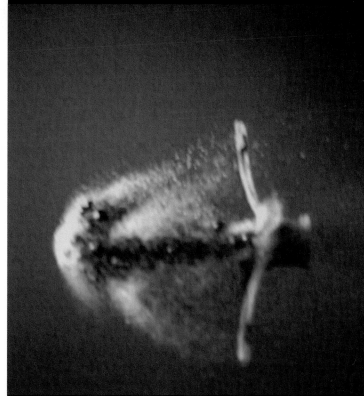

On the question of buffered loads, which, like tungsten, began life among duck shooters, it is advisable to buy lead shot ammunition that makes use of some type of buffering agent, if turkeys are on your menu. Buffer holds payloads together better and also helps maintain pellet roundness when the lead is either a bit soft or isn't hard plated. Even with plated shot, because most plating is just a surface treatment, much like a paint job of sorts, the ground plastic-type buffers tend to help get those pellets downrange as an organized group of round balls, rather than a scattered group of rough lead chunks.

go out and measure off 40 yards, then pattern your combination with care. You want at least 20 pellets in the bird's head/neck region (on a commercial turkey patterning target). The more hits on the head/neck target the better. If, for some reason, you can't find a dedicated turkey target and you're shooting a simple test circle, again, you're looking for that 75 percent in that tight 20-inch inner patterning ring.

FROM ONE TURKEY HUNTER TO ANOTHER

My personal choice in a turkey gun, and even though I own several, is my Mossberg 835 Ulti-Mag.

The author's favorite turkey gun is a Mossberg 835.

The author (below) and a friend (above) working out turkey loads from the bench with one of Brezny's favorite Mossberg's topped with TruGlo fiber optic sights.

In it I run the Mossberg X-Factor .695 turkey choke and a load of Winchester Xtended No. 6 tungsten shot, Remington HD No. 6 if I can find any, or Federal Heavy Weight in the No. 6 shot size. If none of those can be found, I'll make a switch to Hevi 13 shot by Environ-Metal, Inc. That Hevi 13 load selection is also best used in a pellet size of No. 6.

I shoot on average eight to 10 birds a year here in the Black Hills and on industry related events. As such, I have no time for poor performance products. With any of those setups I just mentioned, I don't worry a bit about a bird hung up at 50 yards or having one get hit then running off wounded with this combinations. (I will say that, when shooting Federal Heavy Weight, I will opt for a choke change to a standard Full choke, based on the performance of the Federal Flitecontrol wad used in that load.)

Now, the first turkey I ever killed was the Minnesota State record, an Eastern bronzed-back gobbler. It was the first season for turkey hunting ever in the state, and, by day's end, my 24¼-pound tom had been bested by that from another hunter. Quite a way to get a first season started! I killed that one and my next five birds with my Remington 870 Wingmaster that mounted a 30-inch barrel, bead front sight, and a fixed Full choke. The gun never failed me. Today in the turkey woods, I often carry my old, tight, fixed Full choke 30-inch barreled Winchester Model 97 that has been

The 25-Year Choke

When using a choke that would be considered "balanced" (there's that term again), the choke should take on more then a single load well, and, so, it should be able to perform well against a variety of targets. As a living example of this way of thinking, I have included a short pattern review of my own Dead Ringer choke tube, a design that came together after about 25 years of research and testing. It is performance ported both forward and rear of its ring system. Using head/neck turkey targets from Federal Cartridge and Birchwood Casey, here's what happened at a measured 40 yards. (Weather was mild, low wind conditions; altitude was 3,000 feet above sea level.)

Shot No. 1: Winchester Super Pheasant 2¾-inch 1¼-ounce No. 5 (copper plated)	**37 hits**
Shot No. 2: Hevi-Shot Old Express tungsten 2¾-inch 1¼-ounce duplex No. 3/5	**34 hits**
Shot No. 3: Hevi-Shot tungsten 2 ¾-inch 1 5/8-ounce No. 5	**38 hits**
Shot No. 4: Federal 2¾-inch 1¼-ounce No. 5 lead (duck load)	**31 hits**
Shot No. 5: Kent Game Bore steel 2¾-inch paper wad No. 5 (budget load)	**27 hits**
Shot No. 6: Bluesteel Royal 1³/₈-ounce No. 4 (Mexican-made budget load)	**27 hits**
Shot No. 7: Federal Grand Slam lead 1⁷/₈-ounce No. 4 (worst of the bunch, but still a killer)	**25 hits**

restored to pristine condition. It is only a 2¾-inch chambered shotgun, a "D" model that dates it back to 1897, but it shoots like a dream and everything before its barrel tends to die. I run Hevi-Shot's Classic Double in a 1⅛-ounce payload of No. 6 shot with this gun. Why the old guns with the new ammo? Well, despite my admiration for much of the stellar ammunition and advanced tools on the market today, if you have a favorite scattergun you know can do the job, forget everything I've written here and go for it big time, my friends! Just make the effort to know your setup works instead of assuming.

NEW TOOLS FOR TROPHY TOMS

There are new turkey loads in the works, to be sure. Pinnacle Ammunition had me killing gobblers on several of my hunts last spring, thanks to a very new ultra high-density turkey load featuring .18 density shot. This is off the charts in terms of weight, and it was a head hunter of the first order. Frankly, there wasn't much left for pictures if the range closed to less than 30 yards.

About the same time I was trying the Pinnacle rounds, Remington HD Turkey, another new load, was the primary turkey tungsten shot load a group of us used on a Cabela's hunt, in Nebraska. With a total of 12 birds killed on that hunt, it indicated that Remington high-density shot was able to give a great account of itself afield. Unfortunately, at this writing, the HD is being put on the back burner at Remington, due to the increased cost of pure tungsten pellet material on the open market. By the way, chokes used on all guns for load evaluation were the H.S. Hunter Specialties Undertaker turkey specials, so worth it to seek this one out if you're considering a change in choke tubes.

Last spring, Federal came west out to my area and ran a new special 20-gauge Heavy Weight turkey load on selected trophy gobblers. We were pleased to see it produced the same basic results of a high-performance lead shot 12-gauge load. I know, because I shot a bird with my 3-inch 20-gauge Remington 870 at 45 yards, just about taking his neck and head apart in the process. I also took two more toms, one while finishing off a runner for a friend and the second one on my own tag that popped up. Truly, the new Federal Heavyweight Flitecontrol 20-gauge 3-inch turkey loads are nothing short of outstanding.

Something that doesn't get a lot of conversation, but one that's important to remember when putting together your turkey rig is the move to better sights. Due to those tight patterns going downrange, you really need sights that keep you precisely on target. I like the fiber optic sights offered by TruGlo, though I have one turkey gun that wears a special Bushnell low magnification scope that also works quite well. Really, the days of the plain old front bead sight are about done for, when it comes to today's shotgun turkey hunting.

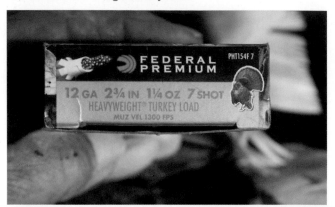

The author with a turkey he dropped at 40 yards. That's a pretty average distance, until you take into consideration that he shot the bird with No. 7 high-density shot.

THE TACTICAL SHOTGUN

This really is an "alley sweeper," a 12-gauge with a drum magazine. They can be a very useful self-defense option, but aren't legal everywhere.

t he modern shotgun has evolved, in fact so much so that, in the past several years, there has been as much if not more attention given to state-of-the-art, combat-style shotguns than nearly any other genre. I base these findings partly on interviews with commercial concerns at each of the national SHOT Shows that have taken place over the past half-decade or so, published sales figures covering new shotguns, and questions regarding new gun development I have taken from readers of my smoothbore articles. To my way of thinking, we are in a transition period with the modern scattergun, and the turn toward the home-defense, military applications, and police-style shotguns has become a dominant force among gun enthusiasts.

For a period of 23 years, I worked both part-time and full-time in law enforcement. As a street police officer, and also by taking on moonlight jobs guarding densely populated, urban "towers," as we called them,

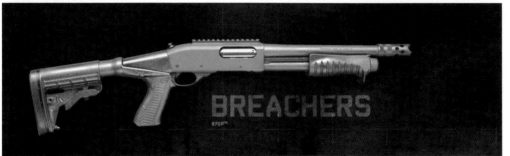

This side-by-side, short-barreled 12-gauge is the author's top pick for a home- or business-defense gun. Many modern iterations of the "coach gun," like this one, come in synthetic stocks and with all sorts of railing for accessory attachment.

If there was a single gun I would totally recommend as a home- or business-defense firearm, it would be a short-barreled shotgun in a very basic side-by-side 12- or 20-gauge design, one equipped with auto (internal) hammers, open chokes, and a couple mild loads of clay target fodder stuffed into each chamber. Why? For one, there's the consideration of lethal force ranges at which I've trained. Say, for instance, someone's in the front yard of your home and mouthing off from a truck or car. Now, you in your house are not in any major degree of immediate threat; the good news is this seems to make sense to most folks nowadays, based on what's demonstrated in a number of shoot/ don't shoot scenarios that have been published. However, when the distance of the intruder closes to the front door and then enters your abode or business with obvious negative intent, the game changes fast, and it's time to consider whether deadly force is required. Shotguns, of course, are basically close-range tools and as such, are well suited to enter the picture I've just painted with a very high probability of success in stopping a threat.

There was a time when I was requested by my supervisor, while on dog watch (late-night shift) to unlock the squad shotgun and cover him as we approached a vehicle that contained an irate and very large man, a guy well over 6½ feet tall, about 3:00 a.m. one Sunday morning. As the huge guy was sent spread-armed over the vehicle's roof, I came across the right side car door with the 870 and racked a round into its chamber. The guy went about limp, at the sound of the gun's action. Sometimes the old alley sweeper can do a fine job just by being pointed in the right direction.

The second example of a shotgun-appropriate defense situation happened when I was working a high-

I got ample exposure to a wide range of violence that involved the use or at least presence of the modern riot gun—your basic "alley sweeper," as some would call it. Shotguns in the urban environment are a way of life to a street cop, for two reasons. First, they safe from collateral damage under most conditions. Second, they are feared by any bad guy or gal with half a brain left in their often drug-crazed head. Shotguns will get the job done when all else fails, and you can take that to the bank.

If you're not wearing a military uniform or a vest that says S.W.A.T. across the back of it, you're not likely to run into this kind of a situation, but the shotgun can be used as a breaching tool (note the inset photo of the lock, which will not be there once the trigger is pulled). In fact, companies like Mossberg make shotguns specifically designed for such applications.

Changing from birdshot to buckshot with a tight choke can extend the distance at which you can effectively engage targets, should the need arise.

rise project at night. Some nut case went out a bought a pump-action shotgun and several boxes of 1-ounce Foster slugs, with the intent of blowing away his cheating wife on the top level of the parking garage, when she got home from work. He almost got the job done. When she got out of the car, the shooting started, but, by the grace of God, she ducked and ran, getting off the upper deck, with the only injuries being that to a bunch of parked vehicles shot up by those big, one-ounce chunks of lead.

Our guys, responding to the calamity, were carrying 9mm handguns chambering Glazer rounds (fine shot in plastic-tipped "bullets"), in an effort to reduce collateral damage with the paper-thin walls of the government housing project, but they were no match for the lead slug-slinging desperado. With the shooter pinned down on the roof, more of our security team and local police S.W.A.T. were called in, and soon 9mm MP3s, police 870 Remington shotguns, and a trained sniper with his Remington heavy tactical .308 Win.

(below) Loads for home-defense are limited only by your imagination and concerns for collateral damage. However, it pays to remember that, when multiple members in your family may need to use the same gun, you should pick a gauge and load that everyone can handle. Also keep in mind that loads for the .410 shotgun can be accommodated in many modern revolvers, adding versatility and options to your home-defense setup.

made a very positive impression on the crazed shooter, and he gave up without anyone being hurt. We were all fortunate it ended that way, because the crazy guy's Foster slugs did indeed have some extended range on their side, initially shifting the balance of that potential gun fight in the bad guy's favor.

Some say the common scattergun is *only* useful in the close-quarters fight. But the basic defense shotgun can become a longer-range tool, with the addition of special chokes. Take, for instance, the Winchester SXP I have used as a review gun for several parts of this book. It mounts Invector Plus choke tubes, so I can screw out the IC tube and install a very tight custom or factory .60 or tighter constriction tube and, thereby, up the game plan for slinging buckshot or at longer ranges. Some testing executed for this book included shooting with the Improved Cylinder choke at 30 feet via the SXP to put 100 percent of the 1³⁄₈-ounce payload of iron shot into an eight-inch circle or a human-figure combat target, then stepping back the range to 60 yards and slapping a 1¼-ounce tungsten/iron Hevi-Shot Dead Coyote load into the same target for a total of 90 hits, all about equaled in the same amount of kinetic energy (or killing shock) on target.

You can go farther. Making the next move to steel flechettes (darts), and now your effective range can jump as far as 200 yards, as was noted in Vietnam against both personnel and thin-skinned vehicles.

Flechette rounds consisting of 20 tungsten darts in a 12-gauge load during that war were very effective against snipers in trees, whereas round

Flechettes are steel darts that can extend a shotgun's range to 200 yards.

shot struggled in its application against the jungle's heavy foliage. Believe it or not, these rounds are still available, as well as legal to purchase. They can currently be found in 12- and 20-gauge and even .410-bore. The .410 flechette rounds maximize the popular .410/.45 Colt handguns by Smith & Wesson, Taurus and others. (www.antipersonnel.net.)

In my stable of munitions, I have a three-sectioned sabot slug of 500 grains, custom loaded by Polywad, that sends the sabot all the way to the target with the slug intact. At the point of contact, the slug separates into three equal projectiles—it is nothing but deadly. Heavy weight and speed also provide some extended range functionality. As varying distance from a threat translates to how you view your personal safety, the shotgun with a mixed "fruit salad" of projectiles can be a handy thing.

A few points about taking up the defense shotgun for the protection of your self, home, or office. First of all, keep it simple. Simple means less weight, in most cases, and that means control and an extra edge in speed, if you get into a gunfight. Those cowboys back in the day shot plain-Jane scatterguns most of the time, not the fancy types you saw in the movies. Some shotguns kept to standard length barrels, while others were cut off as "coach" guns, with nothing added save for a bead on the muzzle, if even that. These guys as lawmen, stagecoach guards, and the like were shooting for their lives anytime those two sections of pipe went off. Still, they kept it simple.

Simple doesn't seem the way these days, but you should try. Systems with flashlights attached may look sexy and are all the rage, but they can get you killed. The light marks *you* as a good target surface right off, when it's attached to the gun. Best to use a handheld light held off to the side opposite of which your gun is cradled. The light can be shot at by a bad guy, but you'll still have your center mass in check, with a good scattergun and a good arm ready to go when it comes time to shoot.

Some people wonder at the merits of having a shotgun in a closed-in location, but using one in such conditions doesn't have to be as awkward as you might imagine. Locate a pre-established defense position in your home, if covering an entry way or door. Use heavy chairs, tables, or even hallway corners as some form of barricade. If you need to expose yourself, stay low and stand sideways to the threat, as you'll then make a small and narrow target. When I teach folks to shoot shotguns for home-defense (and I have worked specially with a number of older members of our Dakota community every now and again), I tell them to set a game plan, factor in what they would do in the event of an intruder entry, and memorize the full layout of each entry area to the house, so that they understand the exact distance the shotgun's payload will need to travel when making contact with a bad guy. What I tell older folks is that even if they are in their late 70s or 80s, they are only five pounds of

(left) This patrol soldier has a very unadorned shotgun. It's quick to use and easy to carry. As a homeowner, you'd do well to keep your own shotgun in such a configuration.

Hard to say this doesn't look kind of cool, maybe even fun, if this was a training exercise, but this isn't real life for the average Joe. You are not a solider, you are not a hero waiting to be one. Keep your shotgun for self-defense simple and minimize the accessories, if any, you attach to it.

trigger pressure away from winning the fight. What they, as well as you, need to do is develop a plan and practice with that shotgun (empty and unloaded with dry runs in the home), if you are going to win the fight, one that's possibly for your life. All you have to go on is muscle memory when you're in a fight, because all the rest of the bull will fly out the window. Believe me, I have been there.

Remember this. A gunfight is only seconds long. That's right, seconds. It is not the big, 15-minute long deal in the movies—*at all*. Range to the bad guy is often under five feet when the situation actually goes down, and the number of fired rounds is usually less then four total—that means both sides of the deal. Sure, there are other situations that have occurred. The street gangs that blast away at each other are a different story altogether, for instance, but, in the case of home-defense it will be close and fast. Count on these two factors and train mentally

for exactly that situation to unfold before you even have time to think.

As a final example of something that actually happened, I will turn to my own family and my daughter, who was 14 years old at the time of this incident. My wife and I had been out for the evening and, upon returning home, found squad cars all over the yard and lights on the house. A call for a possible home intrusion had been put through 9-1-1 by our daughter, and she had barricaded herself with the family dog in the far corner of her bedroom behind the bed, with a police flashlight and my 870 scattergun loaded with 00 buckshot. She had come home about 9:00 p.m. after visiting a friend and, while getting ready for bed, heard glass breaking in the lower level family room. At once she used the pre-established plan—call 9-1-1, put the dog in the room, get Dad's police riot gun in hand (loaded), close the door, and barricade yourself and the dog behind the bed. She had done it all correctly, perfectly, and I was proud as punch.

Because I knew the lay of the house, of course, the local PD asked me to enter the house with them and take point during the clearing process. We were relived to find that a source of extreme heat had caused a two-layer glass window to explode on its own, so there was no actual threat, but my daughter didn't know that and she did the right thing by not investigating. In fact, she did even better, because, when she got on the phone with the police dispatcher, she told them, "If anyone other then my dad or a blue uniform comes through that door, they are dead." I did go through that bedroom door, as there were no other takers that night, and all was well. I believe that the locks on my daughter's doors today, some 30 years later, are there in place to protect the bad guys, not her—and that's the kind of plan it take to survive.

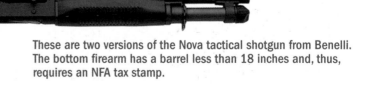

These are two versions of the Nova tactical shotgun from Benelli. The bottom firearm has a barrel less than 18 inches and, thus, requires an NFA tax stamp.

Kel-Tec's KSG – Ultra-Specialized

If there is a new wave of design coming forward in the market-place that will, in time, make a major mark on the basic shotgun as a home-defense tool, it is the innovative examples of the new high-capacity tactical shotguns. These are not sporting guns in the traditional sense and, as such, can't be converted to a bird gun or slug gun with a simple barrel or stock makeover. Due to the design of these shotguns and their ability to retain 12 to 14 rounds in their magazines, these are strictly defensive firearms; when a room entry or small fighting space requires laying down a massive amount of suppressive fire, the new KSG by Kel-Tec or UTS-15 by UTAS, by example, fits the bill nicely.

Being as I have selected various shotguns throughout this book for examples of what I have been trying to say in print, I have elected to use the Kel-Tec KSG for this review, because Kel-Tec was the only company building a new-age, state-of-the-art assault shotgun to respond to my request that a real live weapon be sent for testing. Cold, but true. Here's what I found in my evaluation of this very new combat-style weapon. Pay attention, because we are observing the future of gun fighting with a scattergun in the twenty-first century.

This defensive shotgun is built right here in the USA by Kel-Tec, in Cocoa, Florida. As such, service and parts are close by, if required at any time. It's currently listed on Kel-Tec's website (www.keltec-weapons.com) as retailing for $990, and it is only recently becoming more available after several years of scarcity and hype. The KSG is a "bullpup" design, meaning that the receiver is pushed back into the buttstock so far that the 18½-inch barrel has the gun taking on the look of a much shorter firearm in overall length (26.1 inches). Being a pump-action with a double set of side-by-side magazines that mount alongside the barrel (which has a fixed choke), makes the 18½-inch length pipe street legal, "bullet proof," as it were, when an ATF agent has too short a yardstick and is checking barrel length. Remember, under 18 inches in shotgun barrel length is a *major* violation of BATFE regulations, if you lack the proper federal stamps for owning such a shorty.

Yes, this is a shotgun. You have never seen anything like it before. Made by Kel-Tec, this is perhaps the leading example of the direction in which tactical shotguns are being designed.

Kel-Tec's KSG

The KSG from Kel-Tec may just be the coolest shotgun ever.

With the twin magazines, the KSG packs 12 total 3-inch magnum rounds that are accessed by flipping a magazine switch from one tube to the other as rounds are required. Ejection and magazine function work straight down, rather then via a more traditional side-ejection port. Unloaded, the gun weighs in a 6.9 pounds. Right off I dressed my test gun with a TruGlo red/blue dot glass optic, a sling, M-4 combat light, and the Blackhawk-style AR-15 vertical fore-end grip handle (a broom handle, if you will). With Picatinny rails (Weaver) running the full length of the upper barrel and another shorter section under the tube, just about anything can be attached when making up the gun for a specific task at hand. I test mounted the ATRN Aries 390 Paladin night scope for night work; if I retain the gun, I am going to have the muzzle threaded for Rem Chokes and my .724 Orion 12-gauge suppressor. The bullpup design and the added suppressor will bring the total length of the 12-gauge to the normal length of a street sweeper or standard police/military riot gun.

When testing the KSG, I elected to set up a mini shotgun course using Birchwood Casey "blue man" targets, so as to simulate the 3-Gun competitive element that makes use of a shotgun. With staying power of up to 15 rounds in 2¾-inch buckshot, slugs, or special-

effects ammunition, the new KSG is some kind of fun to run across a series of targets. With a flip of a switch, the shooter can move from one magazine tube (seven 2¾-inch rounds) to another, sending fresh loads down-range in seconds by way of the center section, twin-action bar pump design.

I believe that the new KSG and others on the drawing boards of this type are solidly in the future of shotgun-ning, for those looking specifically for either a speed-shooting action sport gun or one for home-defense. Regardless what the old smoothbore guard thinks, these new fighting designs will hold a solid place among our current war-fighting nation, as well as with future combat-driven audiences.

3-Gun Shooting

I was part of the very first three-gun events, the ones known today as Cowboy Action shooting. Of course, the concept of three guns and one sport has evolved to the genre known specifically as 3-Gun, which makes use of a rifle, handgun, and shotgun throughout a match and over various shooting stages and targets. Why talk about this here? Well, because the shotguns used in the sport of 3-Gun are decidedly on the tactical side of things.

In 3-Gun, shotgun targets can range from fixed, close-range steel fall-down types to clays sent from an automatic thrower. The games I've observed tend to change up often, and about the only thing that can stand in the way of course design is a lack of creativity by the individual setting one up. To address this variety, shotguns for the sport of 3-Gun are designed to hold 12 or more rounds of ammunition by the use of extended magazine tubes on pump-action or auto-loading setups. Many shooters tend to gravitate to pump

The original "tactical" gun, a two-barreled coach gun, here in the hands of Cowboy Action competitors.

3-Gun Shooting

guns for Open class games; the basic Remington 887 is well liked by this crowd, due to the large magazine well on the 3½-inch model, which is beveled and can accept stacked, two-round charging. Beyond the Open class, though, auto-loaders are, in most cases, the preferred shotguns among the professionals, who dictate accuracy as well as fast times on targets. Regardless pump or semi-auto, though, most 3-Gun competitors employ a wide variety of shotguns and specialized accessories if they want to compete successfully. (Cowboy Action as a three-gun event has tighter rules, in terms of specific firearms allowed on course, in keeping with the Old West theme of the sport.)

Shotgun models for 3-Gun have become very specialized. A few that make up some of the choices include FNH's SLP MK I; Mossberg's 590 A-1; Tristar's Cobra Tactical Pump; Remington's 870 Tactical + Magpul, 870 Blackhawk SPEC OPS, and Pro Bore 887 Nitro Mag Tactical; Weatherby's Assault pump, as well as many other basic field guns modified to accommodate 3-Gun. You can make your own, of course. Any shotgun you tag with an extended magazine and other add-ons like scopes or lasers can qualify for some style of 3-Gun event. Many who don't want to soup up one they already own turn to the Russian Saiga 12-gauge semi-auto, tricked out with rails. These guns have a reputation for not shooting worth a darn out of the box, but, with the aid of a good gunsmith, become deadly accurate, super high-capacity 3-Gun elements. Just remember, when selecting or building up a smoothbore for 3-Gun competition, make careful note of exactly what you're tacking on to the shotgun's basic frame. Some rules don't allow add-on elements such as muzzle brakes, for example, so read the rules before you put down

The variation in and courses of fire in 3-Gun are limited only by the match designer's imagination. The guns themselves are also platforms for creativity and innovation.

3-Gun Shooting

your hard-earned cash on a new or project gun.

The sport of 3-Gun is, in effect, a combat-style program that can make the shooter a much more proficient gunner overall. Yes, there's a large group of professional shooters who have financial backing, at times strong military training, and who shoot matches across the country for big money. But there's room for everyone in this sport, and the hobbyist and infrequent recreational shooter can absolutely use the sport strictly for its element of shooting for fun. Try it, it's almost guaranteed you won't be sorry you did.

While it didn't actually take its cues from the sport of Cowboy Action, 3-Gun follows the practice of, as its name implies, the use of three guns in order to shoot the sport.

COMPETITION AND GENERAL-PURPOSE SHOTGUNS
Today's Top Performers

The massive rotating bolt on this Browning semi-auto illustrates the advanced design that has gone into this modern gas gun.

I f I have stated this once, I've stated it at least 20 times: We have never had it so good, when it comes to the variety of different shotguns to select from in the marketplace. With new alloys, stock materials, and dead-on design features, the modern gas, pump, or double gun is a class act, even in a working-class, general-purpose firearm. Truly, the modern shotgun is nothing less then a well-designed, solid piece of field equipment today. Let's take a look at some of the best-in-class coming to retailers now.

TOP-NOTCH SEMI-AUTOS

Starting with the latest in clay target shotguns, attention must turn to the advanced development of the Winchester SX-3 in the Sporting Model. This new breed of shotgun retains a fully adjustable comb that allows the shooter a custom fit, in terms of eye and head alignment to the receiver and barrel. Back-bored to .742, this well-engineered shotgun will produce optimum patterns across a variety of loads, making

The author with a new Browning A-5 . These guns transition easily from the skeet or sporting clays range to the hunting hills.

The author with one of his three Winchester SX-3 semi-autos, this one pulling duty in the turkey hunting field.

As a second entry in the new gun market, the Remington Versa Max is taking hold as a classy clays gun, as well as a field and 3-Gun competition shooting tool. This gun makes use of a special chamber that adjusts for any load by sending spent gas through a layer of ejection ports that line up with the shotshell's overall length. This feature makes operation trouble-free. I field tested the Versa Max over a several months period, both in the States and out of country, with some very solid results. Hard-nosed, high-volume shooting at Remington's ammunition plant trap range also resulted in flawless performance, and this shooting involved the use of very light trap ammunition, which tells me that the gas system is indeed quite flexible. Later, the gun saw everything from slugs to 3½-inch fodder and, again, no failures. The Versa Max can be obtained in a standard format model

The Benelli Vinci, below, is as flexible as you'd expect a gun from this company to be and perfect for a long day in the field where a mixed bag of game is possible.

this gun flexible across the games of skeet, 5-stand, FITASC, or sporting clays events. With a chrome bore, ported muzzle, and a nickel-plated bolt, carrier, slide, and cocking handle, the SX-3 is designed for many years of service in the hands of even the most advanced and avid clays shooter. I own this gun in three different configurations, and have found them all to be totally trouble free. The auto ejection system will not fail the shooter, period. The best part, though, is that the SX-3s are relatively affordable compared to other semi-autos in this class, and, today, that's saying a whole lot, as gun prices continue to advance almost monthly in some areas of the market.

or a dressed up version for whatever clays event you want to put the shotgun up against.

Browning has jumped into their new gun development with the re-introduction of the A-5 autoloader. I got a chance to test this new and very different A-5 autoloader at the R&R Pheasant Hunting operation, in Seneca, South Dakota. Unlike its predecessor, the new A-5 is not a recoil operated system, but is now a short-stroke design that returned flawless function. R&R has a five-station sporting clays range that allowed me to dust off about 175 clays via a Winchester AA clays

(above) Auto-loaders for clay shooting are a favorite. Here a young shooter is learning the skills of hitting crossing targets in a sporting clays setting.

(left) Winchester's SX-3 is a great choice for clays games.

(below) The Browning Maxus with its fore-end removed. This illustrates why the modern gas auto is catching on fast among clays shooters. These designs are nearly foolproof.

Remington's Versa Max, another contender in a gun that works just as well in the field as it does during a day on a skeet or trap range.

(right and opposite) The five-station sporting clays game is one that hunters often use for training before hunting seasons open.

(left and below) Browning's 725 over/under is the latest upgrade in this model lineup. It is a superb all-around gun for those who prefer two barrels.

load. I also ran the brand new Winchester AA TrAAcker shot tracer ammunition through the A-5's action, again finding a solid functioning shotgun. By my estimation, the gun I tested digested better then a case of fodder without giving up a single failure. In fact, on the sporting clays course, I found this hump-backed receiver 12-gauge to perform so well, that it is a dead sure natural to serve as an autoloader that features prominently in this game in the years to come.

The A-5 isn't the only Browning gun to make the cut. The Maxus Sporting semi-auto has now been dressed up for a clays tournament shoot. Maxus makes use of a new gas design, one I've tested over a period of several years. The end result is that they work and work well—it's just not likely you'd lose a target because this gun failed you on the line.

In the Benelli target gun line, the advanced Vinci is the newest kid on the block for this company, but the class act standard must still go to the Montefeltro or M2 in a clays-engineered shotgun. Clays guns are not much different from field shotguns, but they often retain fully adjustable stocks, ported barrels, and longer pipes. These autos are often turned to by clays shooters, as they shoot softer, allow a solid head-to-stock weld when shooting doubles, and are dressed in just about any stock configuration you could ask for.

Beretta's newer Model 3901 semi-auto retains the popular Kick-Off3 recoil reduction system, a key to consistency with these clay bird killers, but the list is endless, in terms of add-on elements with this gun, everything from ISIS recoil reducers and Stock Positioning Systems to special Kick Eez pads. While a hunter sends a few rounds downrange each day afield, the clays shooter can shoot a tournament event that takes hours each day and can involve a hundred or more rounds. In effect, just about any Beretta semi-auto can be turned into a clay target gun by adding a few bells and whistles along the way, or you can buy the complete sport-specific model.

In a lower-priced department, Mossberg offers the 930 autoloader, but, be advised, you can gain some outstanding returns from this choice. Features that cost a whole lot as extras on other shotguns are considered standard on the autoloaders this company sells. I recently sold a Mossberg SA 20-gauge semi-auto to a friend, one who was used to shooting much pricier clay-dedicated target guns. He fell in love with the little gas gun and would not give it up for anything. It hits clays hard and often, and that's what it's all about.

UP AND COMING OVER/UNDERS

In the twin-barrel shotgun department, clay target guns are king. The double gun is the fastest two-shot gun in the world, and it is by far the way most clays shooters go when searching for the perfect target shooting tool.

The Beretta Series 682 is an example of the upper end development in a pure-breed clays shooting gun.

(right) The author and one his favorites, the Mossberg 20-gauge Silver Reserve. Nice gun for the money, to be sure.

(bottom) Note the even split between gas and stack-barrel shotguns among these South Dakota, Rapid City Gun Club 4-H shooters. The learning starts very young.

(opposite) A well-designed over/under makes a well-balanced gun to shoot either for clays or in the field.

This shotgun can also be obtained as a single-barrel trap gun, as a stack-barrel skeet or trap configuration, or as a sporting clays-specific model.

Also staying high on the list of target shotguns, Browning has introduced the Citori 725 Field. I also took this one to R&R Pheasant Hunting operations in South Dakota, where I shot five-station sporting clays over a three-day event with it, then hunted with it for upland game for another six weeks. This Citori is built with a lower receiver height compared to the previous models, and this helps it double nicely as both a field and clays gun. Browning also offers the traditional Citori in the XT Trap gun.

If you want to move *way* up the price line, the Krieghoff K-80 Skeet or K-80 Sporting Clays are top of the pile in target shotguns. I don't own a Krieghoff, but I have shot them in live pigeon competition (out of the country) and, without question, these are very nice shotguns. The Lujtic LM-6, Merkel Model 200 IEL, or Perazzi MX6 trap and skeet round out the very upper end brands of clay bird shotguns. None of these are new, but they all continue to hold favor among the crowds willing to spend many thousands of dollars to be competitive.

If you look at the prices in that last group and feel overwhelmed, turn to Mossberg and its new line of Silver Reserve over/unders and side-by-sides. I own a 20-gauge in the side-by-side and a 12-gauge in the stack-barreled model. Built in Turkey for Mossberg, these are a massive buy for the buck, and fit is nothing less then outstanding on either variation. Fast to point and swing, the stack-barrel in particular fits well on five station shoots, as well as for a full round of trap targets. The great thing with these guns is that I don't have to see my therapist if I scratch the stock.

HOT-SHOT 3-GUN PICKS

The action-packed sport of 3-Gun is definitely catching on and gaining a wider audience with every weekend shoot. Thanks to this evolving combat-style game we have a new generation of tactical shotguns that fit the needs of the 3-Gun competitive shooter. To my way of thinking, just about any gun can be converted to a 3-Gun tool, simply by increasing the magazine capacity, cleaning up the trigger function, and adding the correct sights for the game. But not everyone wants to put a competition gun together. For off-the-shelf buys, Mossberg is the top gun in this area of shotgun development, offering no less then 10

Doubles point like a dream, when they fit the shooter.

(left) A stack of clays, a shotgun, and you're up and running.

The Mossberg 930 Pro, the author's choice for 3-Gun games.

The Benelli M-4, a perfect 3-Gun choice.

models and multiple variations. The gun could be the Rolling Thunder, the 500 Blackwater, or 500 Tactical Tri-Rail Adjustable, to name just a few. I shoot the Mossberg JM Pro Series Tactical Classic, an autoloader that retains a big nine-shot magazine, a special beveled magazine loading well, and a 930-based action. Designed for Mossberg by top 3-Gun shooter Jerry Miculek, this 24-inch barreled competition shotgun is in a class by itself.

The shotguns in the Mossberg lineup aren't the only ones in the game, of course. There are more than a few 3-Gun-appropriate models from FN, Benelli (with its M3 conversion), and the Beretta TX4. Many 3-Gun shooters have also turned to the simple and affordable Benelli Nova, because it can jam two rounds down the loading gate at one time, thereby reducing time on the clock, and the clock is what this game is all about.

As 3-Gun evolves, there will be other entries into this arena of firearms design. Each year we see new ideas coming forth. One example is the reworking of the Russia Saiga AK-47-style 12-gauge. This gun in the rough is not a lot more than junk, and no two seem to even allow a transfer of parts. But, when a good gunsmith gets hold of one of these rugged firearms, it's turned into a high-capacity, auto-loading tactical machine that fits the 3-Gun game well.

(top and above) Remington's short-barreled models fit the tactical look of 3-Gun's shotguns and are highly maneuverable, handy for courses with lots of barricades and small shooting ports.

(left) What's the future going to be in shotguns? Only time will tell for this little shooter.

SHOTSHELL TESTING
It's All in the Details

You cannot connect with a clay disc, a steel popper plate, or sky-high geese without a whole lot of science backing the how, when, and where your shot payload gets to your intended target.

've spent a great deal of this book talking about load development. Why? Those advancements are defining the modern shotgun as much as the shotguns themselves. But, to really understand just what an impact today's shotshells are making in the field and on the target range, and how they're driving gun design, it's important, at least on some level, to know how these state-of-the-art loads make the cut.

I don't care how good a ballistics evaluator you are, or how good a hunter, if you're in the search for a better load in the field, getting your product on live targets is a must. As part of my job as a ballistics expert and writer, there is a defined need to shoot a great deal of ammunition in order to gain a clear picture of exactly what a given load is doing at the target.

Such was my problem at the start of a spring snow goose season, out here in South Dakota. I had no less then five brand new loads to put on warm targets, but two full weeks into the season, I had yet to fire a single shot. I was running out of time.

Change was in the wind, with a call from Tyson Keller, that top gun hunter and photographer I mentioned earlier in this book. Tyson had been tracking and hunting snow geese all the way up the flyway, from Missouri, and he'd dialed in the main migration, in terms of a good chance as to exactly where they should show up in South Dakota. At his call, the marching orders were to get the truck loaded with all my stuff and head east on I-90 until I hit the far eastern end of the state. After that, I'd follow a map he'd get to me and link up with his outfit. H added that his own truck was rolling under flocks of tens of thousands of the white geese moving north. I boogied.

Of the loads I needed to test, I had a new round being marketed by Bucks Run Sports Supply (800-274-0403) called "American E Shot;" a new, uniquely shaped round called "Squounds," by Polywad, Inc.; a super tungsten load offered in a custom package by TSS in a No. 7 pellet; Federal's Black Cloud in a brand new BBB steel; and a final new entry into the market by Fiocchi, a BB steel shot load. Testing all this was a tall order for anyone wanting to cover all the bases on this many shotshell loads, but Tyson was not at all upset by the challenge to find and get enough targets to commit to his decoy spread. Heck, even if he was just a bit apprehensive, he didn't show it at all, as we glassed flock after flock feeding in fields until dark; his cell phone glowed with incoming and outgoing calls to other scouts and local farmers, as they worked to gain permission to set decoy spreads across the region.

Setting up for the first morning's hunt, we selected one of two very good-looking fields, after getting permission from the farmers. The one we picked was bordered by a high and dry dike system that would allow us to get well into it without burying the ATVs and trucks in a foot or two of black spring mud. Our guides hit the field hard about 2:00 a.m., putting out a spread of about 800 Avery snow goose motion decoys, some flyers, other motion decoys of a different design, and the best custom calling sound system I have ever heard over a snow goose set. With layout blinds in place and well laced with corn stubble, at first light we piled in for the first shoot of a three-day event.

Tyson had almost hit the nail on the head with the location, but he insisted that because we were hunting in a late-season snowstorm, we weren't going to do well. Turned out it was maybe the only thing he was wrong about. Geese arrived with the first gray of dawn and, as they clustered up and maple leafed down from 400 feet to ground level, our guns warmed up fast.

I had a box of 25 shotshells for each of the rounds being tested. All were 12-gauge, and all but the TSS loads were 3-inch magnums. The TSS rounds, of nearly pure tungsten, weren't being pushed into the bigger shell, but, at a count of 183 pellets of .18 diameter in No. 7, the load still pushed 600 fps at 80 yards, with pattern densities that were off the charts for such distance. I was prepared to be impressed.

With the outstanding electric calling setup employed by Tyson, as well as those 800 decoys in the spread, I'm here to tell ya, we had geese right in our laps, and they took some terrible punishment, even from the light TSS No. 7 shot. Now, I've hunted the spring season for snow geese from the very first year

You need good numbers of live, warm targets to really determine what today's ammo is capable of. Snow goose hunting, with its liberal spring limits, is ideal for this kind of testing.

the season was implemented (for population control reasons), and never have I witnessed such outstanding decoying by waterfowl.

Our exceptional gunning didn't dry up, but, instead, lasted through all three days of shooting. I got a pile of shot on target, to be sure, and that—suitable

numbers of game killed—is important to your load evaluation.

TESTING REQUIRES NUMBERS

But why? What can you learn about the loads from live field testing? If you're a hunter, either upland

or waterfowl, and you're developing your own loads or testing new factory product, I'd recommend doing what I do and hunt the spring snow goose season if you can, where there's a massive amount to learn about load behavior. This is exactly where a new load can pass or fail for me. Hunting this season, I come away with a huge supply of real time events under genuine conditions. Wind, air temperature, humidity, and altitude all factor into a shotshell's performance, and, with snow geese, their greater size and, thus, harder killability, can make a big difference when it

comes to applying shotshell performance on, say, fall teal and mallards. As conditions change, targets get tougher, the weather gets mean, and loads can turn from pass to fail overnight.

In general, for those of us doing this kind of testing professionally, the "Rule of 100" takes over. What that says, in the field of statistics, is that the closer you can get to 100 examples for review, the better chance you're going to have at making a constructive assessment of the load being tested. That can be a tall order, without question, but, over time, by staying with a

The spring snow goose season, with its liberal limits, is the ultimate proving ground for shotshell ammunition. If you have this season available to you, this is where you want to put both new factory loads you're curious about and your own handloads to the test.

given load, those numbers can pile up and start to show both the positive and negative elements of a load.

So, back to that snow goose hunt for a moment. With a grand total of 134 snow geese recovered during the hunt, I did, in fact, gain a good idea of how those five test loads performed. The heavyweight American E .20-caliber T shot didn't have an upper limit, for instance, while the BB steel shot loads from Fiocchi were effective only to about 55 yards. We also saw that the new and very different Squound pellets, as used by both me and Browning's Scott Grange, developed a

good track record on birds inside 50 yards. This kind of information is important to the manufacturers, so they can ascertain both how to position a certain load on the market and so they know what to adjust if they're looking for something different. You can certainly apply much of the same analysis to your own handload and factory ammo testing.

STATIC TESTING

Static testing of new loads (or even your favorite pet loads run through new guns and chokes), can be done before or after live bird shoots. In the case of every new load shot on that snow goose hunt, the pattern board work had been completed before the hunt; we knew what the potential performance on live game would look like and what guns and chokes worked best with what loads. But, because this is my job, I also wanted to get some samples of the new loads into the freshly killed birds, this time at more normal gunning ranges.

Why do all that? Static re-shooting of downed, dead birds can, at times, reveal issues different from those that surfaced in the live hunt. In such testing, I'll use a chronograph unit set up against board-pinned dead waterfowl positioned downrange, so I can measure the exact velocity of a penetrating pellet. Static testing with penetration media (ballistic gelatin) and those reshot birds can yield a massive amount of solid and well-controlled data to the researcher. Indeed, the total view of what's going on with your gun and load only comes together after the static and field work have run their complete course.

So what do you do with all the information you gather between static shooting and live hunting? At such a point, I know more about a load than I care to know at times, but, all in all, everything uncovered makes for a better understanding as to how and why shotshells do what they do once they leave your shotgun barrel. Let's break down the five test loads I shot on that goose hunt as examples.

In terms of the best energy-delivering load, American E took top honors, because of its density and pellet size. It is just a cannon ball delivery system. Second place went to Black Cloud in its big, bad, BBB pellet size. Backed by its state-of-the-art sabot-like wad, the load had excellent core pattern control and velocity retention, and its hard-hitting

iron shot pellets reach the target at almost any and workable range limit.

The unusual No. 7 shot from TSS cuts a mean alleyway into a flock of waterfowl, with massive pattern density from the 187 pellets in its 2¾-inch hull. If anything slows this load as a top choice, it would be a lack of general availability at the retail level. Not only is it tough to fine, when it can be located, the price of tungsten may have it languishing on store shelves, too pricey for most shooters.

Finally, Squounds loaded to 1⅜ ounces of roughly .17-caliber "B" shot in a 3-inch hull, and the 3-inch 1¼-ounce BB Fiocchi run close to each other, but top damage goes to the Squound shot's hollow shape. All around, all of these loads get the job done well—but I wouldn't have known that, nor where the limitations within each load lay, without doing this kind of work. The charts on the next page break down these five test loads into usable information. It's easy to do something like this yourself, even for just one or two loads.

Freshly killed birds or freezer birds thawed and rehydrated are hung against backstops to measure new load hit energy and penetration.

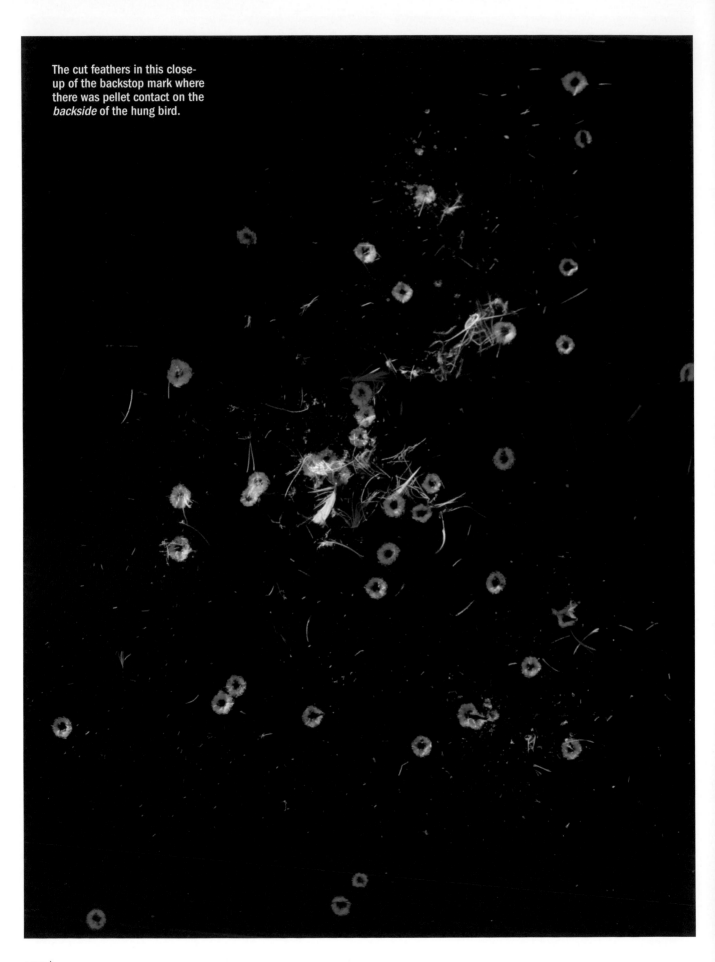

The cut feathers in this close-up of the backstop mark where there was pellet contact on the *backside* of the hung bird.

Field Data Recording

Load:	Handloaded 12-gauge 3-inch, 48 pellets of American E ("T" shot size)
Muzzle velocity:	1,330 fps
Shot Density:	.11
Bore Safe:	Yes
Pattern quality:	Good, through a "standard" choke Browning Gold
Effective range:	nearly unlimited (field kills recovered to 70-plus yards)

Comments: With a layered snow goose flock, a bird was hit and killed in the upper layer at more than 100 yards straight up. This was a shoot-through situation, rather than an intentional shot, but it happened and was duly recorded as such. No other loads, all the rest being of standard steel shot, were capable of this much energy/velocity retention. Subject bird was dead in the air and became a flat-out lawn dart after being hit.

Load:	Federal Black Cloud, 3-inch, 1 3/8 ounces BBB
Muzzle velocity:	1,450 fps
Shot Density:	steel/common iron
Bore Safe:	No, use steel shot wads
Pattern quality:	Very good through non-wad top chokes Modified through Full in a Browning Gold
Effective range:	70 yards

Comments: Birds were absolutely crushed at 55 yards and sometimes more.

Load:	Polywad, Inc., Squound shot, 3-inch, 1³/₈ ounces "B"-type .17-caliber steel
Muzzle velocity:	1,330 fps
Shot Density:	steel/common iron
Bore safe:	No, requires steel shot wads
Pattern quality:	Good to 50 yards with Pattern Master, Wad Wizard, or Dead Ringer wad stop chokes (recommended)
Effective range:	50 yards

Comments: With the 50-yard limitation, this is a decoy or modified pass-shooting load.

Load:	Fiocchi Of America, 3-inch, 1¼ ounces, BB steel
Muzzle velocity:	1,330 fps
Density:	steel/common iron
Bore safe:	No, use steel shot wads
Pattern quality:	Good with Pattern Master, Wad Wizard, or Dead Ringer wad stop chokes (recommended)
Effective range:	50 yards

Comments: Best for use as a decoy load. Restrict shooting to inside 55 yards.

Load:	TSS, 2 ¾-inch, 1 ounce of No. 7 (pellet count 1,283 of nearly pure tungsten iron)
Muzzle velocity:	1,420 fps
Density:	.18 or higher
Bore Safe:	No, steel wad protection required
Pattern quality:	Good through a Light Modified steel shot Rem Choke.
Effective range:	80 yards, when the pattern will hold together. Recommended maximum 55 yards.

Comments: This is a unique, but effective decoy load.

The Georgia Project

For as long as I can remember, ballistics types both amateur or professional have wanted to understand more about what a payload of shot, a single slug, or heavy buck pellets is doing after it leaves a shotgun's muzzle. Now answering some of those questions, the Georgia Project is one of this writer's most important shotshell ballistics studies to come along in a very long time.

Science is allowing a much clearer window to understanding just what a payload of shot does after it leaves the gun barrel. Polywad, Inc., in Macon, Georgia, is at the forefront of this science. It provided the platform for bringing together some of the most sophisticated measurement equipment in use today by military, civilian, and scientific labs that analyze objects in motion. Paramount to this project, and shipped in from Denmark, was a highly sophisticated Doppler radar machine built by Weibel, Inc. The unit, known as a 15028-P, was designed to track military artillery shells, tank rounds, and medium ordnance for miles. Taking on shot clouds or a projectile that would range to only several hundred yards was small business for this tracking system, but, in terms of a ballistics lesson for me and the others involved, the project would turn out to be priceless.

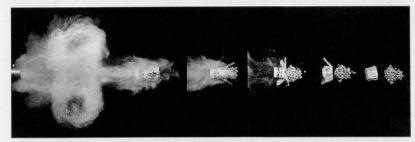

(left) This photo sequence shows how the shot develops from the muzzle and into an effective pattern.

(below) Initial tests on ducks with the odd-shaped "Squounds" from Polywad showed they were quite lethal.

Engineered Shape Steel Shot
12 Gauge 3" 1-1/8 Oz. #3 Steel

Designed For 15-40 Yd. Shooting

Wider Patterns With Superior Distribution

Enhanced Pellet Killing Power

Pre-Production Samples

**POLYWAD, INC.
"SQUOUNDS"**

Engineered Shape Steel Shot
12 Gauge 3" 1-1/8 Oz. #3 Steel

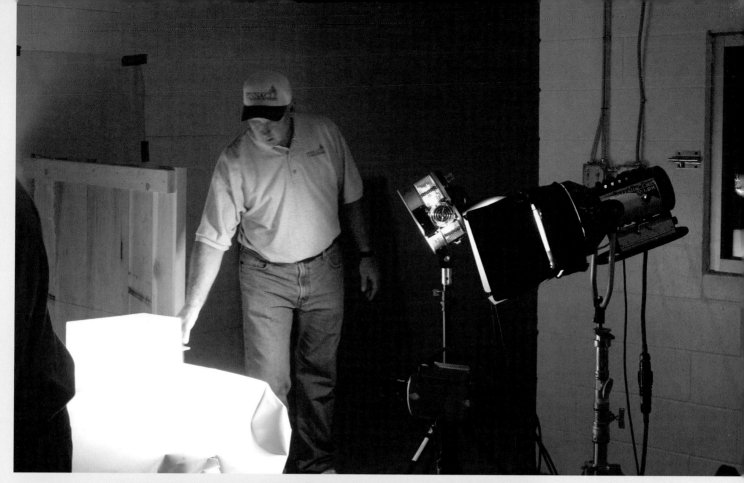

Alan Corzine, head ballistician of the Georgia Project, setting up testing equipment.

Headed up by ballistician Alan Corzine, the Georgia Project was funded by a new shotshell manufacturer dubbed Pinnacle Ammunition. Not to get too far ahead of myself, but, in the early findings of the experiment, I saw that, for the most part, all the high-end loads by Winchester, Federal, and Remington are very strong products. But Pinnacle Ammunition, being the new kid on the block at that time, was running these tests to see what it needed to do to out-perform these rounds. To Pinnacle's way of thinking, if it don't know where to start, they weren't going to move very far forward. This was especially true because Pinnacle wanted to incorporate both Bismuth shot and standard iron pellets in a high-performance load (eventually to be called "Arrow Steel"), and the company strongly felt it needed to get inside the competition's products before it could perfect its own.

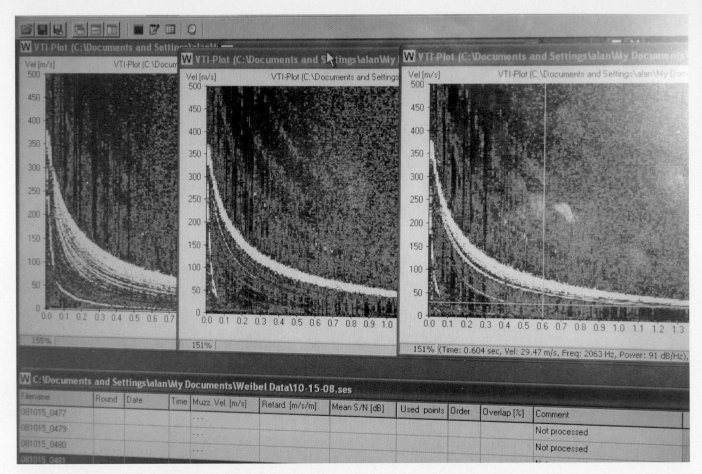

Filename	Round	Date	Time	Muzz. Vel. [m/s]	Retard. [m/s/m]	Mean S/N [dB]	Used points	Order	Overlap [%]	Comment
081015_0477				...						
081015_0479				...						Not processed
081015_0480				...						Not processed
081015_0481										

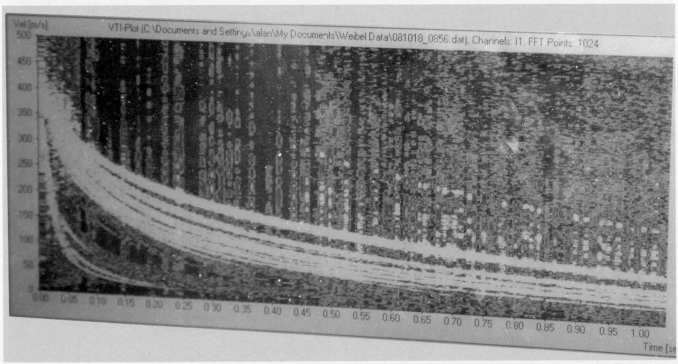

(above) The reverse arc of the Doppler radar as it traces a shot payload from muzzle (far left of the big white curve), lining out across the screen from left to right as the pattern expands. The small, lower white arc is the wad dropping away from the shot payload.

(top) Side by side comparisons of steel loads currently offered by Winchester, Kent, and others proved that they are indeed far beyond where they started when steel was first mandated for waterfowl hunting. They've come a long, long, way.

The first round of testing occurred at a lake lodge near Macon, Georgia, that housed our staff, computers on a screened back porch, and the radar system itself, which overlooked a 200-yard-wide body of water and ended its tracking search out over a large wooded area that acted as a good backstop for our projectiles, as they were tracked across the sky in a long, arching trajectory. Now, Doppler radar won't produce a tracked image of shot moving through the air, rather it sets a tracking curve that needs to be interpreted by a knowledgeable observer. We had a technician on hand from Weibel to teach us about what we were observing, as rounds went downrange and trace radar images appeared on the computer screens.

Alan had brought together almost all the current shotshell ammunition in use today, everything from deer loads to duck and turkey fodder. The majority of interest in the testing was directed at waterfowling loads, as these are the loads that have seen the biggest advancements in recent years. During testing, we turned to the Remington 870 and 11-87, usually equipped with a standard .724 bore and a Modified Rem Choke, as we covered about 350 rounds during each day's experiment. Indeed, the total number of loads fired was nothing less then massive, as, again, we had on hand almost every shotshell produced by the industry today.

At about $180,000, the Doppler radar is as modern as shotshell analysis equipment gets. When a round goes downrange and the system tracks it, there forms a reverse arcing line that starts with the load's actual velocity, drops away to send a line off the screen representing the discarded wad, then lines out each individual pellet in the pattern as velocity falls off and energy drops away. At any point, this payload can be measured for exact velocity and energy generated.

To understand what's going on when viewing the computer images, I learned this. When the radar sends out wide, ragged lines on the computer screen, the payload is becoming open and rough on the edges. A tight line with few wrinkles indicates energy generation and a tighter pellet mass moving away form the muzzle. Uniform wad release was a key element to the testing, as were uniform and sharp trace lines on the computer screen.

Want to know what we found? What I can now say for a solid fact is that those duck hunters who gave up the ship when lead shot went the way of the buffalo were just plain nuts! Even basic steel loads, like Winchester Xpert, Kent Fast Steel, and a few others tended to return great looking tracing through the radar. Energy held up well at acceptable bird killing ranges, and patterns were also dense enough to be lethal. Yes, there were those loads that tended to get a bit "sick" at times, but, thanks to testing like this, we now know that kind of performance is often the result of a choke selection poorly matched to the bore. Gun barrel size also tended to play a part in performance. For instance, we found out that the supposed "do-it-all" back-bored barrels are not always what they claim to be.

Naturally, we wanted to know how good tungsten would prove to be—was it good enough to justify its price? Shallow, almost flat lines were generated by a Federal heavyweight 3-inch load. Hard and heavy tungsten shot just won't produce the sky trail we saw with other shot material, and the degree of drop, or lack of it, was clearly evident to us. Its clean-cut pellet trace line is evidence that such a payload is running very tight to the target and also fighting off gravity quite well. Did we know that all the time? Yes, but it is nice to actually see it. Can't refute this evidence at all, and old lead shot shooters paid attention at this point.

Back to chokes for a minute. The Georgia Project testing revealed that wad-stop chokes like the Pattern Master or my own personally designed Remington thread-based Dead Ringer, for example, do well with some loads, but stay away from frangible pellets with these chokes, and don't shoot saboted wads like Federal's Black Cloud with them, either. I watched frangible shot like the sintered pellets in Dead Coyote loads turn to powder, when going through a wad reduction choke. The radar returned a broom bristle effect, or the look of a star burst fireworks round. What we were seeing in such images were individual pellets leaving the core pattern, in other words a shotshell pattern falling apart.

In terms of the best universal or general-use choke, it is without question the Modified tube. We can play games with everything else, but Modified will get it done and done well, when targets are at normal ef-

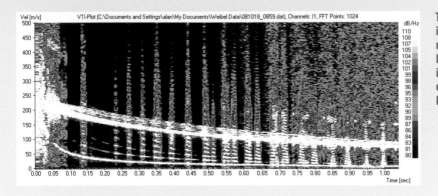

VTI-Plot [C:\Documents and Settings\alan\My Documents\Weibel Data\081018_0859.dat], Channels: I1, FFT Points: 1024

The tight grouping of the white lines on this shot indicate what you think they would, a tight pellet mass. In this case, we were reviewing a tungsten load. The shallow curve here shows that the load is not only staying together well, it's also fighting off gravity. Think what you can do with that kind of knowledge when your shots are long and high.

fective killing ranges of 40 to 45 yards. That this kind of information can be gained through this kind of testing is invaluable, to say the least.

Have you ever wondered exactly what a payload of shot looks like as it contacts soft tissue or while exiting the muzzle of a shotgun? By getting together with other Georgia Project technicians away from the radar tracking station (some of these techs bring you *Myth Busters* and several other television shows that make use of high-speed photography), a continuation of our first week's ballistics testing opened some new windows in terms of what we thought we know about shotshell loads in flight. By way of a special camera with lighting that produces photos at a rate

of 25,000 frames per second, new answers to some age-old questions started to surface.

During this second testing phase, we set up that special high-speed camera, along with special light bulbs that ran about $8,000 each. These lights would help slow down the image of a shot cloud, the wad, and even pellet penetration into soft tissue material for the camera. From the time a payload of wad and shot leaves the muzzle until the camera completes its run of photos, a fraction of a second has passed and the payload has traveled only a few feet across the photo field. This short distance is captured across roughly 300 frames of digital imaging. With Alan Corzine, the chief ballistician of the test event heading up this

phase, we were finally enabled with a frame by frame study of shotshell pellets and wads in flight.

Though fascinating in and of itself, one of the most revealing pieces of information to come from this photographic study, at least in terms of my work, was the fact that the term "wad stop," which I coined years ago, doesn't exist at all. I was dead wrong about it, and I do mean I could not have been farther off base in how I thought chokes of such designation performed. What we have found by viewing a payload of shot moving out of a wad stop-style choke (Pattern Master, Dead Ringer, and other ring-style chokes), is a series of events that go something like this:

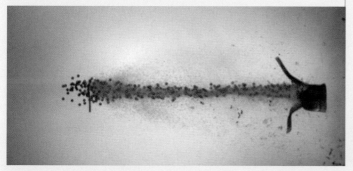

Shooting loads through my own Dead Ringer choke, which was thought to be a wad-stop design by way of a full 360-degree interior choke ring, the payload, while still encased in the plastic wad, becomes trapped. But the wad isn't stopped, rather the edges of the wad petals hit the ring and are turned inward, developing a crimp of sorts that holds the shot inside the wad. As that crimp is forming, the pellets are forced backwards in the wad shot cup and the center of the cup starts to bulge. So, we now have a wad-encased column of shot that will fly as a slug for a short distance from the muzzle (really only a few feet). Compared to the shot payload released from a standard choke, the supposed wad-

(left) A special high-speed camera aided by a bevy of $8,000 light bulbs can shoot a payload of shot leaving the barrel of a shotgun at 25,000 frames per second.

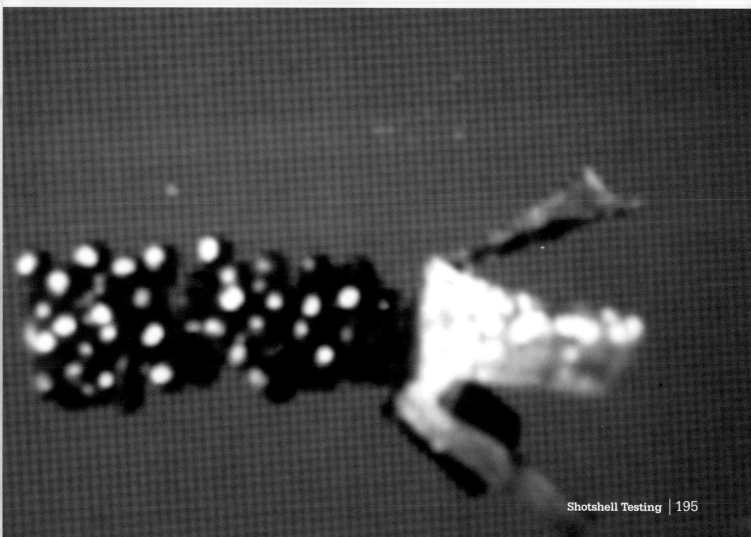

effects of muzzle gas and tend to hold shot tighter to the target; at 10 feet away from the muzzle, the payload has not exited the sabot, thus, that payload is, for all intents and purposes and for a short time, a complete slug.

One way to combat the problem of uncontrolled muzzle gas other then the noted Flitecontrol system, is to use buffers in the shot payload. The buffer blends into the column of shot and act as a soft barrier against the gases, which would otherwise force the payload apart. Observing a Turkey Full

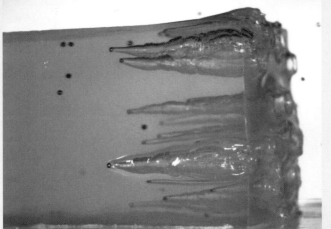

shot string photo, we could see the buffer flowing back and around the shot.

During testing and more work on my part back at my small mountain test range in South Dakota, large amounts of ballistics gelatin were used to gain information about physical penetration and energy cavity shock delivered by various types of steel, lead, and advanced alloy materials. The photos here, for instance, of a prototype "Aerosteel" shot, show how the energy increases when shooting No. 4 in mass against BBs, back to back, into clean blocks of gela-

(left) Federal's Flitecontrol wad effectively keeps muzzle gases from disrupting the pattern by keeping the payload together far from the muzzle.

(below) Shot fired into ballistic gelatin can tell you a lot. In the right picture, a prototype shot known as Aerosteel was fired in No. 4 shot size. The left gelatin block shows the same prototype in BB size. The comparison clearly shows how much deeper the BB penetrates, as well as the more clearly defined "wound channels" it cuts.

tin. The No. 4s kill differently, with mass energy dumping, while the BBs penetrate well and produce larger energy channels, but there are fewer channels (naturally) then there are with the No. 4s.

From Gelatin to Field— Does it Translate?

Someone once said to me that ballistics research applied to actual field-work (hunting) was nothing less then a subjective event. Well, friends, that is about as far from reality as one can get.

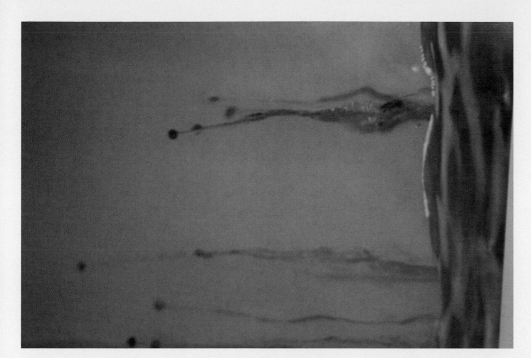

Another picture of gelatin testing, this time Pinnacle's shot in No. 2. Its performance on game proved to be stellar.

Washington state and the northwest corner at Bellingham Washington offered up their surf scoter sea ducks to our guns, so that we could take our radar and photo data and press it into action.

Hunting salt water ducks with Alan Corzine, our guide Duke LeVan, cameraman Bill Saunders, and fellow hunter and founder of Final Approach Ron Latschaw, we pulled up anchor on Ron's outstanding "Willie," a custom built, 21-foot, big water sea duck boat, and headed out onto the clam beds of Bellingham Bay. With good weather, save for some light rain, and a decoy spread fit for king set out by Duke in the chase boat (man and dog set to the outside of the decoy spread a half-mile off the gunning), we were loaded and ready to test much of the Pinnacle non-toxic ammunition that had been the very impetus for the Georgia Project from the beginning.

As I changed up chokes against the fast-moving and very rough surf, white wing scoters flew low over the water. I made careful photos and gunning notes of the pellets shot by others in the party, as the shot made contact against the waves on their way out to the mostly crossing targets. With that water contact, I could see that what we'd witnessed in the research was coming together, in terms of payload reaction to the choke being used.

After my choke change, I put down the camera and notepad. My Remington 11-87, now mounting my

Dead Ringer choke, plastered a single spot on the water with No. 2s. Even at 40 yards, the shot hit the water so hard that it looked like someone had dumped an entire bucket of shot in one place. A standard Modified constriction Rem Choke produced a wider pattern (by far), but, again, most of the shot got downrange in a reasonably tight mass. However, a run with a Full choke sent strings of shot boiling across the blue sea, sending up spikes of water high into the air in long rows, as pellets slammed into the wave tops.

Based on my observations, it is safe to say that, when short shot string patterns hit ducks, those birds died faster and with less after-shock trauma then did the birds gunned with more choke, (and their longer shot strings). If a target is coming straight at you (zero lead) and you get all of that string into the target mass, yes, a load run through a Full choke will be devastating. But how often do you get shots like that? Really, it's the crossing and angle shots we see most of the time—and now I know why I tend to hit several teal crossing in front of me when I'm shooting a Full choke and trying for the lead bird. Now it makes sense! In effect, that long, 14-foot or more string of pellets acts like a whip across the edge of the whole flock, and so one-shot doubles can be the result, even though they won't be at all planned that way.

I once killed a full limit of ducks with two shots, when leading a big flock of teal. My partner at the time, wet-bird writer M.D. Johnson, talked about that shot for almost ever. It truly looked like stupendously lucky and good shooting. Now I know that it was just a long shot string going to work (okay, there was also that pile of luck). It's also the same thing I now know happened when I dropped four giant Canada geese coming into decoys, with just two shots from my SP-10 a few years later. Shot string, and a whole pile of pellets, is what that deal is all about.

In terms of additional knowledge, lets just say the job is never done. I have recently been researching and writing about several very new hyper-velocity loads that are in 10-, 12-, and 20-gauge that absolutely defy description, in terms of the energy they are capable of delivering downrange. Of course, these won't be the last new shotshell loads to come to market. Every year, new wad designs, propellants, and other shotshell components come to market

in an ongoing effort to make better, more effective ammunition. But it's not just the sporting industry that's driving this boat. The military has some responsibility in these areas to be sure, with far more emphasis on the shotgun as an urban war fighting tool than has occurred in some time—and what goes on in the military eventually will arrive as something new in the civilian marketplace. No matter its origins, though, rest assured that American companies now manufacture some of the very best shotshell ammunition in the world today.

What happened in the Georgia Project is only the very beginning. To be sure, in time, additional reference will be made to the Georgia Project, as new and old loads are evaluated, and various elements surface that will require additional study both on paper and in the real world of smoothbore hunting. To my way of thinking, there is no substitute for field success, but we're all lucky to have people doing this kind of work.

BIRDS AND CLAYS, CLAYS AND BIRDS
Improving the Act of Shooting

I didn't cover much of anything about shooting technique in this book. There wasn't much need to.

First, this isn't a book about the basics. Second, the established methods of pull-through, sustained, and pull-away leads to accomplish a broken target or killed bird are just that—established. You should understand them all and you should be proficient in them all so you can address the widest variety of shots with the most success, but there's nothing really new here that would qualify as "modern" material. Third,

there are ample resources available on shooting technique already on the market—DVDs, books, and magazine articles are available in proliferation from a variety of sources, and there are dozens of well-recognized shooting schools, public shooting ranges, and private gun clubs where you can

The author says he generally does well on birds when the shooting comes naturally and instinctively, as a reaction to the target, such as it is with the small windows in which crows present themselves.

seek out instruction for whatever shotgunning skill you wish to acquire. But there is one facet of shooting I think needs to be addressed.

Perhaps because I'm kind of late to it and late to perfecting it, instinctive shooting has become a subject I'm more and more curious about, even after 40-plus years behind a shotgun. It's not a beginner's skill. It is one you see talked about from time to time, but there's never been a tremendous amount written about the subject, nor are there a lot of folks around who know how to teach you how to shoot this way. Call it an old dog learning new tricks, but I think that says something about including this subject in this book and why I think this is something that can take your shooting to the next level.

This past spring, with the opening of crow season out here in the Black Hills of South Dakota, I took off early one morning in the season, loaded up my ATV with an electric calling machine, a few boxes of Winchester 20-gauge Featherlite subsonic ammo, and my 870 Remington with a low-sound Metro Gun extension (to be covered in a later chapter) tacked onto the Remington's choke.

Moving up a ridge to about 5,000 feet above the valley floor, I drove the Polaris RZR into a group of dense pine and set up my Hunter Specialties Prey Master Wireless with the call of a wounded crow, followed by a very upset hawk. The call was always good in this area, as hawks and eagles were everywhere and the common crow was always getting his tail kicked by one brand of winged predator or another. This time, however, the predator was going to be me. With about five minutes of calling time, the first pair of black bandits came rolling in low and fast over the treetops. The pines here on that ridge are only about 25 or 30 feet tall, and the birds were right over the tips of those trees as they approached the electronic caller.

Now, in most cases, I regard myself as a shooter of the sustained lead method, due to a dominant eye problem and being trained, as a kid, with more rifles then scatterguns. Point, track, and develop a gap between the target and the gun's muzzle prior to slapping the trigger has always been the rule, but in the past few years I have started to notice even more of a difference in my shooting when given the sudden opportunity to just spot-shoot my flying targets (a faster version of the maintained lead, would be the method if you broke it down, where the muzzle of the gun is inserted in front of the target at what the shooter believes to be the correct lead and the trigger is pulled virtually as soon as the gun's stock is set on the shoulder and cheeked). This change in style has to be regarded as a turn to an *instinctive* style of shooting, and it's one that was born of necessity rather than intent—a tiny shooting window that precluded time to "get on" the target and swing. But am I on the right track here?

Back on that ridge line with the pines, I got down low beside a tree truck, dressed in Mossy Oak Break-

Up top to bottom, including a face mask and gloves. Those first arriving birds would be toast if they passed a small gap above me through the pines. Here again I would be just moving the barrel as fast as possible; I wouldn't even really be seeing my target at the time I touched off a charge of No. 8s through the pine needles. Sure enough, the pellets slashed through the pines and a black-feathered rag came tumbling though the tree limbs.

At the shot, the partners of the now deceased bandit wheeled around and made a second pass almost over the very same position at which their buddy had died. Again, *thu-thud*, as the 870's silencer muffled the sound of the shot slicing up and into a bird hit, then falling and, with a final round, this one almost at ground level, my second crow tumbled into an open snow field below me, rolling as it met the ground in a cloud of snow and drifting feathers.

Shutting down the electric caller, I reloaded the 870, then sat back and gave the ridgeline a short rest. I could hear crows in the distance on their way to my location, but I wanted them to work at finding me, so as to give them a real reason to bomb in like their counterparts had done. Within about a minute's time, it was game on and, as the caller blasted its wounded crow call, three more big adult spring birds came flying up the valley and straight into the barrel of my scattergun. In a wheeling torrent overhead, one more bandit died, while another took enough shot to also record him in the history column for the morning.

In all that fast and furious shooting, I don't think I was able to do more than mate the gun comb with my cheek, as far as how long I had my barrel moving on and with a target. Reflex reaction was in complete control during the whole event, and the only way that would change would be to select a second calling stand with more open air space that allowed for a more traditional measured lead and target track gunning.

Here's another example of when such shooting works. Now, just as I wouldn't tell you that I'm a world-class clays shooter, I'm not about to tell you that I can tell the difference between hens and drakes at first light, the ducks appearing like mere silhouettes at those times. On one such morning, I was waiting for the day's first ducks at a seven-acre stock tank with friend. That friend has 30-year-old eyes that beat my substantially older pair, and he'll ID drakes from hens for me in those early minutes of legal light. Still, it's hard even for him to tell what's what in such poor light, so his IDs are what you might call last minute. As I, with so little available light, don't have the ability to even get a clean fix on the front bead of my shotgun, I will pull up on birds my partner has indicated are greenheads, using, again, that instinctive swing and trigger slap. Thus partnered, I'll run an almost uncanny average, in terms of the number of birds I connect on under these low ambient light conditions.

So what's happened here? For me, the external

stimuli—clear mid-day light, a wide-open sky—that would normally have me looking down a barrel to note the indicators involved in employing a sustained lead have been removed. I am forced to adapt a different shooting style if I want to make the shot. That adaptation to instinctive shooting can produce a high degree of success.

I'll give you yet another example. Take those ducks that come in low across the water and in the very dark shadows, then suddenly rise up dead ahead, moving spastically right or left. Those are the shots that never allow enough time to swing and lead. If you want to make the shot on those ducks, you'll almost never see enough target against which you can adjust a sight picture. Yet my average on such ducks is up in a strong 75- to 80-percent category. In fact, I have such good luck at this pre-dawn gunning that I can often fill my three or four bird bag before full daylight has arrived and I have transitioned back to use a "normal" sustained lead method of shooting.

While crows, because of how you set up for hunting them, are great game for adjusting and refining instinctive shooting techniques, and while ducks can also turn the trick for this faster and more natural method of gunning, nothing in the world of wingshooting can come close *requiring* instinctive shooting like the deep woods ruffed grouse. Sharptails and sage hens allow time to get on target, and ringneck pheas-

ants are about a fast as a heavy coal train leaving Wyoming, but the timber grouse isn't much more than a flash of gray when flushed at a point-blank range.

The flush, a faint glimmer of gray, and the shot often happens so fast you don't truly realize the gun has been mounted. How tough are these birds? Some say a good day of ruffed grouse hunting is a bird in the bag for about every 15 rounds. Some even say it's a bird out of a box of shotshells. The surprising thing is that, when you get " hot," when that something clicks in that instinctive department, by day's end you have connected on enough of those gray streaks of feathers that a limit of the birds will be brought to bag.

When I was a whole lot younger, I tended to hunt black alder swamps, wearing hip books in knee-deep water all day long. During those grouse hunts, I often carried a just legal, 18-inch, sawed-off H&R Topper in 12-gauge that chambered a homegrown handload of No. 7½ in a full two-ounce payload. This was a buck brush swamp load, and with the cut-down pipe, a light sling, no sights at all (yup—no sights, not even a bead!) and oversized recoil pad, the gun was a grouse killer next to none. Why was it so special? Because this gun was built for speed shooting with an eye toward the total dedication of an instinctive shooting system. (When I gave up those kinds of hunts years later, the scatter-

Gil Ash going over hard focus with the author at the Ash's OSP school.

gun ended up with a liquor store owner who kept it as a last ditch defense tool behind the front counter. You could say that he tended to like the gun's handling speed as well.)

LEFT-BRAIN/RIGHT-BRAIN ACTIVITY

You should have a good picture in your mind of how a moment of instinctive shooting looks, how it feels. You've probably even had some of those moments yourself. But how does it work? How do you get there?

Some time ago, I was watching the History Channel, when the subject turned to just how fast an archer can loose his arrows, if trained as ancient Mongol warrior had been. It was determined by actual hands-on experiments using the world's best instinctive shooting archers that, by way of a Mongol-style recurve bow, no sights, and a dozen arrows at hand, the archer could hit flying targets *to the number of the full dozen in only a few seconds*. From mounted horseback at a full gallop, those archers could also take out six moving (flying) targets in about 12 seconds flat using the same system.

What those demonstrations illustrated was that those mounted archers and cavalry of days gone by were able to take out massive numbers of the enemy in short order, due to the speed at which they could accurately send arrows up to 300 yards away. The system they used was instinctive shooting, and it required, according to a study, the use of the right side of the brain, versus the usual cognitive (deliberate) processes involved in left-brain function. In other words, taking time to *think* through a skill set of movements like those involved in shooting slows you down. That thinking can also block your success when the process starts to become too involved. For instance, I've observed a deadly accurate trick shooter, one who could consistently drill holes into quarters thrown into the air with his .22 rifle, go totally cold on ringneck pheasants. His problem? He'd developed a skill set for one very specific area of shooting and, when pressured and changed, his skill level dropped like a rock.

This past summer, I took it upon myself to give some time to trying to actually train for instinctive shooting techniques. To be sure, these were my own homegrown methods of training and I am not about to say they either parallel anyone else's methods or are a part of any advanced training program set up for clay bird training. However, clay birds are the key here but you don't even need a full sporting clays course. I managed to improve my instinctive shooting with the aid of a simple spring thrower that I can activate with my right foot to send singles at any angle I choose. I can shoot from the gun down position, then force myself to stay off the shotgun's front sight, instead shooting for speed in a snap shooter's instinctive style.

My overall method was quite simple. Taking a low-grade, low-priced promo load of No. 8s or 9s, I selected

a shotgun that would allow me to drive up a little speed in terms of my basic swing. Loading the thrower with a single clay, I set the throwing arm to send the bird at a low velocity straight away from my position. Now, without looking at the area at which the bird would appear (like you would if you were anticipating the clay in a regulated clay bird game), instead keeping my eyes on the ground, I set off the trap, *then* looked up to find and break the bird.

Results were mixed in terms of making clean hits on clay birds—but this is why this was training. At times, I seemed to have the system down pat. Other times everything seemed to just go south on me. My problem was and always has been fighting off that tendency to *think* through the shot versus just letting go and allowing that instinctive process to take over. The correct mindset, as the trendy phrase goes, is "I didn't see that coming." Applied to instinctive shooting, it's that moment when a live bird or clay target comes into view and you react to it, rather than thinking about move-mount-shoot. In fact, in such shooting, you will often be quite surprised by the fact that you made a clean hit! In such moments, what will have taken place is that autonomic system left-half brain shooting control. There's no

Gil Ash with another student during some of the instruction at the Ash's OSP school.

plan or program, just the pure act of the shot itself.

My overall approach to fixing my situation was quite simple. Taking a low-grade, low-priced promo load of No. 8s or 9s, I first selected a shotgun that would allow me to drive up a little speed in my basic swing. Next, out in the field, I loaded the thrower with a single clay andd set the throwing arm to send the bird at a low velocity straight away from my position. Keeping my eyes on the ground instead of looking at the area at which I knew the bird would appear, and with the gun in the low ready position (carried as if I was hunting), I set off the trap thrower with my foot, then looked up to find and break the bird.

Results were mixed, in terms of making clean hits on clay birds. At times I seemed to have the idea down pat, but, at other times, everything seemed to just go south. So what to do with that. I know that my problem was and always has been fighting off that tendency to think through the shot, versus just letting go and allowing my instinctive process to take over. You have to kind of be of the mindset of "I didn't see that coming," if you want to be able to instinctively connect on either live birds or clay birds. When you do not have time to think about taking the shot—analyzing the target speed, thinking through a proper mount, gauging the lead required—quite often you will be surprised by the fact that you made a clean hit. When that happens, hat has taken place is that autonomic system of instinctive action, and that's pure left-brain shooting control. There's no plan or program, just the pure act of the shot itself.

IT CAN BE TAUGHT

So as to again be very clear, regarding my background with shotguns, I need to commit to the fact that, for the most part, I am not a major player in terms of clays gunning—at all. That said, what I have been and still am to date, is a wingshooter with a fairly sold background of success. As such, I've held my own from the dove fields of South America to the rim of the Arctic Circle. With a lifetime of national and international hunts in the bag that include both upland to waterfowl, as well as some shooting on several world-class gun clubs across the country, my wingshooting record has taken care of itself over many years of gunning.

It is in the area of clay targets that I have tended

Vicky Ash keeps her student's attention with her vivid teaching.

to come up a bit short at times. Steady and progressive improvement has tended to elude me all of my life and, until the early summer of 2009, I had no real idea what the problem was exactly. Oh I've tried, and I've worked with some of the very best in the business. But it's a rough day when a world champ tells you, "I have no idea," after I've missed a simple left to right crossing clay bird.

All this would change when I met with Gil and Vicky Ash, the husband and wife team that hands on teaches their OSP (Optimum Shooting Performance; www.ospschool.com) shooting system as they travel around the country each year. In effect Gil and Vicky have been two of the first to break the ice, so to speak, in terms of aiding me toward developing better skills in the clay bird shooting department.

I was, for the most part, self-taught, as were many of you, and so habits have been the end result. But perhaps more importantly, I'd been told, almost forever, to use the shooting method that says you should track a bird with the gun barrel, pressing forward through the bird to establish the lead and eventually slapping the trigger for a clean-breaking target. While all that advice sounded great, and did work for me sometimes, the fact is that, on some shots, the left to right crosser being the worst of the examples, I tend to miss far more often then I put shot on the bird.

I was thinking about all that, when I put my first and very direct question to Gil Ash

"Why can I hit the daylights out of live birds all day long, and turn right around a miss even some simple drifting clay birds on a sporting clays course?"

Gil pointed out, right from the very start, that some things with me needed to change, beginning with understanding that clay birds, unlike real birds, don't maintain velocity after being sent aloft. Second, and also unlike real birds, clay targets don't have a physical wing beat that becomes the focus of the shooter (something that often totally subconscious with bird hunters). Since clays are not feathered flying targets, a completely different approach needs to be applied to hitting them with consistency.

Talking with Gil, I felt that I'd been hit straight between the eyes with a realization. I had never thought of clays as a totally different target, rather only as any other moving target in space, real birds included. This all may seem oversimplified to you tournament clay shooters, but before meeting the Ash training team I had not a clue as to understanding what was actually going on in terms of the differences between clays and feathered targets. To confuse the situation even more, at times I have completely outshot some topnotch target clays guys, when taking on fast flying teal at first light or surf scoters in a high wind on a rolling sea platform. That's not to make light of the situation at all, because I realize that clay bird shooting is not an easy thing, but neither is taking wet birds under dreadful field conditions. But, when I get down to it, all that back and forth failure and success ever did for me was further confuse the whole issue of shooting performance. Now, with that target difference realization stuck solidly in my head, I was able to start working with Gil and Vicky Ash under a reasonably clean slate.

At the OSP school, there was a whole lot of conversation prior to shooting. Then, Gil asked a shooter to step up and take on a few crossing clays, making use of the OSP system. This shooter had previously been through the program and was taking a refresher course of sorts. When the shooter started to break clays each and every time, Gil asked the shooter to concentrate on the clay bird and, just before pulling the trigger, close his eyes completely. Believe me, Gil had *everyone's* attention at that command. The next bird that lifted out of the thrower from far left to right and was picked up by the shooter and cleanly busted with his eyes close at the shot. According to Gil, it was that hard concentration on the target that gave the shooter the edge. In fact, it had programed the hit well ahead of the action itself. Needless to say, but I was impressed.

On the day we ran through the OSP course I was paired with Vicky Ash and several other new or problem shooters. I was the test program for this school's direction, because I came into it with a problem that needed to be fixed (or at least addressed in a constructive manor). First in order was to check for a correct gun mount. In two of four shooters in my class, gun mount needed to be fixed. As Vicky said, mounting a gun is like an essential movement in an activity sport, you're your golf swing or how you throw a football. You must get the gun correctly set in place before trying to work on any other aspect of clays training.

After a quick check of my natural mount, I was informed that I passed the tested, and now the next step was for me to start looking at the target and not the barrel of my gun. Believe me this was not only the first step in the OSP way of shooting, but a very major step for me period. As a western states rifle hunter and cowboy action shooter, I've been welded to sights all my life. (Out West, we even know exactly what open and iron sights are, something lost on a lot of shooters these days.)

Vicky asked me first to not just look at the clay bird in flight as a whole, but to pick a spot on the bird and shoot for that specific location. Starting with some lazy left to right shots from the five position course on the skeet field, I quickly got the hang of this method of sighting. By watching the leading edge of that crossing clay and, therefore, taking my mind off the gun, I was told the lead would take care of itself. I was also informed by Gil, prior to actually shooting, that this kind of target focus was the reason that I had always been very successful on pre-dawn, incoming ducks that offered only a silhouette over the decoys. After all, I couldn't even see the gun barrel at those times, so I *had* to look at the bird.

With a correct mount and, now, watching the bird,

which, to my surprise, seemed to actually be slowing, something I hadn't noticed before, I was automatically reducing my forward allowance and barrel speed to match the degenerating velocity of the clay bird. Because many hunters aren't cognizant of the decelerating flight of a clay bird, compared to the accelerating flight of a live bird, like I've done, they maintain a swing to consistent with the degenerating target velocity of the clay bird. And so they miss, just like I had. But now I had information, and I was hitting clays. And not just

Vicky Ash keeps her student's attention with her vivid teaching.

any clay bird, but my worst nemesis, the left to right floater presented to a right-handed, left eye dominant shooter. (More the eye thing at a later time.)

SIMPLE SHOOTING RULES

When I worked through the OSP program, one thing that stood out was that the training was based on a few simple elements. The school didn't clutter my brain with one pile of unnecessary material. After some time had passed, I started to think of my wingshooting in some very basic rules or systems that have

worked well for me. Much in the way that the Ashes' simplified teaching process helped me with clay birds, I believe some similar basics are warranted for improved shots on live game.

The first rule is to keep the muzzle of the shotgun ahead of the moving target at all times. In most cases, missed clays, birds, or running game have had the shot delivered behind them.

So keep your barrel in front and you're halfway home.

My second rule regards having a bad day in the field. We all have them. So, if you're missing birds

flat out, go to lunch and then start over. Don't let the whole deal get to you. Most shotgunning and rifle shooting is about 80-percent mental training. Mess with the brain, start *thinking* about missing, and you will.

Some old mates of mine often bring up a sore subject with me, reminding me of the day a single crow came flying in a circle around my owl decoy set in an opening surrounded by heavy timber. I stood at the field edge and proceeded to pound out two full magazines—*12 rounds*—at this bird, which paid no attention to my shooting at all. Finally, the bird just flew off, completely unscathed. What I had done was have a shooter's brain crash of sorts; when I missed the very first golfer's " gimme" shot at point blank range, I lost it, and everything went downhill from there.

That day always reminds me of another occasion. I was shooting a new Benelli UltraLite at the Las Vegas SHOT Show during the writer's day hands-on program. I was in a very good mood having just landed a contract for some research writing. Along with several buddies, I was just sort of clowning around, but pounding the daylights out of straightaway and angling clays. When I pulled off the gun, I had shot more than 30 straight, the trap puller waiting for me to go cold. I never did, and in that mood or mindset I think I could have shot at or close to 100-percent all day long.

I had that better, second event in mind, when I took on a new shotgun, one I had never seen before, at the massive Remington Arms corporate clays range a few year ago. Yet, over the course of a 25-round string managed to connect on three chipped birds. Not even a clean break! What went wrong? A shooter's brain crash, complete with about 40 onlookers and someone in the background saying, "This guy can normally hit anything." Wrong folks, and, at that point, I moved to the rifle range, where I proceeded to have a much better day with a sniper rifle and machine gun. See what I mean? When it goes bad, give it a rest.

The final rule I try and follow can't take place all the time, but, when I can, I simply switch guns for a short time. For me, changing guns can make for a quick fix much of the time, when my shooting goes south on me. It's kind of like your workout at the gym. Every once in a while you've got to step outside your normal routine and try something totally different to get out of your plateau or rut. Same with the gun.

While these three basic ideas work for me much of the time (and while the muzzle in front of the bird should work for everyone), I understand that each shooter is different and, as such, you may need to search around to find the combination that works for you in terms of hitting clays or warm targets. But no matte what you find to work for you, remember there is no better training then time over the receiver of your shotgun. Shooting as much you can and on a regular basis will improve your gunning game.

Tailor-Made Clays

As I've said, I'm not some world-class shotgunner. While I have been known to slap a duck or goose, maybe a coyote or fox at some fairly long ranges from time to time, I am not and most likely never will be a top money-making clay bird shooter. The clays games, however, are an important element in shotgunning, because we all need to train on moving targets so that we understand what lead is required on them at various distances, and so that we have an understanding of what the load we are shooting can do against that clay or warm target.

There are many different areas of specialization, when it comes to clay target games. Each of them tend to direct attention to a specific set of requirements. Trap shooting, for example, is all about the target moving away from the shooter (and at varied angles), while five-station sporting clays or a walk-about full sporting course will give the shooter more hunting-style targets to challenge them. In this latter game, for instance, high overhead shooting can be accomplished by using clays launched from a tower, thereby simulating pass shooting of geese coming in over decoys. Military and police, on the other hand, will set up events where clays fly straight at the shooter, part of attack simulation. I once observed the Navy S.E.A.L.s shooting alley-sweeper scatterguns at a flurry of clays coming at them all at once and from unknown directions. The whole thing looked like one big pile of fun and, in that case, those well-trained gun fighters were indeed having a blast taking out dozens of incoming red disks at eye level.

I set up something like that S.E.A.L.s' drill years ago with a friend who was having real trouble on incoming shots. The clay bird-throwing machine was positioned behind a hill directly in front of the shooter. Using radio communication between the shooter and machine operator (who was safely out of view and shot range, birds were sent over the hill to arrive nearly right on top of the shotgunner. This was a major

aid in teaching that shooter to pull the trigger when he blocked out the target with the muzzle of his shotgun. Some years later, I got the chance myself to shoot a full-blown flurry clays event and, to my amazement, I shot it with to-the-letter perfection. Gone was any apprehension about getting on target, because those clays were coming out of the automatic thrower *so fast* and in *such numbers* that all any of us could do was pass the muzzle by the bird, slap the trigger, and watch the clays turn to dust.

The lesson here is to find ranges and targets that cater to how and what you do with your shotgun. So hunters who chase ducks would be well advised to find a tower setup on a clays range, if at all possible, while "ditch chicken" (pheasant) hunters need to press their efforts on trap or skeet clays much of the time. In general, though, any and all clays events will be helpful in getting down your timing, proper lead, balance, footwork, and proper feel with your shotgun of choice.

Subsonic Shotgunning

You've seen lots of mention of my Metro Gun system throughout this book, and for good reason. Almost forever, it seems, people have tried to suppress a shotgun's report, but due to several factors, including the massive .724 bore size of the 12-gauge gun, there hasn't been much success in the area of suppression development. It was an area of shotgunning that fascinated me, and I spent a lot of time dedicating my own design efforts to perfecting such a system. The results were Metro Gun, now almost 15 years in business. Metro Gun (www.metrogun.com) is a noise reducing shotgun configuration that, basically

(above) Yes, this is a shotgun, and yes, that's a very long barrel on it. Not a new concept in noise reduction, but one not known to many shooters, the extreme length and appropriate porting bleed off excess gas and greatly reduce the noise normally experienced with a 12-gauge round shot through a barrel of normal length.

(left and opposite) Crows are notoriously wary birds and will scatter to the wind once the shooting begins. The author's Metro Gun and Orion suppressor can definitely help keep them coming into the call.

explained, uses a very long choke that is ported in such a way as to bleed off and thereby cool all excess muzzle gas, which in turn reduces the sound of a 12-gauge round being shot.

The extra-long barrel design the Metro Gun uses, while unknown to many shooters, has actually been around for many years. Such barrels, to those who knew about them years ago, were often referred to as "Long Toms." We had one of these special guns in the family on my wife's side. It was the meat taker, home protector, and life giver on Nebraska's Platte River at the turn of the century. Still in operation today, that Sears and Roebuck

The author with an ancient "Long Tom."

The author with a shotgun equipped with his Orion suppressor.

38-inch barreled single-shot 12-gauge mounted a "long range" choke, a tight full choke measuring more than .40 in constriction. Upon close examination of the big gun, I realized the extended shooter was not only driving shot at maximum velocity, but, if handled correctly, it could cool burning gasses off the payload and thereby act to reduce the impact of the heavy muzzle blast associated with *all* shotguns. Thus was born the long-barreled gun system labeled Metro Gun. Proper porting and a few other classified elements have made this BATFE stamp-free system the workhorse for many

The business end of the Orion "can" shotgun suppressor.

Author L.P. Brezny says his Metro Gun system has found favor with a good number of turkey hunters, especially those hunting close to populated neighborhoods. The results with this gun are plainly displayed.

The Metro Gun long barrel can be added to a variety of guns, including pump-actions. This one produced excellent duck-killing patterns at 35 yards, perfect for small water holes where noise reduction can help keep the ducks coming back in.

commercial animal control operations, sportsmen who want to shot quietly on a small home-based duck pond, and turkey hunters who want to dust off a gobbler and not tear up the neighborhood doing so.

Today, Metro Gun now offers a second development, the .724 Orion, a full-house "can" suppressor system for the 12-gauge. With this long barrel and the suppressor combination, I believe shotgunning is on its way to a new day in the business of keeping muzzle report sound down, when required. Already, in its first year, the Orion has been picked up by several airport commissions, as well as a number of private contractors. My associates at West River Machine, in Rapid City, South Dakota, are also offering the finished Orion product for use on a wide range of 12-gauge gunning systems. This 17-inch by 1¾-inch suppressor can reduce decibel rates to under 72 Db units, when subsonic ammunition is applied to the task at hand; the average shotgun returns over 130 Db units when un-suppressed. Being that even a single decibel unit increase is massive in terms of *perceived* sound, this system is a major breakthrough in silencer design.

The following are the results of actual terminal (at target) velocities measured when both full-house velocity ammunition was shot back to back against subsonic silencer designed loads loaded with Poly-One shot. For the most part, subsonic loads in standard lead or steel are effective to about 40

SHOTdata
Standard Muzzle Velocity: 1,400 fps

Range (YARDS)	Velocity (FPS)	Energy (FT/LBS)	Effectiveness
40	866	14.2	Very
50	790	11.9	Very
60	728	10.1	Very
70	674	8.1	Very
80*	N/A	N/A	Effective*

*Data was not run to 80 yards, but, based on 70-yard velocity and energy, it would appear that Poly-One would be very effective to the last range listed.

Shot size: BB Poly-One Shot
Sub-Sonic Velocities Through
Metro Gun System "Quiet Gun"
Muzzle Velocity: 850 fps

Range (YARDS)	Velocity (FPS)	Energy (FT/LBS)	Effectiveness
20	717	9.8	Good
40	615	7.2	Good
50*	570	6.2	Fair

*With the subsonic velocity in hitting just under 600 fps at 50 yards, this would be the limit of this load's effectiveness on large waterfowl (geese), but it would still be quite effective on duck-size targets.

yards, or the basic range associated with a muzzleloading shotgun. Currently, silencer designed 12-gauge ammunition is offered by me at Metro Gun Systems, as well as from Federal, Winchester, and Remington Arms company.

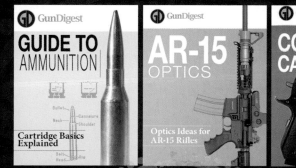
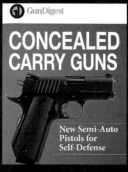

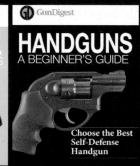

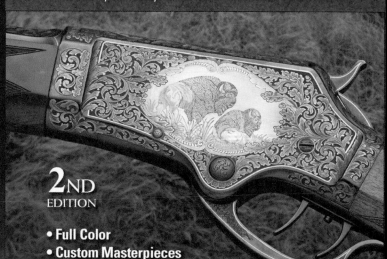